OH, HAMPDEN IN THE SUN . . .

Oh, Hampden in the Sun...

PETER BURNS
AND PAT WOODS

MAINSTREAM
PUBLISHING

EDINBURGH AND LONDON

First published in Great Britain in 1997 by
MAINSTREAM PUBLISHING COMPANY (EDINBURGH) LTD
7 Albany Street
Edinburgh EH1 3UG

ISBN 1 85158 911 2

A catalogue record for this book is available from the British Library

Typeset in Cheltenham
Printed and bound in Great Britain by Butler and Tanner Ltd, Frome

For Edmund Burns (father)

and Tommy Tomasso (uncle)

For James and Jane Woods (parents)

and Pat Woods (uncle)

Contents

Acknowledgements

The authors wish to thank the following:

Ex-Celts John Donnelly, Sean Fallon, Willie Fernie, Billy McPhail, Bertie Peacock and Sammy Wilson for sharing their memories of a famous Celtic triumph. Thanks also to ex-Celt Roddie MacDonald for putting the authors in touch with Sammy Wilson.

Jim Divers, Rikki Fearon, Frank Glencross, Jack Murray, the *Daily Record*, D.C. Thomson Ltd (especially David Walker and the library staff) and Scottish Media Newspapers Ltd in connection with illustrations used in the book.

The Scottish Football League, particularly David Thomson, for access to their archives and for permission to reproduce sections of the 1957 League Cup final match programme.

John Rowlinson of the BBC and the BBC's Written Archives Centre at Reading (particularly Sue Knowles and Jacqueline Kavanagh) and Sir Paul Fox (former editor of the BBC's *Sportsview* unit) in connection with the 'Case of the Missing Film'.

Joe Bole, John Bonnar junior, Bob Crampsey, Joseph Cummings, Tony Cummins, Jim Friel, Chris Goldie, Eugene MacBride, Kevin McCarra, Kevin McKenna, Tom McGouran, Jacky Meehan, Danny Mooney, Paul Murphy, James O'Kane, Tom O'Neill, Allan Pender, John Sawers, George Sheridan, Gerry White and John Woods for their assistance in various ways.

Tommy Bole, John Boyle, Edmund Burns, Fr Lawrence Byrne CP, Paul Byron, Gerry Campbell, Tom Campbell, Paul Cantley, Tom Carruthers, Bill Cassidy, Liam Clarke, Joe Connelly, Harry Conway, Hughie Corbett, Jim Coughlan, Alex Coulter, John Eadie, Andy Gillen, George Gillen, Willie Goldie, Gerard Hamill, Charlie and Mary Harvey, Gerry Heaney, Michael Hutton, Jimmy Jordan, Jim Kavanagh, Patsy Keane, Tommy and Eileen Lanigan, John Lindsay, Paul Lusk, 'Jock' McAulay, Robert McAulay, Roy

McGuinness, John McGuire, John McKechnie, Billy McNeill, Ian Murphy, Seamus Murphy, Gerard O'Donnell, Larry O'Hare, David Potter, William Provan, Betty Solis and Peter Sweeney, without whose personal testimonies this book would not have been possible. Thank you.

P.B. and P.W.

Preface

'7–1'. Even 40 years on, an air of incredulity still surrounds any reminiscing about one of the most remarkable scorelines in the history of football, all the more so for it being the result of a match in a major cup final between two of the deadliest rivals the game has ever known. The authors, therefore, believe it essential not only that the story of this singular event be told as fully as possible, with due regard for both the footballing and social contexts of its occurrence, but that the telling of it also bears witness as frankly as possible to the living memories of this cherished piece of Celtic folklore which have been generously contributed to this book by supporters of the club. It is thus inevitable – if such an account is to reflect honestly those supporters' perception of a rivalry which has always generated strong (some might say elemental) passions – that terms such as 'Huns' and 'Tims' crop up in the text when those supporters give their recollections of what it meant to follow Celtic in the 1950s.

Although the origins of these expressions are still obscure, it would be absurd to deny that they have been common currency among the broad mass of Celtic supporters for several decades when 'characterising' their bitter rivals (Rangers FC, their players and their supporters) and their own favourites and fellow supporters respectively. (The distinguished sportswriter Hugh McIlvanney describes such expressions, accurately, as 'street synonyms'.)To exclude such an authentic voice would diminish a presentation in which the authors have striven to incorporate a wealth of fresh material (not least, the viewpoints of Celtic players who took part in a unique occasion).

By way of explanation, it should be pointed out that the term 'Huns' has obvious parallels with – and one common theory points to its

11

derivation from – the demonisation of the enemy ('The Hun') in British press coverage of World War I; while 'Tims' (an abbreviation of 'Timalloys' or 'Tim Malloys') apparently derives from the name of a Catholic gang operating in the Calton district of Glasgow – close to Celtic Park – in the earlier part of this century. (The identity of Tim Malloy himself – if indeed he existed – has proved elusive. An alternative theory suggests that the name was a generic one used to refer to Irish immigrants to Glasgow.) One plausible explanation has it that the gang's name was adopted as a nickname for Celtic supporters and, by extension, the team itself, on account of its rhyming with an existing nickname for the club and the team, 'The Bhoys'. Interestingly, Charlie Tully, one of the most famous Celtic players of the 1950s, uses the term 'Timalloys' when talking about an Old Firm clash in his autobiography, *Passed to You* (1958).

The authors have made some slight editorial changes to the original written or oral contributions from fans which make up a good portion of the book, mainly for reasons of style or to correct identifiable errors in their recollections (the memory does indeed play tricks from time to time).

The authors found three books useful with regard to certain aspects of Celtic's history in the 1940s and 1950s: *Glasgow Celtic 1945–70*, by Tom Campbell (Tom Campbell, 1970); *Celtic: A Complete Record 1888–1992*, by Paul Lunney (Breedon Books, 1992); and *An Alphabet of the Celts*, by Eugene MacBride and Martin O'Connor, with George Sheridan (ACL and Polar Publishing, 1994). Finally, our thanks to Cathy Mineards of Mainstream Publishing for her diligence and patience.

P.B. and P.W.

CHAPTER ONE

October Revolution

Oh, Hampden in the sun
Celtic 7, Rangers 1;
That was the score when it came time-up,
The Timalloys had won the cup.[1]

PROLOGUE
A former Celtic goalkeeper recounts the following memory:

> I live in a village near Glasgow, and there was once a worthy of the village called Paddy L. who was a fanatical Celtic supporter, and a man who was also blessed with appearances from the Lord from time to time. I remember Paddy telling four or five of us of his experience one particular night:
> 'I was asleep, when all of a sudden I was awakened by a great bright light in my bedroom. I said, "Who is there?", and a voice answered, "It's the Lord, Paddy." I said, "Lord, it's three o'clock in the morning, what are you doing waking Paddy at this time for?" And the Lord replied, with a lilt in his voice, "Haw Paddy, dae ye mind the 7–1 game?"'[2]

At just after 4.25 p.m. on Saturday, 19 October 1957, Jack Mowat blew his referee's whistle to signal the end of the Scottish League Cup final. Most of the terracing at the King's Park (eastern) end of the vast Hampden bowl was still bathed, as it had been throughout that afternoon, in limpid sunlight. All across its classic slopes, men, women, boys and girls in their thousands were still struggling to take in the events which had unfolded before their spellbound, disbelieving eyes during the previous 90 minutes

13

of football. Their amazement was only exceeded by their delight. Celtic had just played 'The 7–1 game'.

FOLKLORE AND HISTORY

Astonishment vied with joy among the Celtic supporters present at Hampden that day, and although joy would ultimately win that contest of emotions, astonishment must still – 40 years later – be considered an apt reaction in the circumstances. The game remains for all with an affection for Celtic FC a magical, almost mythical highlight of the club's folklore. So much so that it seems that folklore is a more appropriate category in which to place this particular football match than the more mundane one of mere 'history' – hence Paddy L.'s tale of his nocturnal Visitor. But the match, and the people for whom it meant so much, deserve a history as well as a folklore. This book seeks to provide it.

Celtic's remarkable victory over their arch-rivals Rangers – still the most emphatic win recorded in a national cup final in Britain – brought the club its last major trophy prior to the appointment of Jock Stein as manager in 1965. With Stein at the helm, a glorious period in Celtic's history ensued, during which they were crowned Champions of Europe and attained a prominence and a reputation in the game which has never been matched by the Celtic sides of other eras, before or since.

As a result, Celtic today are a club indelibly marked and challenged by the standards set during Stein's reign as manager. He transported Celtic to pinnacles of achievement – and hence the supporters to levels of expectation – which have irrevocably redefined the club's sense of itself and of its place in professional football. Despite the generally depressing run of results and lack of achievement in the 1990s, the aspirations of the vast majority of those connected with the club continue to be based on the accomplishments of Celtic sides during the 1965–75 period.

It is easy, then, to forget how the club and its supporters thought of themselves prior to that 'golden age'. While several extensive histories of Celtic have been published in recent years, thus providing for the current generation of supporters a vastly more intimate and reliable knowledge of the club's history than was previously available, a strong case can be made for placing a more intensive focus on the 1950s.

In the first place, it is a period within the living memory of many who still follow Celtic's fortunes today. Of course, there are some supporters who go back further than that, to the days of Delaney, McGrory and 'Happy Feet' Napier, to John Thomson and even Patsy Gallacher. But time has thinned their ranks considerably. There are, however, a good many not yet collecting pensions who can still recall the 1950s. Secondly, that decade was a time of vast change in both football and society at large, or at least saw the beginning of such change. From football tactics to popular music, from geopolitics to the cultural mores of youth, the transformations in the intervening years have been dramatic. Hence, the contrasts are all the more sharply drawn when set beside the continuities provided by living memories, such as those recorded in this book. Finally, the 1950s were a particularly romantic period in Celtic's history. Major successes were sufficiently few in that decade to render them especially precious in the minds of the Celtic supporters who witnessed them, and the club's ups and downs were such as to induce in its followers something akin to the lovesickness which afflicts the characters portrayed in fictional romance. The path of true love never does run smooth, it is said, and it certainly didn't for Celtic supporters in the 1950s.

Those supporters had a particularly colourful group of players upon which to pin their affections, among them Charlie Tully, Bobby Evans, Sean Fallon, Willie Fernie, Neil Mochan, Bertie Peacock and Bobby Collins. The great victory of 1957 – the 'October Revolution' – was these players' last hurrah. Injury and departure broke up the team within a year of their most spectacular triumph, while age crept up on others. In a sense, the era of 'Celtic in the '50s' ended with the break-up of that team, to be replaced by a long line of youthful and mostly less fortunate recruits to the Celtic cause. In football terms, the 1960s arrived all too early and finished all too soon for most of these youngsters, dubbed 'the Kelly Kids', although some were destined to attain true greatness later in that decade.

The supporters themselves were a no less colourful and exuberant group than the players. At a time when British society frowned upon demonstrative behaviour in public, the Celtic fans were renowned for their enthusiasm and noisiness, although they also possessed a less welcome reputation for rowdiness.

David Potter (now resident in Kirkcaldy) recalls the Celtic fans of that era – and their reputation:

> It was always a great event in Forfar when Celtic were at Aberdeen, for supporters' buses stopped in the town to stock up on bridies and beer for the game. Occasionally there was trouble – one day they passed through early in the morning and there was not a milk bottle or a 'herdie poke' [bag of rolls] left on the Brechin Road – but more often they were friendly, as befits the extroverted Glasgow Irish community, full of good cheer and offering you a lift to Pittodrie to see the game on their bus. I was too young to be able to go, but I remember the buses with the green scarves, flags, pictures of the players and cardboard cut-outs of the Scottish Cup . . .
>
> Celtic continued to dominate my childhood, although I was genuinely appalled by the bottle-throwing which the supporters frequently indulged in in those days. I even made jokes that they should wear 'bottle green'.

The vast majority of these supporters, of course, lived in solidly working-class environments and partook of the distinctive West of Scotland version of working-class culture. Incomes were generally very limited, and most fans – especially the older generation – were still innocent of the burgeoning new consumer technologies. A television set was the prime consumer durable which the masses either aspired to own or had newly acquired. But British television programming was still in its infancy, and mishaps were common. Unfortunately, one infamous mishap deprived Celtic supporters of television pictures of one of their happiest-ever days.

Celtic supporter Jim Coughlan (now resident in Irvine) captures the moment in this story about his grandfather, Harry Reynolds senior:

> The story goes that due to work commitments he was unable to attend the match, and for a man who had witnessed the last 'Double'-winning team in action, as well as the Coronation Cup final, this was of great concern. But he consoled himself in the knowledge that if the Bhoys should win, he would be able to relive the glory thanks to the modern miracle of television, because he was now the proud owner of a new television set and highlights of the game were to be shown that Saturday night. After completing his shift that afternoon and with his thoughts firmly directed towards Hampden, he made his way home. On reaching his house he, along with the rest of the family and some neighbours, turned on the radio and waited patiently for the second-half commentary to begin. With the score broadcast at 2–0 in favour of the Bhoys, the family and friends celebrated and settled down for the second half. As the goals crashed in and the score mounted, the only person showing concern was my grandmother, worried in case the shouting and cheering and jumping up and down to celebrate each goal would either bring the roof down or send them crashing through the floor into the downstairs neighbours' living-room.
>
> As the match drew to a close and the result of 7–1 in favour of the Bhoys was now a fact and matter of record, my grandfather, uncle and several others set off to their local, comfortable in the knowledge that when the pub closed they could wend their way back home and settle down to watch the historic event on television. I am told by an uncle who was in the pub that night that the match reports of the [Glasgow] *Evening Times* and *Evening Citizen* were read time and time again with great relish. And as the beer and whisky flowed, the numbers invited back to watch the match at 22 Dalserf Street in Barrowfield grew by the minute (the close and flat still stand and can be seen from Celtic Park). The hour of ten approached and the happy throng led by my grandfather made its way home . . . Oh, the wonder of television, that it gave you the opportunity to watch what you had missed!

16

The company now sat on all available seats with drinks replenished. The first two goals were greeted with great cheers and handshakes all round, and with the expectation of more to come the party atmosphere got into full swing. Then the unthinkable happened. The football stopped and the presenter appeared, stating that due to a 'technical fault' they did not have any coverage of the entire second half and apologising for the inconvenience caused. The silence which greeted this announcement was stunning – from a party atmosphere it turned into the setting of a morgue. Then voices were raised in protest. 'Write in and complain,' said one. 'It's a conspiracy,' said another. 'March on the studios and sort them out' was the most extreme comment.

All through this my grandfather, who up until then had been the life and soul of the party, sat in silence. Then, with the swiftness of a Shawfield greyhound, he rose, raced towards the television and lifted it up all in one movement, and made towards the window. Family and friends, at first shocked by the suddenness of his movements, initially made no move themselves. But then, realising his intent was to throw the television set out of the window, they rose as one and threw themselves at my grandfather in an attempt to stop the planned retribution on the hapless TV. After what seemed a considerable time – although it was probably only a few seconds – he was thwarted, thanks to several strong pairs of hands and arms, amid chaotic scenes, with drink, chairs and those people less mobile being knocked over. This, needless to say, was the end of the party and my grandmother (now protecting the TV) stepped in, ordering my grandfather to his bed and the rest of the throng out of the house, with the comment, 'Yon television will be nothing but trouble.'

To the day my grandparents had both died, any time Celtic featured on the TV in a cup final, the story of the League Cup final night of 1957 would always be brought up, and I, along with all the other grandchildren, would listen in awe as the scene was described again and again.[3]

THE BRITISH SOCIAL CONTEXT

As the foregoing story illustrates, television was still a very new phenomenon in 1957. It was the year during which independent commercial television began to broadcast in Scotland in, initially, mild competition with the BBC. The new medium was soon mirroring the profound changes affecting British society.

Britain had emerged from World War II victorious and intact, but distinctly war-weary. The immediate post-war years were marked by official austerity, and rationing did not end until 1954, meat being the last item to 'come off the ration'. The Labour government which had won a massive Parliamentary majority in 1945 at Winston Churchill's expense presided over a radical restructuring of public policy, the main aims being to ensure full employment and to provide a comprehensive system of social security for all citizens. The National Health Service had come into being in 1948, thus relieving much of the economic insecurity threatened by ill-health. Guaranteed basic rights to an income and to education were strengthened. Social services were expanded, and while most people were still far from affluent, the economic terrors of the pre-war Depression years were confidently and gratefully viewed as gone forever. By the late 1950s, however, a measure of affluence was being experienced by some sections of the population. In January 1957, Harold Macmillan became Prime Minister following the resignation of Anthony Eden, whose stock had plummeted in the aftermath of the Suez Crisis of the previous year, when British troops had tried to prevent the nationalisation of the Suez Canal by the Egyptian nationalist leader, and the country's president, Colonel Gamal Abdel Nasser. The British intervention had ended in failure, and it was widely regarded as another indication of the decline in Britain's status as the pre-eminent imperial power. Perhaps to deflect concerns arising from that perception, Macmillan focused public attention on Britain's increasing domestic prosperity.

In July 1957, 'Supermac', as he was becoming known, told a cheering rally of Conservative Party workers at Bedford, 'Let us be frank about it – most of our people have never had it so good.' The phrase, though misquoted, was to be his most enduring campaign theme, and it helped the Conservatives to win their third successive election two years later (having regained power from Labour in 1951).

Underpinning this sense of economic security was the low level of unemployment experienced in Britain during the 1950s, the result of policies pursued by both main parties under a consensus which towards the end of the decade became known as 'Butskellism' (after the Conservative politician Rab Butler and the Labour leader Hugh Gaitskell). Under this consensus, the Conservatives publicly accepted the legitimacy of the newly created welfare state and the goal of full employment, while Labour pulled back from the old socialist dream of taking all capitalist businesses into public ownership. In the early '50s, on average only three out of every 100 Scottish workers were searching for a job. By the mid-'50s there were twice as many vacancies in Britain as people to fill them. (By 1987, the picture had changed dramatically; one Glaswegian male in four was seeking employment.) The average weekly wage for a man rose steadily through the 1950s, doubling by the end of the decade (from £7.28 in 1950 to £14.99 in 1960).[4]

Growing affluence was reflected in the vogue for foreign holidays. Britons were attracted by package tourism to Spain in particular. In 1957 one could stay in Spain's newest holiday resort, Benidorm (hitherto an

18

'unspoiled fishing village'), for the princely sum of roughly £1 per person per night. 1957 was also a pivotal year for mass travel in another way – it was the first year that as many people crossed the Atlantic by plane as by ship. The growth in air travel was also demonstrated by a huge increase in the number of passengers being carried by BEA (British European Airways) – from 10,000 per month in 1946, to 10,000 daily ten years later. By 1960 BEA had five million passengers annually.

Most people, of course, were still not affluent enough to be flying across the Atlantic. More modest signs of prosperity were the new labour-saving devices for the home. Cookers, washing machines and vacuum cleaners were becoming more widespread, demand being stimulated by hire-purchase facilities (or the 'never-never', as it was less officially known). The discovery of new detergents and synthetic fibres saved housewives long hours of drudgery. (As late as 1954 it was reckoned that the average British woman was spending at least five hours a day in the kitchen.) The seeds of 'women's lib' were being sown by these and similar developments, although 'liberation' from work in the house was generally followed by new forms of servitude in factories, offices and shops.

Shopping was becoming more convenient with the appearance of supermarkets. In 1947 there had been less than a dozen in Britain. Ten years later they were opening at the rate of 50 per month. There were still many more traditional, family-owned stores and corner shops, but the writing was on the wall as the retail revolution got into full swing. Car ownership was another sign of the new consumerism, almost trebling during the decade. But a car was still a luxury item for many people, and even by 1960 the ratio of cars to people was only 1 to 9.3. The first stretch of motorway, however, was opened in 1958 (the eight-and-a-half-mile-long Preston bypass).

What would nowadays be called the 'feel-good factor' was evidenced by the success of the Conservatives in being returned to power at three successive elections in the 1950s, with increasing Parliamentary majorities. Their popularity was such that for the first, and only, time they held a narrow majority of Scottish Parliamentary seats (36 out of 71) in 1955, following that year's general election.

But warning signs that all was not well with the British economy were evident too. Barely a decade after being defeated in war, West Germany overtook Britain in car production and exports, and Britain's share of world trade was on the decline. While British productivity grew by rates of 40 per cent, those of West Germany and Italy grew by 150 per cent, and Japanese productivity rose a massive 400 per cent during the decade. British management failed to invest sufficiently in new equipment, and an innate British caution and conservatism hindered overall economic growth. Much of British industry clung steadfastly to outdated machinery and working practices. Confronted by a management which was often complacent, self-serving and lacking in vision, strong trade unions not surprisingly sought as much of the cake for themselves as possible. This pattern would lead to the trend for growing trade union militancy in the 1960s, which in turn would be met by a backlash of confrontational, blatantly pro-capitalist policies in the Thatcher era.

Charlie Harvey of Simshill has a vivid recollection of the mood in Glasgow's workplaces at the time in the 1950s:

There's a big shortage of labour just now and the wages aren't bad. The Commie shop stewards tell us to grab all we can and salt it away because the bosses will shite on us from a high level when things are back to normal. They're from the past, like their war stories about Spain [the Spanish Civil War of 1936–39]. The bad old days can't possibly return – the press barons Lord Beaverbrook and Lord Rothermere have assured us! It's a comforting thought when the fitba' depresses me.

Britain's aloofness and its sense of empire were still sufficiently marked that the country stood aside when the Treaty of Rome was signed by six nations in 1957, establishing the European Economic Community (popularly known as the Common Market). Contemporary mistrust of the European idea is nothing new! Britain was content to hold on to its Commonwealth links deriving from an Empire upon which the sun was fast setting. Much of Britain revelled in insularity – an outlook captured in the fabled (perhaps apocryphal) newspaper headline which read 'Fog in Channel – England Cut Off'. There was also a certain smug racism abroad, typified by a remark of the (English) Football League secretary Alan Hardaker, who opposed participation in the new European club competitions on the grounds (privately expressed) that it meant involvement with 'too many wogs and dagos'. But probably an equally significant reason for British reluctance to embrace Europe was a fear that Britain was simply not geared to thrive in the competition generated by a Common Market. Hence, the treaty of accession to join the EEC was not signed until the early 1970s.

Prime Minister Macmillan had no compunction when it came to hiding the truth about the economy from the British people. Cabinet papers for 1957 released in January 1988 under the 30-year rule showed that the country's financial situation was in fact precarious, hurt by the flight from sterling in the money markets following the Suez Crisis. In response, the government considered cutting family allowances, introducing hospital pay beds, imposing higher dental charges and dearer school meals, and scrapping RAF Fighter Command as means of restoring order to the public finances. Chancellor of the Exchequer Peter Thorneycroft in some ways anticipated the later Thatcherite assault on the welfare state, and in August 1957 he proposed a dramatic tightening of monetary policy in the face of a rumoured devaluation of sterling and fears of inflation. The resultant financial squeeze, including a shock overnight 2 per cent rise in the main interest rate (known as the Bank Rate), meant that unemployment began to rise in the late 1950s, with Scottish jobless figures eventually doubling to over 116,000 by the end of the decade. The economic 'boom' years of the '50s ultimately only served to mask Britain's relative decline in the global economic league table.

> Behind his confident, ebullient exterior, Prime Minister Macmillan was in fact distinctly worried about the state of the country. He confided to his diary in March 1957 a fear of a looming general strike, so strong was the mood in the shipyards, engineering works, railways, coalmines and power stations. He had already briefed the Emergency Committee of his Cabinet on plans for troops to take over from strikers in key industries, and thought was also given to introducing legislation restricting trade union rights. This idea was not pursued on the grounds that many trade unionists had begun voting Conservative, and because — in accordance with the new 'Butskellite' consensus — the Tories wished to present themselves as a national party capable of drawing support from all sections of the community.

Allied to its relative economic decline was the country's gradual loss of imperial status and power, already signalled in 1947 by the end of British rule in India. But it was undoubtedly the Suez fiasco of 1956 which epitomised this loss in the public mind. An episode later described by Anthony Nutting, then, in 1956, Minister of State for Foreign Affairs, as 'a mad imperialist gamble', it exposed Britain's declining influence in world affairs. With the connivance of France and Israel, Britain had invaded Egypt following the decision by President Nasser to nationalise the Suez Canal. But without the backing of the United States, the move was doomed to failure, and eventually the British were forced to make a humiliating 'tactical withdrawal'. The débâcle later resulted in the resignation of Prime Minister Anthony Eden, ostensibly for reasons of health. The British representative at the United Nations lamented in his diary that his country had now been reduced to the level of a 'third-class power'. It would, however, take some time before the truth sunk in fully, not least in the corridors of power.

This reluctance to accept Britain's waning geopolitical influence was perhaps exemplified most strongly in the determination of the political élite – on both sides of the House of Commons – to retain the country's status as a nuclear power. At the Labour Party conference in the autumn of 1957, the Shadow Foreign Secretary Aneurin Bevan, a veteran 'firebrand' socialist, shocked his former left-wing friends by pleading with the delegates not to vote for nuclear disarmament, 'not' – as he melodramatically put it – 'to send the British Foreign Minister naked into the conference chamber'. The 1950s, of course, were very much the peak years of the Cold War, and nuclear weapons were regarded by the British political establishment as a vital symbol of national virility. The *Daily Express* echoed this attitude when it exulted over the successful testing of Britain's first nuclear bomb near Christmas Island, a Pacific atoll, in May 1957 with the headline 'It's OUR H-Bomb!'. ('H-bomb' meant the hydrogen bomb, a more potent type of device than the older atomic or 'A-bomb'.)

The first British nuclear power reactor, Calder Hall in Cumberland, was opened in 1956 ostensibly for 'harnessing atomic power for peaceful purposes'. But in fact it was also used to provide plutonium for military ends. So secretive was the government about the nuclear industry that it suppressed the findings of an inquiry into a serious fire at the Windscale plant in Cumbria in October 1957 – an incident characterised 30 years later when the truth emerged as a 'potential Chernobyl-style disaster'. The Windscale fire released a radioactive 'cloud' into the atmosphere which drifted over 200 miles of the surrounding countryside and prompted the authorities to consider the wholesale evacuation of local people. Heavily contaminated milk was poured into drains, thus carrying pollution into the Irish Sea. To improve its image after this near catastrophe, the plant was later renamed Sellafield. The official report (The Penney Report) into the incident was rewritten on Macmillan's orders lest the public lose confidence in the burgeoning nuclear industry.

Some acknowledgement of Britain's reduced status had been signalled in the spring of 1957 when a Defence White Paper called for the phasing-out of National Service by 1962, largely on the grounds that it was too expensive to maintain, and a waste of manpower resources. An earlier report had concluded that those called up – nearly 700,000 were in uniform in 1956 – tended to regard their two-year stints in HM Forces as 'an infliction to be undergone rather than a duty to the nation'. The last batch of medically fit 18-year-olds who were eligible for service (some categories were exempt) received their call-up papers in November 1960, by which time opinion had swung round decisively in favour of an all-volunteer, fully professional military.

GLASGOW

Glasgow, in 1957, could no longer boast – as it had done for over a century – that it was the 'Second City of the Empire', having been pushed into third place by Birmingham following the publication of the 1951 census figures. It still had a population of over one million, however, making it one of the world's forty most populous cities. But Glasgow was on the verge of radical change. Glaswegians in the 1950s were one of the last generations of Clydesiders to be put in large numbers to the 'hard but rewarding work' of building ships, forging metals and engineering fine tools. Apprenticeships could still be found in abundance, and there was no real prospect then of workers young and old being 'thrown on the scrapheap'. But drastic reductions in employment within Glasgow's traditional industries were not far off. In addition, large parts of the city were destined to be bulldozed following a report in 1957 which proposed major housing redevelopment – 'slum clearance' was the term much in vogue then – aimed at reducing population densities from 450 persons per acre on average to 164. This would require the demolition of over 90,000 dwellings in the following two decades and the consequent removal of 60 per cent of the population from the designated redevelopment areas, much of the 'overspill' being redirected to the new towns of East Kilbride and Cumbernauld, as well as peripheral estates such as Drumchapel and Easterhouse. The redevelopment would be marked by a switch from high-density low-rise dwellings to multi-storey tower blocks, 200 of which would be constructed by 1970, in an expansion of high-rise housing unmatched in any other British city. The human costs of such a massive social dislocation were not imagined in the late 1950s, however.

Those decamped from close-knit, lively neighbourhoods such as Anderston, Townhead and Cowcaddens often found themselves in housing schemes bereft of basic amenities such as convenient shopping areas, recreational and leisure facilities, and safe public spaces. One Drumchapel resident memorably complained that it was like living in 'a desert wi' windaes'. Problems of dampness, vandalism and a soulless layout of the buildings, as well as the depopulation of inner-city districts, would later become an indictment of the original plans and planners.[5]

In the late 1950s, however, the City Fathers were motivated by good intentions, of helping the more disadvantaged sections of the populace, and by a desire to overcome the rather grim image Glasgow then had in the rest of the country. The latter was in part a result of the very squalid housing conditions many Glaswegians then endured, typified by the dilapidated, soot-covered tenements which disfigured much of the city, their grime-encrusted exteriors the legacy of decades of smoke belching from coal-fired chimneys. It was thus not unusual in the early winter evenings for fog to blanket the city, producing, as the poet Edwin Morgan once recalled, 'a silent wall of impenetrable grey. There were no buses, trains, taxis or cars to be seen or heard. It was a stricken, immobile place.' Glasgow's 'pea-soupers' were justly notorious, although other cities such as London also suffered from them. They were to become largely a thing of the past following legislation passed in 1956 which required people to burn smokeless fuels in their grates, or use alternative methods of heating to the traditional coal fire.

Charlie Harvey recalls the day of the 1957 League Cup final:

Until I die I'll remember the weather on that late autumn day. It was perfect, and with a unique quality of light that seemed to penetrate everything it fell upon. I would next experience its like on the day Pope John Paul II came to Bellahouston [1982], and never since. There was no danger that day in 1957 of smog, a poisonous industrial filth that tore your lungs apart several times a year.

I had a girlfriend then who worked at the Vicky [Victoria Infirmary]. She said that the smogs killed thousands each time they appeared but the Government wouldn't let the media tell anyone about it. She said they were scared of the cost of cleaning up the air. Hard to believe — after all, we live in a democracy! Still, she was adamant — every time a smog was forecast the mortuaries would go into disaster mode. On the day of the final I was thinking, 'Glad we've missed the smog today, though I'll probably be sorry when the game's over. A berth in the morgue might seem attractive later on!'

Coal, of course, was still the most common domestic fuel in use in 1957, and it was often sold from horse-drawn carts that made their way around the tenement districts which, in the words of one observer, were populated by 'neighbours who gossiped and squabbled' in gas-lit closes. An *Evening Citizen* columnist of the time, gently parodying the city's reputed naming after the Gaelic for 'dear, green place', called Glasgow a 'dear, dirty old place'.

Nor was life in the close-knit tenement communities as rosy as some of the sentimentalists have portrayed. In 1957 Glasgow had, officially, 11,000 'slum-dwellings'; unofficially there were many more. Alastair Borthwick, writing in the *Citizen*, asserted that there were still 17,000 families 'living under conditions in which a reasonably progressive farmer would hesitate to keep his cattle', although he acknowledged that 'there are warm hearts and neighbourliness in the slums which are hard to find elsewhere'. He described a visit to a building in Grace Street in the Anderston district where he watched a woman 'trying to cope with five children and her husband's dinner' in a one-roomed house where the only water flowed from a single cold tap. 'The oldest child,' wrote Borthwick, 'was 11 and the youngest was a baby who looked at me from a box-bed in the corner, the bed in which all the children slept. The walls were damp, the plaster was crumbling and the flagstones of the close outside were so worn they might have come from a medieval dungeon . . . The place was rotten through and through. It had the unmistakable slum smell that no woman can ever scrub out of her home, however hard she tries. There were 15 other houses like it up that single stair. It was, of course, scandalous. It should not be possible, in a city which calls itself civilised, for children to be born in such a room' (19 August 1957). Borthwick noted that the family had been on the Corporation's waiting list for a new house since 1945 and was only now on the point of being rehoused because their present abode was about to be condemned.

Another factor in Glasgow's poor reputation within Britain was the supposed proneness of its citizens to drink-fuelled violence. The razor gangs of the 1930s – immortalised in the novel *No Mean City* – were still fresh in many people's minds. That this perception was unfairly overdrawn is beyond question. But Glasgow was a heavily industrial, overwhelmingly working-class city in 1957, and it suffered from all the social problems which attend poverty and social deprivation. Among these were poor health, to which both the social and physical environments of the city greatly contributed. The unhealthy environment was underlined by the launch in March 1957 by the city's Medical Officer of Health, William Horne, of a five-week-long campaign to screen over 700,000 people (nearly three-quarters of Glasgow's population) for early signs of pulmonary tuberculosis, the dreaded 'TB', which caused more deaths in the city than anywhere else in Britain.

Despite its many problems, the city was very much a bustling centre of commerce and industry. Getting to and from work meant that a familiar sight in Glasgow in 1957 was that of trams clanking through the busy city-centre streets as they hauled passengers to and from the outer districts. But as the year drew to a close, it was becoming clear that this much-loved form of transport, seemingly a permanent feature of Glasgow life, was doomed, only awaiting the formal announcement of its demise.

The tram system had served the city well for many decades, and as late as 1955–56 had borne a total of 367 million fare-paying passengers. But such was the congestion in the streets, particularly in the city centre during rush hour, that it reduced the average speed to only seven miles per hour (according to one calculation by a Corporation

Transport official in September 1957). Cost was another factor in the decision, as replacing worn-out trams and maintaining tramlines were proving very expensive. The *Glasgow Herald* noted that the rails and cobbles made the streets bumpy and dangerous for other vehicles, while one critic described the 'caurs' as 'misshapen monsters who roamed the streets, rattling and rumbling along like fugitives from a museum'. The tramcars may have been viewed with great affection in retrospect, but the authorities had had enough of them. A final ceremonial procession of 20 trams of different types would take place on 4 September 1962, watched by an emotional crowd of 200,000 despite torrential rain. The 'caurs' had wound their way round the streets of Glasgow over the previous 90 years. Many of them were used, of course, by Old Firm fans to make their way out towards Hampden Park on 19 October 1957.

Charlie Harvey presents a vivid recollection of the city-centre scene on League Cup final day, 1957:

A stop at the Argyle Street corner just to watch the world go by. Very enjoyable on a sunny day. Every building in sight is as black as the Earl of Hell's waistcoat. Why did they build such an ugly, depressing city? Even the sunlight can't penetrate this gloom. Really old people tell me the stone was originally a beautiful cream colour. Sometimes the City Fathers talk about renovation but the experts say we'd be back to square one in a couple of years.

Argyle Street is jammed end-to-end with tramcars. Slow bloody things! Each one brings a street to a standstill every time it stops to pick up or drop off passengers. They've got people wasted. They won't walk anywhere. I could ask anyone here, 'How far to the Cross?' and the answer more often than not would be 'Four stoaps on the caur'. The caurs are on the way out. Five years the planners give them. I'll believe it when I see it. The caurs were here before the city!

A sight I can't get used to is the shop windows crammed with goods. It's only a wee while since they were empty and you had to queue, ration book in hand, for whatever was given to you. Now people look quite prosperous and well dressed. Maybe at long last we can put the war firmly behind us. Up till recently the powers that be exhorted greater effort with the slogan 'From austerity to prosperity'. Have we finally and really made it? Hard to accept . . .

Despite the efforts of the local authorities to improve its image, Glasgow retained its reputation as a hard-drinking city. In 1957 it boasted over 1,000 public houses, most of them spartan establishments whose grimness merited the sobriquet 'spit and sawdust', and where female drinkers were viewed with suspicion if not downright hostility. They were concentrated in working-class districts such as the Gorbals, which had a staggering 112 licensed premises for a population of 40,000. The Gallowgate, the thoroughfare linking the city centre with the Parkhead district where Celtic Park is located, had 66 pubs along its two-mile length.

And Glasgow was still 'dancin' daft'. In the mid-1950s Glaswegians frequented as many as 30 licensed dance halls, a higher proportion relative to population than anywhere else in the United Kingdom. It was not unusual for people to attend ballrooms four or five times a week (the biggest, the Dennistoun Palais, had room for 1,700 dancers).

However, a new phenomenon, 'youth culture', was making its presence felt and beginning to undermine the traditional pastimes. For the first time, British teenagers (the word was unknown at the start of the decade) were experiencing a degree of freedom and affluence which made them an easy marketing target for new forms of popular music and fashion. The new mood was personified by one Elvis 'The Pelvis' Presley, a former truck driver from Mississippi, whose stage performances were having an electric effect on audiences in the United States. The *La Crosse Register* (Wisconsin) reported in May 1956 after he appeared locally that he 'somehow picked out a bit of teenage spirit and tucked it into his whanging geetar. You don't have to understand it. Just listen to it and the kids will tell you – this boy is crazy, man, crazy.' The air of hysteria surrounding the newly appointed king of popular music was such that by the autumn of 1957, a phenomenal 28 million of his singles had been sold worldwide. His impact spread to Glasgow, and traditional local dance bands, used to playing jazz, were suddenly inundated with requests for 'rock 'n' roll' music. British singers such as the young Cliff Richard soon adopted the new musical genre inspired by Presley's immense success. However, British pop stars and fans were not fully caught up in the new flamboyance being imported from America. As one observer noted of BBC TV's *Six-Five Special*, 'Lonnie Donegan, top artiste of skiffle, England's derivative answer to rock 'n' roll, grins his way through a number, while his audience, wearing long flared skirts and poplin blouses and blazers, hands clasped, faces blank or slightly pensive, gaze at him as if he were giving them a lecture on personal hygiene.' It was a decade, after all, when young men in Britain prided themselves on not having a hair out of place, with Brylcreem pressed into service to that end on a daily basis.

But there was a new tempo sweeping the country in 1957, and a young

Glaswegian named John Stephen gave another sign of things to come. Having previously been a menswear assistant with the Glasgow Cooperative Society, he moved to London where he opened (at the age of 21) a shop in Carnaby Street, a side street which at the time had only one other retailer. He was soon catering for young trendsetters who bought 'way-out gear' to a backdrop of the new pop music. By the middle of the following decade the street would become synonymous with the 'Swinging Sixties'. Another young Scotsman had also taken a step in 1957 which would eventually lead to another, footballing version of the 'Swinging Sixties' – Jock Stein took a coaching job with Celtic FC after being forced out of the game by injury . . .

Tommy Lanigan (King's Park, Glasgow) recalls the mood of the city:

In 1957 there was a great buzz about Glasgow. I had finished my National Service and I was happy to be back amongst it. In Bridgeton a man was either for Celtic or for Rangers – there was no in-between. We were definitely in the minority. Following Celtic every week was a major part of my life, one which I still consider to be a privilege. I would never dream of missing a game. I would meet my mates in the local pub, The George, before setting off. We would end up back there after the game and we'd have a few more, sometimes a few too many. The bloke who owned the pub, Charlie Deeney, had a line into Celtic Park. His sister was Jimmy McGrory's secretary and this lassie married Willie Fernie. Charlie Deeney loved to gossip, and so The George was always alive with news and rumour from Parkhead.

I was 23 at the time of the 7–1 match and had followed Celtic since 1938. I stayed in Bridgeton, within sight of Celtic Park. It was really tough following Celtic in those days, especially in Bridgeton. Celts always had great players and you usually saw a good game but they never seemed to win anything. (I even missed the Coronation Cup in 1953 through National Service in the Army.)

Rangers were always a very bad memory. Except for one occasion when Tully destroyed them 3–1 it was a nightmare even thinking about a game with Rangers. They seemed invincible. That was the true state of mind of all the 'Tims' on the morning of 'The 7–1'. About 30 of us met in our usual Bridgeton pub, The George in Muslin Street. It was also home to the local 'Tim' gang, 'The Muzzy'. I drove a milk-delivery lorry then – hard work, but the money was good. I could clear £10 a week. To put it in context, the top price of a pint was 1/6d [7½ pence] so a man, if he so wished, could easily get stoned and have change from a quid.

I put a couple of pounds on Celtic, at long odds. I think it was 7–2 but it may have been 5–2. Bookies' shops were illegal then and you risked your liberty to put on a bet. The Black Maria was liable to turn up and cart everyone off to Tobago Street police station. If that happened the bookie would pay the fines and give everyone ten bob [50 pence] compensation. Although we backed the Celtic with our money, in our hearts we didn't relish the game, but we were always optimistic.

As often happened in those days, the driver of an open lorry told us all to jump on board, and on that beautiful sunny day we set off for Hampden in style, in good voice and with banners flying . . .

Despite the buzz about Glasgow, and the changes sweeping through British society in the late 1950s with the arrival of rock 'n' roll, 'Teddy boy' fashions and the new youth culture, the abiding impression of Britain as a whole in 1957 is that of a rather staid, conservative society, resistant to change and still ruled by a complacent, somewhat blinkered Establishment, as the following two cameos suggest. In 1957 Lord Altrincham provoked only angry outrage in the press, not genuine debate, when he accused Queen Elizabeth in an issue of *The National and English Review* of being 'surrounded by a highly unrepresentative circle, making her remote from her people and the Commonwealth' – a criticism that would not have elicited such a blindly reactive defence of the monarchy four decades later when, in the wake of various scandals, public confidence in and support for the British Crown would be greatly reduced. But in 1957 'rocking the boat' was still an alien philosophy for most people. In defence of the status quo, if only obliquely in support of the Queen's position, Dr Geoffrey Fisher, then Archbishop of Canterbury, effectively vetoed the establishment of full diplomatic relations with the Vatican on the grounds that the presence of a papal internuncio in Britain would have, potentially, 'repercussions in some parts of the country and [would provoke] a revival of religious controversy'.

There was an echo of this Establishment stance north of the border when, in November 1957, the Church of Scotland magazine *Life and Work* carried what Hugh Delaney, the general secretary of the Celtic FC Supporters Association, described as a 'bigoted and vicious attack' on the club and its supporters. The writer of the article did ask the question, 'When did Rangers last sign a Roman Catholic footballer?', but the main thrust of his analysis was directed against Celtic. 'Is it right,' he asked, 'that one club in the Scottish League should have predominantly Irish Catholic associations and draw to itself the support of the vast majority of Roman Catholic football supporters? It is no doubt natural that in a Protestant country Catholics should seek their own kind in sport and social affairs. But provocative demonstrations of their solidarity only lead to trouble. To the ordinary rivalry of the football field is added an ugly religious bigotry. It is doubtful if a Protestant club would get such freedom in a Catholic country. In fact, it's a dead certainty it wouldn't!' We can safely assume that neither the Archbishop of Canterbury nor the writer of this article was on the slopes of the 'Celtic end' at Hampden on the afternoon of 19 October 1957.

Liam Clarke (now resident in New Zealand) vividly recalls a divided Glasgow:

It's 1957 and I'm on my way home from school, Our Lady and St Margaret's in Kinning Park. Turn left at the bottom of Stanley Street and on to Paisley Road West; trams are clanking and there are people everywhere. The tenement buildings seem huge to my ten-year-old eyes, and every 50 yards there is another pub . . . The Old Toll Bar . . . The Quaich . . . The Grapes . . . The Doctors . . . get home at last, 133 Maclean Street, Kinning Park.

We live on the top floor of this grey tenement building. There are no tiles on the walls of our close (I was later to find out that the colour of the building – grey, or red sandstone – and whether the close walls were tiled or not signified your position on the working-class social scale). We live in a room and kitchen. The toilet is on the landing, and we're lucky as we only have to share it with another four families. Me and my big brother sleep in the small room, Ma and Da in a little alcove in the kitchen. The rest of the kitchen consists of a coal-fired grate and a 'wally' sink complete with brass taps. You can look out of the kitchen window on to the 'middens' or from the little room on to Maclean Street. A rag and bone man is blowing his bugle and kids are getting a 'hudgie' on the back of his horse and cart.

We're Catholic, so we support Celtic. My big brother and me go to all the Celtic matches. The three main things in our lives are surviving, Celtic and the Catholic Church. It's Mass every Sunday in the old church attached to our school. Everybody goes to chapel, with the priest promising hell and damnation unless we mend our ways. Being 'respectable' is drummed into us from an early age – you must always be seen to be 'respectable'.

Ibrox Park is a mile from Maclean Street, just along Paisley Road West. That's where the Proddies go to support their team Rangers. There's this huge Union Jack that flies above the main entrance. My Da says they won't sign Catholic players – something about élitism, and our Irish background. He doesn't seem angry about this, just rather hurt and sad. My Da (God rest his soul, educated by the Marist brothers at St Joseph's College, Dumfries) talks about the Masons a lot. This subject does make him very angry, telling me they got all the good jobs and that we are discriminated against. (In later years, after reading many books on the subject, I don't think the problem was nearly as bad as he suggested.)

After Mass on Sunday we catch the tramcar and go to visit Granny

Clarke in Dennistoun. She's an old Irish woman who lives there with my uncle Tom and two aunts. Their red sandstone tenement has a tiled close, and they have an inside bathroom (can you imagine such luxury?). After tea we go into the big front room where records of Irish rebel songs are played. It's there I learn of Robert Emmet, Kevin Barry and other Irish patriots. The conversation quickly turns to Celtic: Isn't Charlie Tully the greatest?! Who can compare with Willie Fernie? Then they would discuss events in the Irish Republic, or the 'Free State' as they sometimes called it. It was described in the most glowing terms. To a young kid like me, everything seemed better there. It was the true homeland . . . Erin.

Life was economically tough in Glasgow during the 1950s. Britain was 'skint' after the war and it took a long time to recover. People were poor, but how do you measure poverty? I don't know. If I was to sum up in one word the Glasgow of the '50s, it would be 'vibrant'. There was bigotry and discrimination during this period, and no doubt there still is today, but the lasting impression I take from this period is of 'wee wummin' standing outside their closes talking to their pals, clanking old tramcars – and a deep sense of belonging.

ENDNOTES

1 The full background to this song will be given in a later chapter. 'Timalloys' (or 'Tims') was a nickname in this period for Celtic and/or the club's supporters.

2 The goalkeeper who contributed this story was Willie Goldie. He was a third-choice guardian in October 1960, when he was picked up by the Celtic team bus on its way to a match at Broomfield, where he was selected to play on arrival at the ground. Willie had been out with his wife dancing until 3 a.m. on the Saturday morning, but was chosen because of injury problems affecting the regular keepers, and because – apparently – Celtic chairman Robert Kelly was impressed by Goldie's obvious devotion to Celtic as he stood in his green and white scarf waiting for a bus (public transport, that is) to take him to Airdrie as a spectator, intent on supporting the team from the terracing.

3 The full story of the missing television film will be explained at greater length in a later chapter.

4 Decimal equivalents of pounds, shillings and pence – the 1950s' British currency – are used throughout this book.

5 The 1957 report said that Glasgow needed 100,000 new houses for its people, a notable reason being the huge pressure of post-war council housing applications resulting from newlyweds looking for their first home (the related post-war baby boom was an important factor too). By the 1970s Glasgow was being dubbed 'Britain's high-rise metropolis' and 'the city of towers', one well-travelled commentator remarking that he hadn't seen a city skyline so dominated by high-rise accommodation outside the Communist bloc. In its defence, the city had little option but to 'grow upwards' within its boundaries given land pressures, reflected most notably in 'green belt' planning restrictions on its fringes.

    The ex-Celt Bertie Auld, raised in a tenement in Panmure Street in the working-class district of Maryhill, once passed – when manager of his boyhood favourites Partick Thistle – a typically blunt verdict on this redevelopment: 'If they'd given Hitler the contract, he couldn't have done a better job!'

CHAPTER TWO

Five Sorrowful Mysteries

I see Tully running down the line;
He slips the ball past Valentine.
It's nodded down by 'Teazy Weazy',
And Sammy Wilson makes it look so easy.[1]

AND WHEN THE WAR IS OVER
Celtic emerged from the shadows of World War II in a state of considerable disarray, most notably symbolised by the dilapidated condition of the club's ground when hostilities ceased in 1945. Football, of course, had been assigned a much reduced status for the 'duration', but even the vital, momentous task of defeating fascism had not been able to hide the disconcerting fact that during the 1940s Celtic FC was plunging into the darkest period of its history. Neglect of the stadium had been matched by a similar neglect of standards on the field of play, as former club trainer Alec Dowdells recalled in later years: 'Most clubs made good their losses [of playing personnel] by taking on as many guest players as they could. The Celtic management, on the other hand, decided to rely as far as possible on their own resources. We must have passed up dozens of players who would have jumped at the chance of wearing a Celtic jersey' (*Weekly News*, 25 May 1957). It was clear to the supporters that Celtic's directors were not interested in making much of a challenge in wartime football, and no real attempt was made to field a consistently strong side despite the best efforts of then manager Jimmy McStay.[2]

Rangers, by contrast, adopted a far more purposeful stance and completely dominated Scottish football during these years, winning all the unofficial league championships and amassing a total of 25 out of the

34 trophies they competed for during the war. The only honours Celtic collected during the same period were a Glasgow Cup in 1940, a Glasgow Charity Cup in 1943 and, at the war's end, the Victory-in-Europe Cup in May 1945, which was won 'on corners' after a 1–1 draw with Queen's Park at Hampden.[3] Celtic's record in wartime matches against the Ibrox club was abysmal; the Parkhead men won only three out of 12 league encounters and emerged as victors only once in 13 matches in various cup competitions. More importantly, Celtic's half-hearted attitude to football during World War II also had the consequence that Rangers, and to a lesser extent Hibernian (assisted by Matt Busby's influence), were in a much stronger position to compete effectively for honours once the war was over and full-time professional football restored.

One little-known episode typified both the dearth of ambition and the niggardly sentiments prevalent in the Parkhead boardroom during this unhappy chapter in the club's history, namely, a near strike which almost resulted in the cancellation of an Old Firm game. When the Celtic players gathered at St Enoch Square in May 1942 to board the team bus for the semi-final of the Southern League Cup match at Hampden, they were incensed when manager Jimmy McStay told them that no complimentary tickets were available, and that instead arrangements would be made for friends and relatives 'to be passed through to the enclosure'. This announcement seemed to be the last straw for players already disillusioned by shabby treatment in several respects at the hands of the management, most notably the board's refusal to stump up the financial 'extras' the players knew were being used as inducements at other clubs.[4] When the players reached the Hampden dressing-room, they refused to obey trainer Alec Dowdells's instruction to strip. It is significant of his lack, indeed abdication, of authority that the manager does not appear to have been present in the dressing-room at any time before the match. A few minutes before kick-off time, and shortly after the referee (Bobby Calder of Rutherglen, later a noted scout with Aberdeen) had departed with a quizzical look in the direction of the Celtic trainer after checking the players' boots, the Celtic chairman Tom White threw open the door, having somehow got wind of the fact that something was up. White, a rather portly, somewhat rakish figure in his Raglan coat and bowler hat and smoking a Corona cigar (all in all, the archetypal football club director of popular imagination until recent times), proceeded to lay down the law, telling the players that they were 'not going to hold a pistol to his head' and that they had to start stripping 'now – and be sharp about it!' He then turned on his heels and marched out without saying another word, but all too aware that his message had sunk home. To no avail, it should be said, at least in terms of the result – Rangers won 2–0. White's performance may have been the perfect illustration of the classic master–servant relationship, but it was no way to run a football club.

Little wonder, then, that not only were Celtic conspicuously unsuccessful in wartime, but the club's outlook forced the eventual departure of its most prominent player of the time, Jimmy Delaney, to Manchester United in February 1946.

John Eadie, then living in the Gorbals, now resident in Los Angeles, recalls:

> We were all upset when Jimmy Delaney left. I remember when he scored at Hampden a couple of months later in the last minute to beat England in the 'Victory' international match — we were all proud because we still regarded him as a Celtic player. But Celtic were making a lot of bad decisions then and we had a poor team. I remember being at the Kelvin Hall with a school team. Celtic and Rangers players were there for a five-a-side tournament. One of the Celtic players was the centre-forward, Joe Rae. [Some wags at the time called him 'Doh' Rae.] Bobby Hogg was there too, and Ugolini was in goal. I always remember one of the boys shouting at Rae, 'You're a diddy, Rae, a big diddy!' I always remember that!

By September 1946, the Celtic Supporters Association, formed towards the end of the war by Willie Fanning of Caroline Street, Parkhead, had grown sufficiently in organisational strength and self-confidence – and concern over the state of Celtic – that its executive committee placed before the Celtic directors a series of pertinent and telling questions. Had Celtic made plans for the signing of new players? Had the club organised an adequate scouting system? Was Celtic's training and fitness programme adequate? Were the wages and bonuses paid by Celtic on a par with those of other clubs? Did manager Jimmy McGrory (he had replaced McStay in 1945) have full authority as regards team selection? But it was not until the start of the 1948–49 season – after an inglorious brush with relegation the previous spring and a continuing trophy famine on all fronts – that a new beginning was heralded. Although recovery from the doldrums of the wartime and immediate post-war slump would continue to be painfully slow and stuttering, a key step was taken with the appointment of Jimmy Hogan as first-team coach in August 1948. Hogan was renowned throughout Europe for his coaching talent, and his recruitment was an imaginative move (for once) on the part of the Celtic board. The task facing him was a daunting one, however, as Hogan himself soon realised after initially telling the press that he felt he had come to his spiritual home (in a footballing sense). He confided to a *Daily Record* journalist that he sensed an air of suspicion, if not hostility, among his new charges, as if they thought, 'What can this old codger show us?' (Significantly, it was the chairman, Bob Kelly – not manager Jimmy McGrory – who introduced Hogan to the players.)

Hogan was actually quite shocked to find that the distinctive, short-passing style of play he had imbibed from his Scottish team-mates when he was a professional at Fulham in the early years of the century – and which he later propounded as a coach in Holland, Austria and Hungary – had all but disappeared in the land of its birth. By the time Celtic employed him, the club was perceived to be relying far more on sheer effort and desperation than the trickery and craft for which the Celtic name had in former days been renowned. Indeed, in the previous few seasons Celtic had resorted to an uncharacteristically 'physical' approach which had drawn adverse comment in the press. But despite the shortage of real talent at his disposal, Hogan enjoyed some initial success in getting the team to put into practice his belief in controlled passing and methodical approach work.

Tom Campbell (now resident in Edinburgh) recalls the impact of the new coach:

> Hogan was a tremendous figure in football, and the signs of his arrival were evident in various ways on the field: defenders trying to pass the ball, the use of the goalkeeper to start attacks, innovations at free-kicks, and a dramatic improvement in the play of Bobby Evans. Unfortunately some of the more senior players largely ignored Hogan. After he left, Celtic began to deteriorate again. There was little method in their play. We would enjoy territorial advantage in every game, but lacked penetration until Mochan came in 1953.

In addition to the appointment of Hogan, the club had also made a significant foray into the transfer market. The brilliant if somewhat wayward English inside-forward Wilf Mannion could not be persuaded to come north, but the name of another inside man – equally brilliant and equally wayward – would soon be on the lips of every Celtic supporter in the country.[5]

CHARLIE TULLY
John Eadie recalls:

> I left school in 1948 and that was when Tully came. That was the change for us – us young ones. My uncles had always talked about the great players from before the war. But Tully – he was something else. That 3–1 game, that was the greatest thing I ever saw. He was fantastic. A great brain he had.

Ask Celtic supporters to name any well-known player for the club from the 1950s and the odds are that most will instantly recall Charlie Tully. Charles Patrick Tully signed for Celtic from their ill-fated Belfast cousins on 28 June 1948 for a reported fee of £8,000. He was in the starting line-up from the beginning of the new season (1948–49) and was instrumental in the winning of Celtic's first post-war trophy, the Glasgow Cup on 27 September 1948 (3–1 versus Third Lanark), watched at Hampden by a record crowd for the tournament of 87,000. But it was his performance in a match played two days previously which made Tully's name in Scottish football. 'Tully dribbled about at will . . .' 'The miraculous Irishman bewildered, badgered . . . mesmerised Rangers. Every time he got the ball . . . three Ibrox men were with him and none dared to tackle . . . he kidded McColl, Cox, anyone who came within his orbit . . . he brought repose to Celtic, panic to Rangers . . . and goals as well.' 'Tully trailed half the Rangers defenders with him, gesticulated to Paton exactly where the pass would go and served him perfectly.' 'There were occasions when the Irishman beat three would-be tacklers in the space of as many yards – and each time by a different manoeuvre. His ability was tantalising, although that did not excuse the lunges made at him.' Tully, whom the *Glasgow Herald* match correspondent praised as 'undoubtedly the cleverest forward in the last ten years of Scottish football', had humiliated Rangers' famed 'Iron Curtain' defence and masterminded Celtic's 3–1 victory, moving Willie Thornton, Rangers' star centre and a fine sportsman, to congratulate the man of the match with the words 'A wonderful game, son'. Tully's was indeed an unforgettable performance, full of footballing 'cheek'. Of course, from then on he would be a marked man.

One of Tully's victims that day, Rangers defender Sammy Cox, would exact a nasty revenge on 'Cheeky Charlie' almost a year later at Ibrox. In another League Cup sectional Old Firm contest – the clubs had been drawn in the same section for the third year running – he and Tully were jockeying for possession on the Rangers byline, and well inside the penalty area. Cox won possession, and turned as if to clear the ball upfield. But in full view of the packed 'Celtic end' contingent in the crowd of 95,000, Cox ignored the ball and landed what looked like a deliberate kick in the upper part of Tully's groin. To the astonishment of the spectators, and the fury of those supporting Celtic, the referee, Mr R.B. Gebbie, not only failed to award a penalty kick but appeared to wave play on. The mood at the Celtic end swiftly changed from the clamorous to the violently indignant, with bottles being thrown, spectators fleeing for cover, and arrests being made. If Celtic and Tully were aggrieved at the referee's decision, they were positively incensed by the actions of the Referee Committee of the SFA, which met a couple of weeks later to consider the incident and the resulting crowd trouble. Its members issued a judgement which blamed both players equally, and ordered identical punishments for both clubs, yet decided to take no disciplinary action against Mr Gebbie. Despite a request from the secretary of the Players' Association, the committee refused to provide a transcript of its proceedings. The *Daily Record* described the committee's actions as 'a shirking of a straightforward duty'. The full Council of the SFA later approved the committee's report by 25 votes to five, despite strenuous protests from Celtic chairman Robert Kelly. Adding insult to injury was a remark by the chairman of the Referee Committee, Mr Angus Forbes (Inverness), which suggested that Tully had been more or less guilty of play-acting. To Tully's folk-hero status among the Celtic support was now added that of a martyr.

Charlie Tully was the principal reason why in the first few months of the 1948–49 season Celtic consistently played to massive attendances. But it wasn't just Charlie's remarkable football skill which attracted the crowds. If ever there was a player for whom the overused title of 'a character' was invented, then Charlie Tully was that player. He possessed a sharp wit both on and off the field, and his sayings (and those inspired by him) were collected as 'Tullyisms'. Tully, indeed, was something of a one-man public relations industry in an era when such a thing was virtually unknown in Britain. As one Parkhead official observed, 'the moment Charlie Tully stepped off the Irish boat, somebody pressed a button and the first Charlie Tully story started circulating. Before he was a week at Celtic Park they were coming off the assembly line faster than Ford cars.'

Like practically everyone else who knew Tully, Sean Fallon has a 'Tullyism' to relate. He chuckles when recalling a Celtic match against Aberdeen in the early 1950s. Tully produced a complimentary admission ticket from the waistband of his playing shorts during a game in which he was getting the better of his immediate opponent, the fearsome full-back Don Emery. He then cheekily handed it to Emery, with the observation, 'Here, would you not be better watching from the stand?' Another Celtic team-mate of Tully's recalls a later occasion when, on entering the foyer at Ibrox, Charlie spotted the home side's captain, Bobby Shearer, dressed in his club's formal blue, white and red blazer, and, with the 'edge' of a man born in the Catholic and Republican heartland of Belfast's Falls Road, remarked, 'Bobby, you look like a Union Jack!' Again in later years, following a match at Ibrox in which Willie Fernie had given Rangers' Sammy Baird the proverbial 'run-around', Baird emerged from the main entrance and looked right and left, prompting Charlie to remark, 'Hey Sammy, if you're looking for Willie Fernie, he's sitting on the Celtic team bus.'

Charlie was always a jester and he got a chance to meet a professional one when he shared a joke with American actor/comedian Danny Kaye before kick-off at the Charity Cup final at Hampden in 1950, in front of another tournament record attendance of 81,000 (who saw Celtic defeat Rangers 3–2 in an entertaining match); he sang along with crooner/film star Bing Crosby on board the SS *Royal Albert* en route to Ostend; and he was among the Celtic party which had an audience with Pope Pius XII in Rome later on that 1950 Continental trip – this last encounter prompting the joke, 'Who's that in the white suit up there with Tully?' In 1958, Pius XII's death coincided with an unexpected recall for Tully to the Northern Ireland international squad. Asked if he was surprised at getting another cap at this late stage in his career, Tully replied, 'Surprised? I was walking down Argyle Street and noticed the newspaper bills. One said "Holy Father Dies in Rome". The other was "Tully Gets Another Honour"!'

Against Aberdeen in the St Mungo Cup final played in the summer of 1951 – the tournament was Glasgow's contribution to the 'Festival of Britain' – the goal which inspired Celtic's fightback resulted from a piece of sharp practice on Tully's part: he grabbed the ball from the hands of the Dons' tough full-back Shaw as it was being handed to him to take a throw-in, then knocked the ball off the defender's back for a corner kick which he took himself. W.M. Gall, writing in the *Scottish Daily Mail*, described Tully's corner-kick-taking in the match as follows: 'The ball, piloted at low trajectories, appeared to have a deceptive turn on it.' When the Irishman placed this one, 'the ball swerved past friend and foe until it reached the uncovered Fallon', leaving the latter with a simple task to net Celtic's opener (match report, 2 August 1951). The winner was scored in mildly controversial circumstances after Tully chipped over a cross from a position which the Aberdeen players claimed lay beyond the byline; referee Jack Mowat would not entertain their plea since he perceived that the linesman had been in a good position to observe the incident. Not that the Dons' complaints would have bothered the bold Bhoy from Belfast. Perceptibly enamoured of the success of his earlier ruse, he was in no mood not to take advantage of every break going.

John Eadie recalls the occasion of Celtic's victory in the summer tournament:

> Now listen, that was the best thing I ever saw. That night there was an Irish dance in the St Mungo's Halls [public halls at the corner of Ballater Street and Moffat Street in the Gorbals] – we all got in, a big crowd of us. We were all singing, all up on the stage. That was a great night. We were all drunk, all on the wine.

Earlier that year, Tully had given another scintillating performance against Raith Rovers in the Scottish Cup semi-final, inspiring Celtic to a dramatic 3–2 win after the Fifers had twice fought back to equalise. In the final, Tully was again on hand as Celtic collected their first major trophy since the war, beating Motherwell 1–0 in a tense and rather disappointing match, the only goal being scored by John McPhail, who had enjoyed an inspired and inspiring campaign at centre-forward. He, along with Tully and the rest of the squad, was mobbed by a near-hysterical mass of

15,000 supporters at Glasgow Central station when they returned in July from a tour of the United States (where they had also shown off the Scottish Cup 20 years previously). Celtic fans, starved of success for so long, were now in an almost uncontrollably exuberant mood, and Tully was, along with McPhail, a principal object of their adulation.

John Eadie recalls:

> At the time of the cup final in '51 I worked in a furniture place, and I asked the boss to let me away early so I could go to the game. So he let me away that day at 12 o'clock instead of working through till 6 o'clock. And John McPhail scored that great goal. We watched the bus coming down with all the players on it with the Scottish Cup after the end of the game. It was fantastic. To see us winning in a final was just fantastic, you know, because Rangers had always won this and won that.

David Potter adds:

> The day of the big gale in 1953 saw me in Wull Neave's barber shop in North Street, Forfar. It was a Saturday afternoon, and as the weather had put paid to the football, the shop was full of men talking about the Scottish obsession. An amiable drunk whom I later got to know quite well was havering away about Celtic and John McPhail – or John Mc-Never-Phail, as he put it.[6] At the age of four and a half, I was intelligent and precocious enough to say that McPhail played for Celtic and that they wore green and white jerseys. 'Nor' Prophet, as the drunk man was called, immediately rewarded me with half a crown [12½ pence] – a colossal sum in those days.

Despite the twin trophy breakthrough of 1951, Celtic struggled to find any consistency in the league championship, and the following two seasons were very disappointing in that respect. However, Tully could still be relied on to provide moments of supreme entertainment. The most legendary of these occurred in a Scottish Cup tie at Falkirk on 21 February 1953 when Celtic fought back from two goals down to win, but only after Charlie had scored direct from a corner kick. That it was no fluke was proved by the fact that the kick in question was a retake, ordered by the referee after Charlie's first effort had also sailed directly into the Falkirk net but been ruled out on account of the ball not having been within the corner arc markings when the kick was taken. Tully had also scored direct from the corner flag the previous year when playing for Northern Ireland against England at Windsor Park, scoring both his side's goals that day in a creditable 2–2 draw. At the start of that match, Charlie asked his would-be marker, Alf Ramsey, whether he enjoyed playing for his country. When the future Sir Alf replied that he did, Charlie retorted, 'Make the most of it today, then – it may be the last chance you get!' Tully proceeded to give the proud Englishman something of a roasting.

Roy McGuinness, formerly of Glasgow, now resident in Cambridge, Ontario, recalls the Tully magic – and the Tully foibles:

> I'd say the greatest player I have ever seen would be Charlie Tully. Even with very ordinary players around him, he made them look good. At the same time, I don't know how he would last, or if he would last, with the rules today, as he could be quite dirty and did things like shy a ball off an opponent's back because nobody else was up for the throw. At Brockville in the Scottish Cup, I saw him score direct from a corner, being made to retake it, and scoring again. Then there was the Sammy Cox–Charlie Tully incident – Sammy was a hard-tackling full-back but Charlie could be one of the greatest actors of his day. They often had their scuffles, those two, but on that particular day, the bottles rained down from the Celtic end.

Tom Campbell, a noted Celtic historian, has similar recollections of the player:

> One of Charlie Tully's team-mates described him as a player who never wasted a ball. He never tried anything outrageous and failed at it. Sometimes he would deliver a pass with a scissors-kick, but the pass was completed and he never fell flat on his face attempting it.
>
> Charlie would be guilty of a stream of silly, petulant fouls in a game, and then he'd dribble up the wing and cross the ball for the winning goal. In some ways he was a symbol of Celtic's lack of professionalism in that era – he was a poor trainer, by all accounts.

Tully always seemed to reserve something extra for games against Rangers: 'The man who made most of the difference to Celtic was . . . Tully. Sometimes his trickery ends in the deception of himself and his team-mates, but when he uses the ball, he really uses it. As he prepares to cross or pass he seems to say, "Put your head and foot to scoring position and I'll not be an inch out with the ball"' (*Glasgow Herald* report on Celtic 3 Rangers 2, 23 September 1950); 'So long as such immaculate ball-players as Thornton and Tully are permitted to display their skill, a game cannot be dull' (*Glasgow Herald* report on Celtic 2 Rangers 1, 20 September 1952); 'Tully made an auspicious return to the Celtic team, and frequently baffled his immediate opponent McColl with dexterous footwork and sprayed inviting passes all around' (*Glasgow Herald* report on Rangers 1 Celtic 1, 19 September 1953); 'The Tully–Collins wing began the match brilliantly. In 19 minutes, Tully's magnificent ball control and pass to the unmarked Collins brought Celtic's goal' (*Glasgow Herald* report on Celtic 1 Rangers 1, 24 September 1955); 'It was manifest that Tully can still be the architect of victory if he has colleagues who can capitalise on the scoring opportunities he can contrive' (*Glasgow Herald* report on Rangers 2 Celtic 0, 19 August 1957). Charlie was to save something special for his penultimate appearance in an Old Firm match in October 1957 . . .

By the mid-1950s Tully was considered to be at the veteran stage. Age and injury had slowed his pace, but he was still an entertainer of note. As had often been the case, though, there was a histrionic streak to some of his play which didn't always help Celtic when the chips were down. His love of teasing his opponents, of inviting the rash challenge, of regarding the rules of the game as mere roadblocks to be ingeniously circumvented and then theatrically pleading innocence when sanctioned – all were part of the Tully act. His was a talent stamped by a highly individual brand of gamesmanship. It was hugely entertaining to the ordinary punter who delighted in Tully's ability to wind up opponents as well as beat them. And, of course, it was hugely entertaining to Tully himself.

Yet the 'Clown Prince of Soccer' had, it seemed, less to smile about in the summer of 1957 insofar as his future as a Celtic player was concerned. Although his popularity as a personality had shown no signs of waning, and his number-one fan, Moira Gallacher – a Donegal-born Glasgow bus conductress who had collected over 300 photographs of the genial Irishman – maintained that 'Celtic just aren't Celtic without Charlie', he was being written off by many among the Celtic support. Two of them, both Glasgow-based, wrote letters to the *Sunday Post* to advocate that he no longer be regarded as an indispensable member of the first team. Tully had, of course, been absent through illness and injury at various times in his Celtic career, and by the mid-1950s his appearances had become somewhat intermittent and his form variable. In the 21 July 1957 issue of that popular 'Sunday', a Mr McTear of Dalton Street, Parkhead, suggested that the veteran 'would be valuable to the second team' (i.e. the reserves), while a Mr Hughes of Preston Street, Govanhill, called for the dropping of the two 'tanner ba'' players, Fernie and Tully. Fortunately, Tully was determined to answer his critics and, buoyed by being restored to something approaching full fitness after ridding himself of the persistent leg troubles which had bothered him over the previous couple of seasons, he rediscovered his impish skills at the start of the 1957–58 season, once again confounding opponents with his knack of producing the unusual and the unexpected. 'He is back', said one writer 'to being the brains of the attack' – sometimes, as so often in the past, one move ahead of his team-mates. He now established himself at outside-right, a berth left vacant by the talented but luckless John Higgins, who had been put out of contention by a nagging knee injury (which, sadly, soon forced his premature retirement from the game). Tully seized the opportunity afforded by Higgins's misfortune, and it was from the latter's erstwhile position that he would play his part in Rangers' terrible downfall in October.

Always a 'chatterbox' on the field of play, Charlie was not slow to give his opinions off it either. He nursed a strong sense of grievance about the conditions of employment for professional footballers of his generation. He revealed that Celtic at the time (the late 1950s) paid their first-team players a basic wage of £16 per week, with a £3 bonus for a win, and 30 shillings (£1.50) for a draw. In comparison, labourers were earning around £10 per week, with the chance of making that up to £15 with overtime. But – as Tully was quick to point out – the average working chap didn't have to 'dress the part,' as was required of footballers constantly in the public eye. 'The men who are cheered on that glamorous football field are probably in as much of a financial struggle as anyone else,' wrote Tully in 1958. Had he still been around four decades later, one can only imagine what his thoughts would have been on the pay-scales and bonuses prevalent at the top level of the senior game.

A CUP OF DESTINY

At the end of the 1952–53 season, Celtic and their supporters were very much back in the doldrums. They had lost out to Rangers in the Scottish Cup at Ibrox following Tully's tricks at Brockville, and had played very poorly in the second half of the season to finish eighth in the league table. Since the happy days of the spring and summer of 1951, key players, particularly John McPhail, had been plagued by fitness problems, and the forward-line permutations were becoming ever more numerous. The habit had grown up among the support of referring to some of the less successful combinations as the 'Five Sorrowful Mysteries', and the search for a consistent strike-force was to become a recurring headache throughout the decade. In seasons 1951–52 and 1952–53 the outside-right spot had been occupied at different times by Bobby Collins, Jock Weir, Jackie Millsopp, Jimmy Walsh, Tony Hepburn, Willie Fernie, Alex Rollo and John McDonald; at inside-right were fielded Walsh, Donald Weir, Collins, Alec Boden, Bertie Peacock, Jock Weir and Bobby Evans; at centre-forward there was McPhail, Jock Weir, John McAlindon, Gil Heron, Jim Lafferty, Sean Fallon, Jimmy McIlroy, McDonald, Frank Whyte and John McGrory. The left-wing partnership was more consistent, Peacock and Tully usually getting the nod, injury permitting; but those positions also saw McPhail, Fernie and Walsh as occasional occupants. The fans were in despair of a consistent scorer, particularly in the centre-forward position. At last the board acted, and Neil 'Smiler' Mochan was purchased from Middlesbrough in May 1953, having been bought by the Teessiders from Morton two years previously for the then considerable sum of

£14,000. Celtic brought him back to Scotland for the more modest figure of £8,000, and his impact was immediate.

He was fielded in the Charity Cup final against Queen's Park at Hampden and he was an instant success, scoring twice to help Celtic overcome the 'Spiders' before a healthy crowd of 40,600, many of whom had come out to see the man they recalled scoring a hat-trick for Morton at Celtic Park in the league opener to the 1950–51 season.

Tom Campbell recalls:

> Celtic were desperate for a centre-forward, and Mochan was signed in time for the Coronation Cup. It was reportedly one of the few occasions when Bob Kelly's wishes were overruled. Kelly, however, repeatedly over the next few seasons was able to have Mochan dropped – with calamitous consequences. I have a theory about that: there was a rumour, as I recall, that Neil Mochan had supposedly been fined a small sum for failing to have a valid radio licence – and so Kelly felt vindicated on 'moral' grounds for disliking Mochan. Bob Kelly could be a self-righteous, unforgiving so-and-so!

Despite the consolation of an end-of-season win in one of the lesser competitions, Celtic fans were not too confident about their side's chances in a tournament which had been arranged to celebrate Queen Elizabeth's coronation. The press were not shy in suggesting that Celtic had only been invited because of their drawing power, and even hinted darkly at the possibility of a humiliating outcome for the Parkhead club. The other teams were all much stronger on paper. Rangers had just completed the 'Double'. Hibs had won the league championship three times in recent seasons. Aberdeen were on their way to building a side which would soon be one of the strongest in Scotland. Against the pride of Scotland was ranged the might of England: Newcastle United, winners of the FA Cup in 1951 and 1952, as well as Manchester United, Tottenham Hotspur and Arsenal, all formidable sides in the English game at that time. Yes, and all much stronger than Celtic on paper – but then, football is played on grass.

Celtic, drawn to play Arsenal in the first round, surprised everyone with a confident display which brought a more convincing win than the 1–0 scoreline suggested. In the other first-round matches, Rangers had fallen to Manchester United, while Hibs had beaten Spurs after a replay and Newcastle had defeated Aberdeen. In the semi-final Celtic produced another remarkably good performance, with Tully in top form, to dispose of the Old Trafford side by 2–1, Peacock scoring a memorable opening goal from a Tully cut-back. The other Celtic scorer was Mochan, with Tully again the provider. With Hibs having destroyed Newcastle by 4–0 at Ibrox in the other semi-final, the stage was now set for an all-green-and-white clash at Hampden on 20 May 1953. In a famous match, Neil Mochan scored a fantastic goal from 30 yards in the first half, and Celtic goalkeeper John Bonnar produced a fabulous display in the second period when Hibs' 'Famous Five' forward line of Smith, Johnstone, Reilly, Turnbull and Ormond threw everything at him. The crowd of just over 117,000 roared in appreciation of the titanic struggle and the inspired play of Bonnar, yet it seemed impossible that Celtic could hold out against the constant pressure on their goal. But hold out they did, and Jimmy Walsh sealed a marvellous and entirely unexpected triumph three minutes from time. The win was achieved despite Tully's enforced absence through injury, but a most capable deputy on the night was Willie Fernie, involved in the build-up to both Celtic's goals.

Hughie Corbett, now resident in Australia, recounts his memories of the occasion:

> This all takes me back over 40 years to when I was a mere lad of 13 summers, playing fitba' in the back streets of Bridgeton, about 200 yards from Bridgeton Cross. As I was to find out later on, this was the throbbing heart of not only Rangers, but the 'Brigton Billy Boys' – not the best place for a wee St Mary's bhoy to be seen in green! (Yes, the same St Mary's where, in 1888 [some sticklers for historical accuracy say 1887], Brother Walfrid started something even he could not have imagined would become a household name in all four quarters of the globe. To think I stood in the very same room as this famous man!) Anyway, back to that day playing in the street. Me and my pals got caught up in a mob of big, big men covered in green, white and gold (giants, they looked to me). They were on their way to Hampden to see the 'Tic play in a cup final, singing and talking at a hundred miles an hour about this and that player, how it was destiny that they would win this cup, because they were famous for winning 'one-off' cups, and hadn't they won the last one? Someone mentioned the Empire Cup, and at that time the only thing I knew about Empire was the biscuit of that name from the City Bakeries (I used to wallop intae them).
>
> To our tale. Unlike today, kids had nothing to fear from adults sporting their team colours, be it green, blue, red or tartan (except if you went a message fur the man doon the sterr, you only got thruppence instead o' a tanner [6d, or 2½ pence], if you hid on yer Celtic scarf). We walked across Glasgow Green to the [St Andrew's] Suspension Bridge, still singing. By the time we tramped up Polmadie Road to Hampden, I didn't know then that this was the start of me being a dyed-in-the-wool 'Tim'. Then a shock – you had to pay to get in! (2 shillings [10 pence], I think.) But, have no fear, the Celts are here – before I knew it, two huge arms lifted me up and put me over the bar [turnstile]. 'Thanks, mister,' I said. 'No problem, son,' said he. 'Nae

point paying tae watch yer team get walloped,' and he proudly walked away with that swagger that any 'Tim' would recognise. By now you will have gathered I was about to see the Bhoys win the Coronation Cup. To be honest, I don't remember much of the game – my memories are of grown men swearing, foaming at the mouth, blaming the ref. And then going wild at the final whistle – that I will never forget! Not to mention the odd tanner and shilling that came my way. Best of all was the green and white scarf someone wrapped round my neck, which I had for years, and had to hide in my secret plank, because my Dad was a 'Hun' – now there's another story worth the telling!

John Eadie recalls:

My brother Eddie and I went to the Rangers v. Man United game. At Hampden, in amongst all the Rangers fans! Rangers scored first, and the crowd went crazy. Then my brother Eddie starts shouting, 'Come on Rangers, intae these people,' and all that – pretending to be a Rangers fan he was, so we wouldn't get found out. Then Man United scored – he wanted to shout, but had to shut up. Anyway, United won 2–1. As we were coming out the ground, the Rangers fans were all saying, 'Och, this Manchester United team will kill Celtic on Saturday, they'll kill them.' And we just murmured to ourselves, 'Aye, so they will.' Then we went to Hampden on the Saturday. My God, that Bertie Peacock goal – that was something else!

Edmund Burns (Glasgow) recalls:

In 1953 I was going out with my future wife and I had promised to accompany her in making a Novena devotion, which meant going to St Columba's Church on Hopehill Road for nine consecutive Wednesdays. I went to the Arsenal and Manchester United games, but the final against Hibs was the night of the last Novena devotion in honour of Our Lady. I kept my promise and missed the game. Maybe that's why we won!

FANS IN THE '50S

If one listens to the radio commentary of the Coronation Cup final, one is immediately struck by the sounds of the crowd. The cheers and roars sound quite familiar to modern ears, reflecting the ebb and flow of the game. One is especially impressed by the awesome roar which acclaims Mochan's thunderbolt of a goal, scored at the 'Celtic' end at Hampden where the terraces were dangerously overcrowded in the bright evening sunlight.

Short clips of film and some photographs are all the visual evidence we have to go on when examining the nature of football crowds in the 1950s. It is easy to get the impression that they were largely a staid, respectable lot, dressed rather formally in heavy grey coats draped over shirts and ties, and the impression of staidness is reinforced by the black and white imagery. Certainly clothing today is much more colourful than it was in the 1950s – bright red parkas or multicoloured T-shirts were basically unknown then. Many fans of the older generation had gone to matches in the pre-war years wearing the then universally fashionable 'bunnets', and they saw no reason in the post-war years to change the habit of a lifetime. Younger men in the 1950s, however, generally went bareheaded to football matches, despite only the slightest improvements in protection at football grounds from the notoriously inclement Scottish weather. Scarves in the team colours were certainly worn, although they were not quite as common as they were to become in the 1960s and subsequently. At Scottish Cup matches especially, some fans would sport coloured rosettes (some of them homemade), and supporters often chose to wear clothes in colours which suggested in a mild way their allegiances. The effect at an Old Firm game, for example, was that one end of the ground took on a blue hue from the many blue-coloured items of clothing – ties, shirts, raincoats, handkerchiefs and sweaters – while a corresponding fashion statement would be made at the other end, only in various shades of green.

John Eadie recalls:

> When a goal was scored, everybody went forward. They all pushed forward. The kids at the front always got it. And the bottles, too, because they never landed on the park, they always hit the kids at the front. I had bottles nearly hit me a couple of times when I was a youngster.

Celebrations of important goals were certainly noisy, as the audiotape of the Coronation Cup final proves. And pieces of film still survive which show Celtic supporters reacting at Hampden to John McPhail's winning goal in the 1951 Scottish Cup final, to his and Tully's goals in the 3–0 win over Aberdeen at Celtic Park in an earlier Scottish Cup tie that same season, and again when Neil Mochan's deflected shot opened the scoring in the 1954 Scottish Cup final. In all three clips of film, the impression given is recognisable to the modern fan – arms rising in a sudden jolt, punching the air; certain individuals leaping up and beginning a celebratory dance; the packed terracings (the crowds at each of these matches strained ground capacity) convulsed in the moment of joyous release. But one also gets the impression that the celebrations were not quite as uniformly demonstrative as they became in later decades. One factor in this is that there was undoubtedly a far larger proportion of older fans at matches in the 1950s, men in their fifties, sixties and seventies, who were less given to jumping into the arms of their neighbour and hugging each other in a mad dance of delight. They were more likely to content themselves with a hearty round of applause and loud cries of approval. Another factor was probably the lack of television coverage of fans' displays of affection for their favourites. Football supporters in the 1950s had little experience of watching themselves (and the supporters of rival teams) act out the rituals of support and celebration which television later communicated to a mass audience. Hence, there was less of a stimulus for one set of fans to imitate the behaviour patterns of another set. This was particularly relevant to the relative lack of mass chanting and singing at Scottish football matches in the '50s. The practice certainly existed, but was less prominent in those days.

Old Firm matches, however, were then, as now, a category apart. Since both sets of supporters had ample opportunity to observe the 'enemy ranks' in action, there was a good deal of rivalry in terms of singing and display of colours. Such practices were officially frowned upon, and the *Glasgow Herald* newspaper in particular waged something of a campaign against behaviour it perceived to be sectarian and liable to provoke violence. The following excerpts from that paper's reports of Old Firm matches of the period convey both the concerns felt and the crowd atmosphere which gave rise to them:

> The result being of less moment than the manner in which it was achieved, Rangers would have been wholly satisfied with their draw had they not been let down by some of their supporters. It would not, of course, have been an 'Old Firm' match, had everything in the garden been lovely. Rangers had commendably made it clear in the press and in their programme that such things as banners, party-tune singing and foul language would not be tolerated . . .
>
> The outcome was almost incredible, for even when Collins scored his magnificent goal in 21 minutes there was not a sign of a banner associated with Celtic, and yet before and throughout the match there was considerable vaunting of flags at the Rangers followers' end of the ground. We do not know all the party tunes, but we have heard some in the past from Celtic supporters. On Saturday we strained our ears in vain to catch a note in praise of Erin's green valleys, but no extra effort was necessary to pick out from the clamour at the Copland Road end the old Ibrox lyrics. From beneath the orange and blue and Union Jack the faithful promised over and over again to guard old Derry's walls and to follow, follow, even unto Dublin.
>
> Only the waving of a myriad of green and white scarves, a bout of slow hand-clapping that mingled derision almost with dignity and, at

half-time, the necessarily slight variation in the promises to follow, follow, denoted the opposition's disfavour. Thus was the battle of behaviour clearly won by the Celtic crowd, some of whose components in the past have been decisively out-pointed. (*Glasgow Herald* report on Rangers 1 Celtic 1, 22 September 1951)

The disgraceful behaviour of a small section of the 40,000 crowd at Celtic Park almost succeeded in spoiling the pleasure of the vast majority, who could not possibly have expected to see so exhilarating and so skilful a display of football as both teams – and Rangers in particular – provided on a ground that was a sea of melting snow and mud.

When hundreds of spectators were scrambling on the track and even for a moment encroaching on the playing pitch, the players continued to act as if nothing were happening to distract their attention. It is to the great credit of all of them that nothing happened on the field which could have been construed as provocative of the hooliganism at the Celtic supporters' end of the ground. (*Glasgow Herald* report on Celtic 1 Rangers 4, 1 January 1952)[7]

Tully, whose first-half foul on Young was the only annoying infringement, was the man who rallied his side late in the second half through his ability to hold the ball. 'We want Tully,' the Rangers' end had shouted after the Young incident. They may have been sorry, for they probably got more of him than they wished. (*Glasgow Herald* report on Celtic 2 Rangers 1, 20 September 1952)

Policemen on the track and terracing were even more prominent than usual and for the first time in my recollection an appeal was made before the start of the match by the police authorities that banners and provocative emblems should not be flaunted. That appeal was unsuccessful, for Union Jacks and Orange flags were observed at one end of the ground and Eire tricolours – for a section of the Celtic supporters have resumed their ill-advised ways – at the other. The sash was worn a thousand times and the green valleys of Erin traversed just as often, but there was even less happy harmony than there has ever been in the segregated crowd: one felt that the volcano would erupt at any moment. Such are the depths to which we have sunk. (*Glasgow Herald* report on Rangers 2 Celtic 0, 14 March 1953)

The attendance at the Glasgow Charity Cup first-round tie between Celtic and Rangers at Hampden Park was only 44,000 and it is interesting that Scottish football officials are attributing the smallness of the crowd to the fact that the English Cup final could be seen on television in Scotland . . . The average Celtic supporter does not miss his club's game in fine conditions of weather such as applied on Saturday; no more does he treat a game with Rangers as of less importance than others. Rangers too have tens of thousands of supporters who did not attend the Charity Cup tie – and there are many of no allegiance to either club who would not have stayed away had they had any form of guarantee that there would be no trouble.

Celtic and Rangers cannot afford to do without the patronage of all three classes. They can afford, however, to do without the banner-wavers and the sectarian-song singers who enjoyed another afternoon unmolested by the authorities . . . Some will say that fortunately the football season is over and that passions will have cooled during the recess. That may be so, but they will become heated again. Not a day should be lost in exploring every means of eradicating the hooligan element. If that is not done we had better announce that admission to games in which Celtic and Rangers play will be by banner and through ability to voice hatred only, and admit that a few hundred hooligans can hold the city to ransom. (*Glasgow Herald* report on Celtic 0 Rangers 1, 1 May 1954)

Many of the followers of Rangers and Celtic stayed away because of dissatisfaction with their teams' form, but many more were absent because of the risks attached to attending a match between the clubs. Though there was the usual display by ignoramuses at either end of the ground of colours which are not those of the competing teams, and though the repertoire of the age-old sectarian songs was employed to the full, that was the extent, as far as could be seen, of bad behaviour inside the ground, except for one case of a spectator at the Rangers supporters' end compelling the police to make an arrest.

Outside the ground at the end of the match, there was an outbreak of bottle-throwing – the more serious in that it seemed to be indiscriminate and caused casualties amongst those who were not members of the rival factions. Such disorder is the reason for the absence of so many football followers. (*Glasgow Herald* report on Celtic 2 Rangers 0, 18 September 1954)

Some folks got their fingers burned on Saturday at Ibrox Stadium – the fanatics who, a few minutes before the kick-off, set alight a green flag amid the circling Union Jacks . . . Twenty minutes before the end of the match, having suffered a humiliation as never before, the hard core of spectators who disgrace the club they follow had gone, the colours they misappropriate and the musical instruments they favour having vanished more quickly even than the flag that had been burned at the stake as a heretic, as was, of Hibernian lore, the famous flute. (*Glasgow Herald* report on Rangers 1 Celtic 4, 27 August 1955)

Of course, trouble at Old Firm matches was nothing new in the 1950s. Celtic Park had been closed for a month following crowd disturbances involving Celtic fans at Ibrox in September 1941, and there had been fierce clashes too in the inter-war years, with a peak of 120 arrests at a 1936 Old Firm game.[8] What is interesting about these *Herald* reports, however, is that the disapproval extends almost as strongly to sectarian chanting and flag-waving as to acts of physical violence. But the newspaper's campaign for better behaviour went largely unheeded and, if anything, the ferocity of the rivalry between followers of the two clubs grew only more intense in subsequent decades.

Despite the often bitter atmosphere surrounding the Celtic–Rangers rivalry, John Eadie remembers how Old Firm fans in the '50s could also experience a state of 'peaceful coexistence'. (This catch-phrase was popularised by then Soviet leader Khrushchev in reference to a hoped-for soothing of Cold War tensions.) Mr Eadie recollects, though, that there were indeed also one or two individuals of less pacific temperament:

I was born in 103 Florence Street, Glasgow – in the Gorbals, two closes away from where Benny Lynch was born. My mother's family was all Irish, O'Mearas, Boyles and Kellys. My grandparents came over from Ireland. My uncle Eddie and my uncle Tommy, they were real Celtic supporters. I don't remember my first game, but one I do remember concerned another bloke, a Rangers supporter who was the same age as my brother George. His name was Bobby Quinn. His father used to deliver coal all over the Gorbals. And George took him – a Rangers supporter, mind – to a Celtic game at Parkhead. George said, 'Come on, we'll go doon tae the front' – so that they could see better. Well, Bobby Hogg [Celtic's right-back] hit him, this crazy Rangers supporter Bobby Quinn, with the ball, right in the face! Ha ha ha! I'll always remember my brother George talking about that. The Quinns were all Rangers-daft, despite the name. They used to go on the [Orange] Walk and everything. And Bobby Hogg hit this lad Quinn in the face with the ball!

There was never any trouble, mind. They were all pals, Celtic and Rangers fans, even with girls and that; they would even mix at the dances. If you met a girl at a dance, she wouldn't ask you what school you went to, she would just ask what team you supported, and vice versa with them. All the fellas that we went about with, the guys at the corner of Florence Street and Rutherglen Road – there were half a dozen guys among them who were Rangers supporters: the Mackays, the Goldfarbs, the McCormicks. We were all buddies with them, and there was never any trouble with them, you know. We'd talk about the game afterwards. Near where we stayed in Florence Street was the Adelphi Street school – that was the Protestant school. That's where we used to pick up all the good-looking young girls!

The Mackays, they were all Rangers supporters, except for the youngest, David – all his buddies were Celtic supporters, so he became a Celtic supporter. But his older brother 'Dandy' used to wallop him because he wore a green and white jersey. 'Dandy' Mackay, he was one of the hardest men in the Southside. Talking of hard men from the Southside, there was another guy called Louie Kerr. Louie Kerr was Celtic-crazy. He used to go to Friday-night games, junior games – Cambuslang Rangers – and go into the 'Rangers' end and fight with them! I'm no kidding, Louie was crazy. I remember the Friday night before the 7–1 game. We were all at the corner. Louie came along. He said, 'Are you guys ready fur tomorrow? We'll get into these b*******!' We all said, 'Aye, okay Louie.' And as he was leaving, he said, 'Right, I'll see youse here tomorrow at 1.30 p.m., and we'll go right up to the game – and don't forget yer cutlery!' Louie had bayonets and everything, he stood there showing us all. He was mad – I mean, anyone who'd go to a Cambuslang Rangers game and fight with them all just because they were 'Rangers' – ha ha ha! But he was a real hard man, Louie was. We kept away from him the next day.

SEAN FALLON

If Celtic fans today were asked who scored the winning goal in a match which completed Celtic's first league and cup 'Double' in 40 years, it would be interesting to see how many would get the right answer. Some might be able to identify the year as 1954, and some might even recall that the match in question was that season's Scottish Cup final against Aberdeen, won 2–1 by Celtic; but few, one suspects, could name the scorer of the crucial winning goal. It was, in fact, none other than that wholehearted Celt from Sligo (and with the accent to prove it!), Sean Fallon.

David Potter recalls:

> In 1954 I remember my father listening anxiously to the Scottish Cup final on the radio. At one point Johnnie Bonnar saved from Paddy Buckley [Aberdeen's centre-forward] and I slid along the linoleum floor to show how it was done, to the disapproval of my tense father. I was allowed that night, however, to lift the teacup in an imitation of what captain Jock Stein would have done earlier that afternoon.

The difficulty many fans would experience in answering this question points to the self-effacing, wholly team- and club-oriented spirit which Fallon typified (and still does – he enjoys rude good health at the age of

75). In the current era, when the mentality of many players resembles more that of bankers, lawyers, marketing executives and accountants than that of 'good club servants' who play 'for the jersey', Sean Fallon represents a throwback to a bygone and in many ways more wholesome age in professional football. Nor did Sean favour night-time adventures 'on the town', or run-ins with the law. And few players were even less puffed up with self-importance, few less inclined to seek the limelight, and fewer still were more devoted to the cause than this iron-hard full-back and occasional centre-forward.

After spells with various junior clubs in Ireland and then with Sligo Rovers, Sean signed for Celtic from Glenavon on 21 March 1950. The story goes that Joe McMenemy, son of Celtic legend Jimmy (aka 'Napoleon'), saved Sean's sister from drowning in Lough Gill while on holiday in Sligo. Joe and his friends were invited to the Fallon household, and the bond was sealed when McMenemy later sent a copy of Willie Maley's book, *The Story of the Celtic*, and a Celtic jersey. (There may have been a touch of pre-destiny about the gesture, for Fallon, like Maley, was the son of a man who served in the British Army.)

When Fallon joined the Bhoys, he was four months short of his 28th birthday. At that age, few thought that he would be anything more than a stop-gap in a Celtic side still struggling to emerge from the post-war shadows. And, looking back, it is neither disrespectful nor dismissive of Fallon's contribution as a player to agree with his own assessment of his capabilities: 'I was just an ordinary player with only a big heart and a fighting spirit to recommend me.' This remark echoes that of his team-mate and later colleague in management Jock Stein, who, speaking of his own playing ability, once chuckled for the cameras, 'I was ordinary, *very* ordinary as a player.' In many ways the Celtic careers of these two men would be intertwined. Stein was the captain of the 'Double'-winning side of '54, while Fallon was The Big Man's right-hand man in Lisbon and throughout the glory years. Sean bore not the slightest bitterness at not getting the manager's position in 1965, even though he had been groomed for the role by Bob Kelly. When Stein was badly injured in a car crash, it was Sean who took over (sadly, without success). Probably no one in the world of football got a closer insight into what made Jock Stein tick than Sean Fallon. As a Celt to the core of his being, Sean knew more than most what Stein had meant for Celtic.

In addition to that winning goal in the 1954 cup final (struck home from a Fernie cut-back after 63 minutes), Sean made a valuable contribution at right-back in the 1951 final against Motherwell. Sadly he missed out on the Coronation Cup triumph of 1953, but he had already led the line effectively in another 'one-off' triumph, the St Mungo Cup victory on 1 August 1951. His performance at centre-forward in the final against Aberdeen before a Hampden crowd of 81,000, when Celtic came from 2–0

53

down to win 3–2 with Sean bagging a brace, caused Willie Maley, who attended the match at the age of 83, to comment, 'He was out of position but has the same never-say-die spirit as Jimmy Quinn.'

Sean Fallon's courage was never in doubt and he sustained a total of five injuries to his left arm – once completing a match at Brockville despite a fracture – as well as a broken collarbone against Hearts on 24 October 1953. This kept him out of the championship-seeking team until St Patrick's Day 1954, when he returned at centre-forward and celebrated with a goal in a 6–0 demolition of Airdrie at Broomfield. Fallon kept his place for the final six league matches, all of which Celtic won, aided by a further four goals from the Irishman. This run saw Celtic come from behind to beat Hearts in the title race. Then came the cup final against the Dons, and Fallon's winning goal. But Sean was not really a striker, and he eventually reverted to his more accustomed role as a full-back. His most consistent performances were reserved for the left-back slot where his best partner was probably Mike Haughney. But among Sean's 14 goals in 254 appearances for the club were several of the most important in Celtic's slow recovery from the doldrums of the 1940s. The league championship and Scottish Cup won in 1953–54 with Fallon's help would be the last such honours gained by the club until the appointment of the man who captained the 'Double'-winning side – Jock Stein – as manager in 1965.

At full-back Sean Fallon was a hard, enthusiastic but generally fair tackler – although on one occasion he was so incensed by the cynical fouling committed by Rangers' Sammy Baird that he gave Baird an even stronger dose of his own medicine with a crashing tackle that left the Ibrox man prone on the turf and the Ibrox partisans in uproar on the terracing. His uncompromising and singularly courageous displays for Celtic helped bolster the defence with much-needed 'dig' and 'bite'. He was the quintessentially unyielding defender, who provided solidity to the Celtic rearguard for most of the decade. One of his playing contemporaries remembers him as 'someone you could depend upon to head the ball off the line when your goalkeeper was beaten'.

At the start of the 1957–58 season, Sean was enjoying the most carefree period in his seven-year career at Parkhead, in stark contrast to the accumulation of injuries which had dogged him in earlier years. These had included, in addition to his series of left arm and collar-bone injuries, a broken nose, a broken ankle bone and torn knee ligaments. Sean's arm breaks were so severe that had it not been for the fact that his body had a high level of calcium – an agent which helps fractured limbs to knit – he would have already been finished with football well before the League Cup final of October 1957. During the previous season (1956–57) he had undergone an operation on a cyst behind the knee which left him with 12 stitches. Not for nothing was he nicknamed 'The Iron Man', although the sportswriter Malcolm Munro must have suffered a momentary alliterative aberration when he dubbed the player 'The Sligo Slasher'. Munro's ripe prose continued: 'He chews bolts and spits rust. He's a rarin' tearin' son of a gun that all the injuries in the game can't hold down . . . He's got the hide of a rhinoceros, an appetite like a horse, the heart of a lion, and the stamina of a marathon runner' (*Evening Citizen*, 19 September 1957). Notwithstanding the overwritten figures of speech, Sean Fallon was one player Celtic fans could believe would run through a brick wall for the club. Perhaps it was because Celtic had been founded by a fellow Sligo man.

SCOTTISH FOOTBALL IN THE *1950s*

Having won their first 'Double' in 40 years in 1954, Celtic came close to repeating the feat just one season later. In 1954–55 they had the misfortune to finish second to Aberdeen in the league table despite improving on their title-winning points total of the previous year, and then lost to Clyde in the Scottish Cup final after a replay. The first match – which was the first Scottish Cup final to be televised live – was one Celtic should have won before half-time, but they had only a one-goal lead as the final whistle approached. Clyde's Archie Robertson took a corner kick on the right, and the ball hung in the air and then scraped John Bonnar's fingertips before turning and falling into the net. This was the first in a catalogue of disasters which would befall Celtic teams playing in the Scottish Cup over the next ten years. In the replay, Clyde's Celtic-daft winger Tommy Ring stole away to grab the only goal of the game and take the cup to Shawfield.

The disappointment was mingled with misgivings about the team selection for the replay. Collins had been dropped, possibly because Bob Kelly disapproved of a challenge he had made in the first game on Clyde's goalkeeper. This necessitated a series of changes in the forward line. Fallon was restored at centre-forward, but by now he had lost most of his 'shock value' in that position and in any case lacked match fitness after a long spell out through injury. John McPhail was moved to inside-left, and Jimmy Walsh to the right wing. The changes didn't work. In later Scottish Cup failures, even more bizarre selection decisions would be made to the almost universal dismay of the Celtic support.

David Potter recalls:

> 1955 saw Celtic v. Clyde in the Scottish Cup final. The game was on TV, commentated by Kenneth Wolstenholme (who's still around), and Auntie Norah now had a TV. Walsh scored for Celtic in the first half, and I got a little bored by the second half. I went out to kick a ball around by the back door, but told my father to call me in to see the cup being presented. I thus missed one of the Celtic horror stories, for

Clyde equalised with a late corner kick which my hero John Bonnar completely muffed. No cup was presented that day, and eventually Clyde would win the replay. I thus had an early introduction to the 'bitterness of defeat'.

John Eadie recalls the same bitterness:

In the replay, when Ring scored that goal, I was so sick. I got home quickly, two storeys up in a tenement beside St Luke's church. I went into my room, and my mum said, 'What happened – did ye get beat?', and I said, 'Yeah'. I looked out the window on to Ballater Street, and there was Clyde going by with the Cup, the big bus, holding it up. I very nearly broke the window shouting at them! I was so sick because we had it won on the Saturday, you know? But Tommy Ring scored a good goal, so that was that.

John McKechnie, now resident in Chiswick, London, recalls an incident in the aftermath of the final:

I remember, as a 14-year-old schoolboy attending St Gerard's school in Govan, that Harry Haddock, Clyde's captain and an ex-pupil of the school, came to parade the Scottish Cup after Clyde had beaten Celtic 1–0 in the replay at Hampden – a game which I saw from the terracing. The reception for Haddock, even as captain of Clyde, was cool, to put it mildly, as we were all Celtic-daft, and a few choice words were forthcoming from all quarters at the 'cheek' of this man in showing off the Scottish Cup after having beaten the Bhoys! This was the 1954–55 season. John Bonnar, Celtic's goalkeeper, was delighted that the infamous 'Hampden swirl' [a notoriously deceptive wind which often plagued matches at the national stadium] was blamed for Archie Robertson's last-minute equaliser in the first game, which ended in a 1–1 draw. My father took me to that game as a 13-year-old, and I still remember the fantastic camaraderie which existed amongst football fans in those days.

Every supporters' bus then had a sweep or a raffle for whoever scored the first goal. I was allowed to pick one of the 22 names, and I got the Clyde centre-forward Hill, who duly scored a perfectly good goal which was disallowed as the linesman had seen an infringement that no one else spotted – and of course I was delighted to be on a loser!

Gerard Campbell, now resident in Australia, recalls:

I took the Celtic 'bug' from my father, of course. Recently deceased at 97, he was still a season-ticket-holder at 'Paradise' right up to the end.

He attended his first game in 1904 – a victory for Celtic over Rangers. He was taken by his father and the great tradition has continued with myself taking my own son to the 1994 Ne'erday game (my first game since 1979!). His bedroom here in Sydney is festooned with Celtic 'stuff' . . . however, I digress.

My earliest memories of the '50s are of my father and his brothers disappearing off to a home or away game on a Saturday afternoon – I used to feel an intense sense of disappointment at not being allowed to accompany them. My mother thought that the atmosphere would be too 'rough' for me! However, I could sit for hours listening to them talk about the games or the great Celtic players of the 1920s and '30s. Happy days.

I wasn't even in attendance when I first saw Celtic play. The 1955 Scottish Cup final was, I believe, the first to be televised. TVs were extremely rare in those days and I was taken on the Saturday to visit the only household amongst six aunts and uncles which had a tiny black and white TV! This was a game which Celtic should have won. The score was 1–1 on the Saturday and Clyde won the replay on the Wednesday. My only recollection of a player is the Clyde outside-left – Tommy Ring, a great player and Celtic-daft, who played very well. In the first match Clyde scored direct from a corner. And the second game was the first [Scottish Cup] final replay ever to be lost by Celtic. Celtic missed many, many chances in both games. The first of many disappointments in this era.

Another '50s memory is of yours truly scoring a goal *against* Celtic. We had a summer fete about 1956 out at John Ogilvie Hall [the Jesuit primary school] in Langside. One of the 'sideshows' was Johnny Bonnar in a 'beat the goalie' competition (taking penalty kicks). I was first up, and into the bottom left-hand corner it went like a rocket (that's my story, anyway). Well worth the threepenny bit and a pat on the head from JB. I can still visualise the brilliant yellow of his jersey. Incidentally, when playing football at Langside one had to take care that the ball did not go over the surrounding 'stane dyke'. You would never find anyone to throw it back over and the wee yins' increasingly desperate calls went unanswered – you see, the building behind the wall was a Carmelite convent!

*　　　*　　　*

Clyde's 1955 Scottish Cup success, as well as Aberdeen's in the race for the league title the same season, served to underline the democratic aspect which Scottish football had increasingly assumed since the war. In the inter-war years, Rangers and, to a lesser extent, Celtic had dominated the game in Scotland. Only one league flag left Glasgow during those years, when a fine Motherwell team held on to clinch the championship in 1931–32. In the Scottish Cup, Celtic and Rangers amassed six victories each in the 1920s and 1930s. But it was a different story after the war. Rangers were very strong in the late 1940s, but they were soon credibly challenged by Hibs, while in the latter part of the 1950s Hearts were to show that they too were made of championship-winning material.

The rise of Hearts as a force in Scottish football had already been signalled by their winning of the League Cup in 1954–55 (beating Motherwell in the final), and the Edinburgh side were to give further indication of their intentions and abilities when they defeated Celtic in the 1956 Scottish Cup final, the Maroons' first capture of the nation's premier cup competition in 50 years. In this they were assisted by another series of baffling selection decisions on the part of their opponents. Celtic fielded inexperienced youngsters at right-half and outside-right, played Haughney, normally a full-back, at inside-right, and had Frank Meechan at right-back. Meechan's usual post was on the left side, and, indeed, he was not even a regular choice in that position at the time, the final being only his ninth appearance in the first team that season, and his first since March. With such a weakened and inexperienced right flank, it was no surprise that most of the dangerous play in the final stemmed from Hearts' left-winger Crawford, who netted twice before a crowd in excess of 133,000 to help the Tynecastle side to a 3–1 win. With this victory added to that of Clyde the previous year, the Scottish Cup was fast becoming something of a no-go area for the Old Firm. In the next three seasons, the cup went to Falkirk, Clyde again, and then St Mirren. In two of those seasons, Celtic were defeated semi-finalists, despite having knocked out Rangers in earlier rounds. Bitter disappointments in the semi-final and final stages of the Scottish Cup continued into the early 1960s, with the supporters again and again being left upset by bewildering team selections.

Celtic did manage one enjoyable cup success during this period when they beat Rangers 5–3 in the Glasgow Cup final replay on Boxing Day 1955. The first match had been an entertaining 1–1 draw. The issue was settled by Celtic's introduction of a promising young centre-forward named Jim Sharkey, who scored two, or possibly three, delightful goals and played skilfully throughout (in an interview with *The Celt* fanzine Jim claims a hat-trick). Rangers had a player of an entirely different style leading their attack, the South African Don Kichenbrand (rumoured to have been baptised a Catholic as an infant). The contrast in styles provided plenty of talking points for the supporters, but Celtic's traditional belief in a more refined approach was amply rewarded on the day.

Gerard Campbell remembers that match with good reason:

The first Celtic game I attended in the flesh was the Glasgow Cup final on Boxing Day 1955 – 5–3 to Celtic. Sitting high up in the North Stand at Hampden – what a Christmas present! O magic day! Memories – Rangers' centre-forward Kichenbrand, who was quite appositely nicknamed the 'Rhino', and Celtic's deft Jim Sharkey, who seemed to me to score every time he had the ball. A standing joke in my family was the question I put to my father and uncles on the way home in the tramcar – 'Do Celtic always beat Rangers so easily?' I suppose the '90s equivalent of the reply would be 'Aye, right on, wee yin'. Strangely enough, Sharkey seemed to drift out of the game as a Celtic player shortly after this match. Also, this must have been one of Jock Stein's last games for Celtic. My father contended that Jock's ankle injury sustained around this time, from which he forever thereafter limped, was caused by a particularly bad assault from behind by Max Murray, who played for you know who.

The pluralism affecting the acquisition of trophies in the 1950s was further underlined by the remarkable fact that in the first seven seasons of the decade (including season 1949–50) the League Cup was won by neither Old Firm club, and only once did either of them even reach a final (Rangers in 1951–52). East Fife (twice), Motherwell, Dundee (twice), Hearts and Aberdeen had all won the League Cup before Celtic ever made it to the final. But in season 1956–57 Celtic at last broke their duck in the competition. So regularly had Celtic failed even to qualify from the initial sectional ties in previous years, that the competition was widely regarded as a 'bogey' by the support. Only twice before in ten attempts had the team managed to progress beyond the qualifying sections. In season 1950–51 they had lost badly at home to Motherwell in the quarter-final, eventually going out on a 4–2 aggregate, and the following season they were outplayed by Rangers at the semi-final stage and went down 3–0.

But in the autumn of 1956, Celtic at last made it to the final, having shown commendable coolness in eliminating Rangers in the sectional phase, followed by Dunfermline over two legs in the quarter-final and Clyde in the semi-final. In the final they faced Partick Thistle, a clash watched by less than 60,000 at Hampden Park (the attendance, perhaps, another indication that crowds had begun to decline after the peak years of the late '40s and early '50s). The match was equally disappointing, ending in a no-scoring draw. The replay the following Wednesday was attended by barely 31,000 – a clear sign of dissatisfaction on the part of Celtic's supporters with their side's early league form. However, a quick burst of scoring just after half-time brought three goals to Celtic and the League Cup to 'Paradise' for the first time. Although the new signing from Clyde, Billy McPhail, notched a brace, the man of the match was undoubtedly Tully: 'Charlie was full of running and tricks at outside-right, and he was the one personality of the final who had ideas about making position,' observed Andrew Wallace of the *Scottish Daily Mail*. Wallace was less generous in his appraisal of the Celtic side as a whole, deeming it to be 'probably the poorest team from Parkhead ever to win a national trophy' and describing the replay as being 'as dull as a wet Sunday in Kirkintilloch' (1 November 1956). Despite the breakthrough in a competition which had provided some of Celtic's best and worst moments since the war, the mood was one of anti-climax. That would not be the case the next time the trophy was won . . .

Despite the winning of the League Cup, the Celtic support was in a highly disgruntled mood before the end of the season. The club's management had become notorious for continually chopping and changing the team formation, and the promise of the Coronation Cup and 'Double'-winning years had not been sustained or fulfilled. The frustration felt among the support was such that the manager, Jimmy McGrory, and the directors were roundly abused while sitting in the stand (the team manager hadn't yet migrated to the bench) by the patrons in the enclosure below. The central target of their vitriol, however, was not McGrory but chairman Bob Kelly, undoubtedly the real power behind the selection and other decisions which left the fans bemused and angry. Kelly was perceived as an autocratic figure whose influence in team matters was notorious. One *Daily Record* reporter put his finger on Celtic's recent failings after the second of the club's public trials inside four days (just prior to the start of the following season).[9] These were matches played between the 'Green and Whites' or 'Probables' (first-team regulars) and the 'Whites' or 'Possibles' (reserves). The *Record* correspondent remarked that 'there is an abundance of talent at Parkhead. There is a good player for every position, with one almost as good standing by, and it would appear that the management problem is, once again, how best to deploy their forces' (7 August 1957). He was not exaggerating the depth of Celtic's playing resources when one considers that the likes of Billy McNeill, Bertie Auld, Mike Jackson and John Divers were already catching the eye as promising performers in the 'Whites' line-up. But it is an indication of the management's failure to field a settled forward line – widely perceived to be a perennial problem at Celtic Park – that the front five for the 'Green and Whites' in this trial, who were playing together for the first time as a unit (Tully, Collins, McPhail, Wilson and Mochan), would not be fielded again until the League Cup final in October. In the interim, seven permutations would be used in Celtic's forward line-ups, injuries notwithstanding. The old lament about the 'Five Sorrowful Mysteries' was now a reflection not just on the individual players chosen to play, but on the management's seeming inability to work out a settled formation and persist with it.

Nikita Khrushchev beat off the most serious attack on his leadership of the Soviet Union today when he won the support of the USSR's military supremo, Marshal Zhukov, to ensure victory in the full session of the Communist Party's Central Committee. He has now cleared the way to remove key opponents from the ruling Politburo.

Khrushchev's defeat of the faction led by Vyacheslav Molotov, Lazar Kaganovich and Georgi Malenkov was a close-run thing. The three – all opponents of Khrushchev's year-long de-Stalinisation campaign and seeking a return to a more rigid regime – engineered Khrushchev's initial humiliation in a special Politburo meeting vote. Both Molotov and Malenkov were staunch Stalinists who had been shuffled aside by Khrushchev in the period following the dictator's death in 1953. (News item, 3 July 1957)

CELTIC VERSUS RANGERS

Celtic's problems were often highlighted in Old Firm games during these years. The perception among Celtic supporters was, and still is, that Rangers were nearly invincible against Celtic in the 1950s. In fact, that is not quite accurate. Celtic certainly went through a very rough spell in Old Firm encounters in the late '40s. After their 1–0 New Year's Day victory in a Southern League match at Ibrox at the start of 1945, Celtic won only three out of the next 23 meetings between the clubs in all competitions during the remainder of that decade. But there was a definite, though hardly spectacular, improvement in Celtic's Old Firm record during the 1950s. In all Old Firm matches played in the years from 1950 to 1959 inclusive – 44 games in total – Celtic managed 12 wins and 11 draws, and while these are not particularly impressive statistics, the picture looks much better if we exclude Glasgow Cup and Charity Cup matches and concentrate on the three national competitions. In those tournaments, Celtic won ten matches to Rangers' 13, with another seven drawn – hardly evidence of the Ibrox club's near invincibility. One countervailing factor, however, is that, particularly in the earlier part of the decade, Rangers had a habit of winning the 'crunch' encounters; for example, the 1951 New Year's Day clash, when Celtic were mounting a credible challenge in the league race, and later in that year when Rangers won handily in the League Cup semi-final. The Scottish Cup tie between the clubs in 1953 was also won by Rangers. And while Celtic did manage to record a series of league victories over their historic rivals at Celtic Park, they only managed one league win on Rangers' home turf during this decade.

Perhaps the worst experience for Celtic fans as far as Rangers were concerned occurred at the start of the 1955–56 season. Celtic had opened their League Cup sectional campaign convincingly, with comfortable victories home and away over Queen of the South and at home against Falkirk. Celtic then travelled across the city to Ibrox and, with a wonderful display of controlled, attacking football, humbled Rangers by four goals to one in front of a crowd of 75,000. However, Rangers exacted full revenge in the return leg at Celtic Park the following Wednesday night. Once again the Celtic management, not convinced that Fernie was fully fit, opted to field a very inexperienced youngster (Matt McVittie) at outside-right. Rangers opened the scoring early on through Baird. Worse was to follow for Celtic. Ten minutes before half-time, their centre-half and captain Jock Stein left the field in considerable pain following a most unfortunate tackle which would eventually lead to his retirement as a player. There being no provision for substitutes in those days, Stein valiantly resumed after the interval, but at outside-left (from which position he nearly scored with a header). But Celtic's fate was sealed very shortly after the start of the second half when Sean Fallon pulled up in a race for the ball after suffering a muscular strain. This left Rangers' right-winger Scott with an unaccustomed freedom in which to operate. The visitors extended their lead not long afterwards. Celtic were handicapped by a further injury, this time to goalkeeper Bonnar, which prevented him from taking goal-kicks. Celtic were now on the rack and Rangers pressed home their advantage, adding two further scores in the closing stages. Meanwhile Willie Fernie sat in the stand, helpless in his exasperation at the turn of events.

Celtic often seemed to suffer from bad luck in these matches. In the 1951 New Year league clash at a semi-waterlogged, semi-frozen Ibrox, Celtic's inspirational goalscorer John McPhail, whose name was cheered lustily by the visiting support when it was announced on the Tannoy, crashed a shot off the woodwork with the score at 0–0, but then, with less than half an hour gone, injured himself while stretching for a ball that had broken away from him, and spent the rest of the game hobbling ineffectively on the left wing. In the 1951 League Cup semi-final, Rangers had scored a decisive goal while the Celtic pivot Alec Boden lay unconscious on the turf following a collision. In the 1953 Scottish Cup tie, Rangers' goal survived a series of astonishing near misses shortly before the interval, when Collins, then Tully, then Collins again did everything but score. The trend of misfortune had been set at the very start of the decade: 'One had to see the distress of Mallan, the Celtic left-back, after he had completely missed his kick eight minutes before the end of the match at Parkhead, to appreciate the fortuitousness of Rangers' equalising goal.' (*Glasgow Herald* report on Celtic 1 Rangers 1, 2 January 1950)

Tom Campbell recalls this last incident:

> Poor Jimmy Mallan completely missed his kick near the end – nobody
> near him or within ten yards – to give away the equaliser. He lay on the
> ground punching the turf.

Even in matches of lesser importance, Celtic's luck seemed to run out
against the 'auld enemy'. In a Glasgow Cup semi-final replay on 3
September 1953, the *Glasgow Herald* reporter observed that Celtic's
goalkeeper Hunter 'was beaten four times, but had not a single save that
was worth noting. Niven, on the other hand, had the save of the match
after only five minutes' play, and it was from the fourth shot driven by
Evans – a right-half, mark you – in that brief period.' Celtic ended up
losing 4–0, despite having had the lion's share of scoring opportunities,
and the result was described as 'fantastic' in that light, although the
writer added, 'That is not to say that Rangers did not deserve to win.'
They had merely been helped in their task by profligate finishing and a
series of bad defensive errors by Celtic, including a couple late in the
game by Jock Stein. Stein was also at fault a couple of years later in a
Charity Cup semi-final at Celtic Park when his blunder led to the only goal
of the game, again scored late in the proceedings. The *Herald*
correspondent reporting on the match thought that 'Rangers will
probably never have a more fortunate win than they had [last night] at
Celtic Park. The home team, who more or less monopolised play from
start to finish, would with any luck have won by at least half a dozen
goals. Niven was in brilliant form in Rangers' goal, but on four occasions
when the ball rebounded from the framework of the goal, he was in no
position to save, and twice he had his full-backs to thank for clearances
on the goal-line. On other occasions he could do no more than parry the
ball which, however, invariably spun to the feet of a colleague.' (Celtic 0
Rangers 1, 7 May 1955)

In the vital New Year league clash at Parkhead in 1956 which Celtic
went into topping the league table, Rangers again won 1–0, with Stein's
lack of pace against Kichenbrand and Beattie's hesitancy in goal being
responsible for Rangers' winner. Once more the *Herald* noted Rangers'
good fortune: 'Rangers were lucky on several occasions – notably when a
Fernie shot struck Brown rather than was saved by him, and three
minutes from time when Caldow pulled Mochan down from behind in the
penalty area and escaped punishment.' But again the reporter added,
'Celtic were not unlucky to lose,' and he castigated the Celtic forwards for
being 'shockingly ineffective at shots'. Poor finishing and poor defending
often saw Celtic losing out in these contests, much to the frustration of
the supporters. Hence victories, when they were achieved, were greatly
savoured. One of the most memorable for Celtic fans was the 2–0 win at

Ibrox in a Scottish Cup replay in February 1957. In the first match, Celtic had lost a 4–2 lead in the last seven minutes. But they made no mistake in the replay, watched by 88,000. Completely outclassing Rangers, the team gave a sparkling display of fine football on the heavily sanded pitch. But even that deeply satisfying 2–0 victory was tinged with misfortune. Shortly before the end of the match, Celtic's right-winger John Higgins was felled by a shocking tackle – which one journalist judged was worth a dozen penalties – as he was about to shoot. No penalty kick was awarded by Jack Mowat, who would referee the League Cup final between the clubs later in the year. Higgins, though a very fine player, was somewhat injury-prone, and the Celtic players and officials, as well as the supporters, felt that he and other ball artistes like Fernie could have done with far more protection from the match official than they received. This was to become a common complaint in Celtic circles as Scottish football, and Rangers in particular, increasingly adopted the 'power-play' physical approach in the later 1950s. Celtic, under Bob Kelly, resolutely eschewed that style of football as the decade neared its close, preferring to field young, enthusiastic sides dedicated to playing attractive football, even if it meant not always getting good results. But in one match at least prior to embarking thoroughly on his youth policy, Kelly's purist belief in attractive football would be fully vindicated. The Scottish Cup victory at Ibrox on a wintry day in early 1957 was merely a foretaste of an autumnal delight to come . . .

*　　*　　*

Despite the spread of honours to the provincial clubs which was such a marked feature of Scottish football in the '50s, Rangers were still considered to be the strongest club in the country. The Ibrox outfit at the time preferred to be called 'The Rangers' (as per the masthead on the official programme, the definite article being written with a capital 'T'). Similarly, they referred to their home, whose most notable feature was the imposing red-brick grandstand designed by Archibald Leitch, as 'The Stadium'. With its gable ends sporting the club crest of Lion Rampant shield and the 'Aye Ready' motto, the Ibrox stand embodied the club's sense of itself as the quintessential sporting expression of the Scottish Establishment. Not only was it a club and a team possessed of enormous self-belief – regarding success as virtually a birthright – it was by far the wealthiest club in Scotland. Rangers' prosperity was such that following a highly profitable season in 1956–57 (during which they had won the league championship), the directors recommended a whopping 25 per cent dividend to shareholders. An indication of how 'big-thinking' a club it was, even in an era marked by conservatism in football boardrooms, is that in the autumn of 1957 those in charge at Ibrox were considering ways of making the stadium – already an impressive ground by the standards of the day – still more imposing. There was, for example, a plan to divert the railway branch line which ran past Ibrox into the stadium area itself, and construct a sizeable platform to accommodate arriving passengers. The idea was to allow spectators to purchase combined match and railway tickets at Glasgow Central before making their way out to 'The Stadium' in Govan. These plans came to naught after discussions with the railway authorities, but it was an indication of a brand of progressive thinking in terms of spectator comfort and convenience which was not in evidence at the time elsewhere in Scottish football.

John Eadie looks back at '50s-style transportation to football matches, as well as other features of life at the time:

> Most of the fans just walked to the games. Well, you know, you could take a bus or a tram at the time, but most of the time the tram couldn't get moving for the congestion of traffic and pedestrians in the streets! Games like Partick Thistle and Rangers, you'd take the subway [underground train]. But most of the time you'd just walk.

Roy McGuinness recalls his methods of getting to matches as well as his other pastimes and living conditions at the time:

> Most games at Parkhead, we took the number 7 tram from Govan Cross to Bridgeton Cross and walked – there was lots of walking in those days. Hampden, we took the number 12 tram from Linthouse. Away games, my brother Eddie was a member of the Gorbals CSC and I was invited on their bus. I lived upstairs from The Tower bar where two Rangers buses left for every game. I would cadge a ride when they played Celtic! I recall one incident coming home with them when bottles were thrown at the bus coming down the Gallowgate and me waving to let them know I was a Celtic supporter.
>
> As well as The Stag bar in Govan, we drank at The Tower bar, Donnelly's (for a good pint of Guinness) and the Chrystal Bell at Glasgow Cross. A pint was from 11d to 1s/3d [4½ pence to 6½ pence] at that time. 'Woodbine' cigarettes were sold in sleeves of five (single) or ten (double). We never wore colours, maybe because we lived in Govan, or maybe because we did not have money to buy stuff like that! Every Saturday night we had a party, usually at my place, where we sang the popular songs of the day. My Irish pal sang 'Kevin Barry' and other rebel songs, but I did not know them, and I still don't. Strange, but I thought I was Irish until I was 15!
>
> My father died about 1932, one of the few 'Tims' to get work during the Depression (at MacGregors of Renfrew, Upholsterers). We lived in

a room and kitchen with an indoor toilet, in Harmony Row. I got married in 1954 and lived in a 'single end' [one-room flat] in Helen Street. As near as I can remember, I earned about five pounds a week as a lathe turner. The dance halls I remember were the F & F in Partick, the two town halls in Govan, the Barrowland in the Gallowgate, and many small ones. In those days of no television, we would sometimes dance seven nights a week. I grew up in the 'Swing' era, with singers like Bing Crosby, Sinatra, Perry Como, Guy Mitchell, Frankie Laine, Johnny Ray, Ella Fitzgerald, Kay Starr and Jo Stafford – they were the best.

THE SHAPE OF THINGS TO COME

1957–58 was the first season in which interest in European competitions really gripped Scotland. Crowds of 85,000 turned up at Ibrox to see Rangers play both St Etienne and AC Milan in the European Champions' Cup, attracted by the novelty of it all, even if Rangers' 'rummle-'em-up' style was eventually exposed as wholly inadequate by the skilled Italians. The 4–1 rout of the home team was described by one reporter as akin to 'being cut to pieces by an expert with a rapier'. Scottish football fans were beginning to see that a gulf in class existed between their own favourites and the cream of the Continent. It was a gulf that would not be bridged for another ten years, and only rarely thereafter.

Off the pitch at least, Scottish football in the 1950s seems a world away from the game fans know now. Football grounds were characterised by largely terracing 'provision' for supporters, affording little if any shelter from the elements. All-seater stadia were unheard of, at least in Britain, while crowd control techniques were as primitive as the conditions for spectators. The clubs' philosophy as regards the customers was simply to pack as many of them in as possible, with little care for their comfort or safety. Catering was largely limited to pies and Bovril of dubious quality. There were no club shops selling sportswear and replica merchandise. There were no executive boxes. Football was seen as overwhelmingly the game of the working classes, who (although it wasn't stated quite so bluntly) were thought neither to deserve nor to be capable of appreciating anything better than that which the clubs chose to offer them. The more recent broadening of the sport's patronage as a consequence of the 'glamour factor' and 'upmarket' promotional strategies would have been unthinkable in the 1950s. To the extent that commercialisation affected football in that decade, it was but a cottage industry compared to the massive, television-driven enterprise it has now become, at least for the larger clubs. If there appears to be something artificial, manufactured or synthetic about football's modern appeal, back in 1957 the game still had a genuine, spontaneous hold on the imagination of the average

Glaswegian male which was comparatively spiritual or romantic in nature.

The broadcaster Robert McKinnon, in a BBC Home Service radio talk given in August 1959, made the following observation: 'Football in and about Glasgow never really stops. There is a short, official break from late May to early August, but there is no transfer of allegiance to a summer game such as cricket. The true Glaswegian fitba' fan is a one-game man, and in the few weeks of high summer he will give you his views on what is wrong with Scottish football just as readily as he will shout advice from the terracing when the season is in full swing.' As the title of McKinnon's talk – 'King Soccer' – suggested, the long summer days and the school holidays were essentially an excuse for one thing: football and more football, played until you were ready to drop, with jackets for goalposts, in stretches of waste ground, back yards and streets (particularly at night-time, when lamplighting came in handy) – indeed, anywhere where there was room enough to manipulate a ball, even up a tenement close. It was an environment which fostered the last generation of great 'tanner ba' players such as Jimmy Johnstone, a breed unlikely to be reproduced in our contemporary, post-industrial landscape.

ENDNOTES

1 'Teazy Weazy' was a reference to Billy McPhail, who at that time was in the hairdressing business, and who also bore a resemblance to a TV hairdresser with that nickname.

2 The contrast with Celtic's attitude and performance during World War I could not have been more marked. During that earlier conflagration, Celtic dominated Scottish football, adding a further three Scottish League titles to the one they had won on the eve of the war and generally striving at all times to field as strong and attractive a side as possible in the circumstances.

3 It was customary for several decades to decide drawn matches in certain lesser cup competitions on the basis of the number of corners won during open play, the idea being to reward the more attacking side, as well as cut down on replays.

4 During World War II, all footballers were required to be part-timers and wages were fixed at £2 per week 'basic', plus a maximum bonus of £1. But such restrictions often met with less than full compliance and, as has practically always been the case in football, clubs became adept at finding other ways of inducing players to appear in their colours, often using the cover of 'expenses' (for which additional payments were authorised in principle). There is one report of negotiations taking place between three Celtic players (Malcolm MacDonald, Bobby Hogg and John Divers) and chairman Tom White over a £25 bonus per man for winning their inaugural Southern League Cup section in the spring of 1941. In view of Tom White's attitude to bonuses, this special pay-day compels attention more for its rarity than for any question as to its legal propriety.

5 Celtic made a bid of £12,000 for Mannion on 12 September. A month later the club made a renewed effort to land the Middlesbrough star, offering two players and a cash sum for his services, but again the bid was rejected.

6 John McPhail's other nickname was 'Hooky', apparently a reference to an idiosyncratic way he had of propelling the ball.

7 It was the trouble at this match which led to the 'Flag Flutter' controversy, in which Celtic were asked to remove the Irish tricolour which at that time flew on top of the old 'Jungle' roof above the juncture with the 'Celtic' end. The controversy is one which has been covered in depth elsewhere, and so will not be further examined here.

8 There was little chance of that happening at one post-war match, however. It took place on 24 September 1949 at Ibrox, and was boycotted by the Celtic Supporters Association to express their dissatisfaction at the standard of refereeing in two recent Old Firm encounters – the match involving the Cox–Tully incident already referred to, and a Glasgow Cup tie at Celtic Park which Rangers won 2–1 with a late goal of such dubious legality that the Celtic players, apparently at Tully's instigation as well as in response to chants from

their own supporters, almost left the field in disgust. When the Celtic team took the field at the boycott match, reported the *Glasgow Herald* correspondent, 'no more than a few dozen pairs of hands clapped a welcome; not a scarf was waved, not a flag unfurled . . . a smattering of green and white rosetted men who had risked being called blacklegs . . . made violent gestures to try to dissuade photographers from proving that the Celtic team were not entirely on their own.'

9 Gate receipts from Celtic's pre-season public trial matches in this period were donated to charity.

CHAPTER THREE

FIRST STEPS TO GLORY

I see Mochan beating Shearer;
The League Cup is coming nearer.
He slams in an impossible shot.
The Rangers team has had their lot.

THE START OF THE SEASON

Celtic would emerge as the surprise team of season 1957–58. But even before a ball had been kicked in anger, the club's management was still being criticised for a degree of chopping and changing in the line-up which could not be accounted for by injuries alone – a policy that had the supporters in a state of high dudgeon as the new term began. And there was a perfect illustration of Celtic's failure to find the right blend in the opening match of the new campaign, a League Cup sectional tie against Airdrieonians at Parkhead. The home side's fecklessness in front of goal elicited a slow handclap and whistles of disapproval halfway through the second half, before Tully finally manufactured an equaliser (to make it 2–2) by meandering along the byline and then centring the ball to Collins. He in turn slipped it through to Mochan to shoot home. Eight minutes from time Peacock notched the winner, with a low, skidding shot to which the Airdrie keeper Walker mistimed his dive. It could have been a lot worse, for Caven had struck the woodwork for the visitors when they led 2–1, and Sean Fallon had had to clear another shot off the line moments later. Tommy Allan of the *Scottish Sunday Express* suggested that the club's long close-season tour of North America may have blunted the players' customary enthusiasm, 'for here we had a poor, jaded-looking, listless apology for the fighting, go-ahead team we expect from Parkhead' (11 August 1957). The popular ex-Celt John McPhail (brother of Billy), who was now on the staff

70

of the *Daily Record*, delivered a more scathing judgement on a drab performance that matched the miserable weather (which had kept the crowd down to 38,000, thousands of whom sheltered from the monsoon-like conditions under the newly built cantilever cover at the west, or 'Celtic', end). McPhail quoted a fan whose verdict was, 'If that's Tully finished, the others have qualified for a pension!' He agreed that the Irishman was the best Celt on the day, but only in comparison to the deficiencies in the play of the rest. It was not an auspicious start. Even Billy McPhail's fine opening goal was not enough to spare him his brother's lash. John praised his sibling's astute though often unsupported head-flicks, but asked plaintively, 'What has happened to his footwork?', and went on to castigate him for looking 'lost on the ground, lacking in confidence and reluctant to speed through on his own when well positioned' (12 August 1957). Perhaps the elder McPhail felt he needed to show that he could be ruthlessly objective when reporting on the younger.

In the week prior to the start of the Scottish football season, a news item reported that despite Prime Minister Harold Macmillan's claim that Britons had 'never had it so good', the flow of people emigrating from Britain continued apace. According to figures released by the Government on 6 August 1957, a worrying 2,000 people were still quitting Britain every week. While most were leaving for Canada and Australia, both of which were offering highly attractive packages to much-needed qualified professionals and their families, there were also signs that a significant number of valuable science and medical graduates were heading for the United States, where pay levels were much higher than in Britain. This exodus was characterised as a 'brain drain'.

The mood of the rainsoaked fans leaving the new-look Celtic Park that wet summer's day would not have been lightened by the news that Rangers had crushed St Mirren by 6–0 at Ibrox before an opening-day crowd of 55,000, Max Murray and Billy Simpson both helping themselves to hat-tricks. But the large Ibrox following was also drawn to see Rangers' new centre-half, John Valentine, signed at the end of the previous season from Queen's Park as a replacement for the famous George Young, who had finally retired.[1] Valentine came with the reputation of being a solid anchor-man, strong and determined in the tackle, whose only weakness was thought to be a lack of real pace and an occasional waywardness in his distribution of the ball. But these were rough edges which most observers imagined would soon be smoothed over as he accustomed himself to a full-time professional set-up (his former club, of course, being amateurs). Indeed, Hugh Taylor, previewing the new season in the *Sunday Mail* earlier that summer, had stated: 'Rangers will miss George Young. But I'm certain that Valentine, from Queen's Park, will shortly be as bulky a nightmare to centre-forwards as the Big Fella ever was' (21 July 1957). It was a prophecy which must have caused Taylor to squirm with embarrassment a few short months later.

Rangers followed up their demolition of the hapless Paisley 'Buddies' with a narrow 1–0 victory over Partick Thistle at Firhill the following Wednesday night, before another bumper crowd of 35,000. The same evening Celtic travelled to Methil and won fairly comfortably in the end, by four goals to one. Willie Fernie had suffered a knock on the head against Airdrie which required him to leave the field for attention, and then resume out of position on the left wing for the final 20 minutes. Against East Fife his place was taken by a player making his debut for Celtic, Sammy Wilson, signed the previous May on a free transfer from St Mirren. Wilson had not especially impressed in the pre-season public trials, and so had not been risked in the opening match. But with Fernie having experienced double vision following his knock in the Airdrie game, Wilson took over at right-half for the tie at Methil, in line with his new club's perception of him as a wing-half, the role he had usually been asked to perform at Love Street. Eric Smith had not shown sufficient guile on the Saturday and was dropped in favour of Jim Sharkey, a young forward of considerable talent, but one who had struggled to keep his place over the previous 18 months. Sharkey had suffered a series of blackouts after having a ball driven in his face at Cappielow in February 1956, and then had fallen into disfavour with chairman Bob Kelly prior to that year's Scottish Cup final following an alleged misdemeanour at Seamill. Despite making an apology after he had made his feelings known about being dropped for the final, he never regained a regular slot in the first team and his days at Celtic Park were numbered thereafter.[2]

> The top ten UK singles in August 1957 were: 1) 'Love Letters in the Sand', by Pat Boone; 2) 'All Shook Up', by Elvis Presley; 3) 'Teddy Bear', by Elvis Presley; 4) 'Island in the Sun', by Harry Belafonte; 5) 'Gamblin' Man/Puttin' on the Style', by Lonnie Donegan; 6) 'We Will Make Love', by Russ Hamilton; 7) 'Little Darlin'', by The Diamonds; 8) 'Bye Bye Love', by the Everly Brothers; 9) 'Last Train to San Fernando', by Johnny Duncan and the Blue Grass Boys; 10) 'Diana', by Paul Anka. By late October, perhaps as a result of a certain event's impact upon Celtic fans, 'Teddy Bear' had fallen out of the 'Top Ten', while Belafonte's song retained its place; and another ditty based on the latter hit would soon be topping the football charts round Parkhead way!

Against the East Fifers, Celtic's defence was still suspect, although they dominated the opening exchanges. Their efforts were rewarded ten minutes before half-time when McPhail blasted home from eight yards following a Tully corner kick. But if there was any thought that Celtic would seize control of the game having scored the opening goal, it was almost immediately dashed when East Fife equalised through Bonthrone from the penalty spot after a handling offence. The visitors regained the lead before half-time, however, after Bobby Collins capitalised on an error in the home defence. Celtic were still not out of the woods, though, and in the second half survived another penalty claim for 'hands' as well as a missed 'sitter' by Bonthrone (a stalwart of the fairly successful East Fife teams of the '50s). The home side then switched Bonthrone to the wing in a bid to salvage at least a point, but Celtic killed the game with two goals in the closing stages, Mochan beating the keeper to a through ball from McPhail, and then McPhail himself scoring from a 'picture Tully cross'. Despite the goalscoring contribution of McPhail and the reasonably pleasing debut of Sammy Wilson, the best player for Celtic on the night was Bobby Collins, now beginning to form a really profitable partnership with Charlie Tully in a new-look right wing.

BOBBY COLLINS
Bobby Collins had figured in a major controversy in Celtic's history even before he first donned a green and white hooped jersey. An editorial in the Celtic v. Partick Thistle (Glasgow Cup) match programme of 8 September 1948, commenting on the signing dispute over Collins which had raged between Celtic and Everton, stated, 'Bobby Collins will go down in history as the first player to be directed to sign for an English club by the Scottish Football Association – after he had signed for Celtic.' That tug of war had come as a surprise to a prominent scout who had watched the diminutive forward and dismissed him as 'having nae legs' – surely one of the most crass misjudgements ever made by a paid talent-spotter. For within a decade this midfield dynamo was regarded by many as the finest match-winning inside-forward in Britain, an assessment shared by Celtic's other inside-man in the 1957 League Cup-winning team, Sammy Wilson: 'Bobby had such energy and skill that not only could he exhaust the opposition, he was always ready to take on and go at players and create room for others, besides being liable to put the ball in the net from 30 yards!'

The dispute with Everton had arisen after Collins, only 17 years old at the time, had sparked the interest of the Merseyside club while playing with the Glasgow junior club Pollok. Bobby, accompanied by his father, then travelled to Liverpool to discuss matters, but when no one from Goodison turned up to meet them they simply returned to Glasgow, and Collins later signed for Celtic. When Everton learned of this, they implied that Celtic had 'tapped' the youngster, ignoring the fact that he had not signed for Celtic until two months after his fruitless journey to England. But Everton claimed that correspondence with Pollok constituted a binding agreement, and in this claim they were backed up by the SFA, who ruled that Collins must now join the Merseysiders! Collins simply refused. Both he and his father pointed out that neither of them had received any written communication from Everton, and that the player had never received any money from the club either. Finally Everton, in the face of Collins's refusal to join their playing staff, abandoned their interest, adding in a note of pique at the outcome that 'he's not big enough anyway'. The SFA stepped in again at this juncture, giving official recognition to the player's wishes – but not before suspending him for six weeks!

The determination of Bobby Collins to play for the Parkhead club was not lost on the supporters. And soon they were impressed by what they saw. On his debut, a League Cup sectional match versus Rangers at Celtic Park on 13 August 1949 in front of 71,000 spectators, he contributed handsomely to Celtic's unexpected 3–2 victory. Collins, whom the *Glasgow Herald* correspondent noted was deemed far too small – at 5ft 1in – by many in the crowd before the start, left the field the recipient of a congratulatory handshake and a pat on the back from his immediate opponent, the formidable Rangers veteran 'Tiger' Shaw. The *Herald* reporter continued: 'I cannot recall Shaw being able to tackle Collins on more than half a dozen occasions. The outside-right showed fine intelligence in parting with the ball at exactly the correct moment, and to those who recall the feast of crosses that Connolly, Bert Thomson and Delaney used to send into goal, the service supplied by Collins was particularly heartening.' To be placed, on one's debut, against Rangers, in the same company as Celtic's three finest right-wingers of the inter-war period was praise indeed. And it was not long before Collins was catching the eyes of the Scotland selectors. He was picked the following spring to play against Switzerland at Hampden, although an injury meant he had to withdraw. But the first of his 31 full international caps was won only a few months later in a Home International match against Wales in October 1950.

Although Bobby started off his Celtic career at outside-right, many supporters were quickly and firmly of the opinion that his drive and energy would be more effective if he were moved inside from the wing. On the first three occasions he did make the switch to inside-forward he scored, earning rave notices in matches against Hearts and Queen of the South, even though on the latter occasion the change of position was due to an injury to McPhail sustained during the match itself. But the clamour that he be given a permanent berth in a more central position was eventually acceded to by the management, and it was as inside-right that

Bobby won his first major winner's medal, in the 1951 Scottish Cup final versus Motherwell. Had it not been for Bobby's late headed equaliser in the first round at Methil that year, Celtic supporters would have suffered an even longer sojourn in post-war trophy limbo. He was back on the wing when the St Mungo Cup was won a few months later, and for most of the early part of the decade Collins was fielded as a winger, usually on the right. By the mid-1950s he was often filling in at inside- or outside-left. But Bobby was ahead of his time. Nowadays he would simply be regarded as an attacking midfielder, possessed of a tremendous work-rate and great shooting power. The latter was in evidence against Rangers, for example, on 22 September 1951, when he scored a stunning goal in front of 86,000 crammed into Ibrox: 'The remarkable power of the smallest player of the 22 was evident in Collins's sudden shot from 25 yards which Brown may have done very well indeed to have touched.' (*Glasgow Herald* report on Rangers 1 Celtic 1) The same reporter could not resist praising this score several times in different places throughout his account of the match, describing it as a 'magnificent goal' and the 'most memorable feature of a most satisfying match'.

Gerard Hamill (now resident in Liverpool) recalls:

I grew up in the Parkhead area at the time. In fact, my school, St Michael's, moved from Salamanca Street to Springfield Road, right behind the old Rangers end, just at the end of the period – I think it was 1960.

My first match must have been about season '54-'55, Bobby Collins was definitely playing because all I remember, apart from being shifted from shoulder to shoulder of Dad and a series of uncles, was everyone shouting for the 'Wee Barra' – and me looking everywhere for this little barrow and not being able to see it!

My dad, Phil Hamill, used to be at all the matches apart from the Rangers games. I don't think he ever even set foot in Ibrox, except for a cup semi-final we lost to St Mirren.[3] He, like most men then, had his chosen spot at Parkhead. It was in the middle of the 'Hayshed', as he always called it, although it was far better known as 'The Jungle'. He and many of those men had to move out around the early '70s because a lot of 'headcases' started moving in. I grew up on the back wall that used to run along the 'Hayshed' before it was replaced by the new 'Jungle', built in the '60s. It was a great place for a wee boy to watch the game and it saved a lot of pain for the men, if they were lifting kids all through the game. They would probably also have got a lot of abuse from other supporters wanting to see the match. The 'Hayshed' was also always a safe place. No matter how notorious 'The Jungle' might have been, I never wanted to be anywhere else watching Celtic.

Bobby Collins was appointed Celtic's penalty-kick taker and became one of the few Scottish players to score a hat-trick of spot-kicks (in a home league match against Aberdeen on 26 September 1953). His brilliant form was one of the highlights of Celtic's Coronation Cup success earlier that year, and it was his goal direct from the corner flag which saw Celtic through the first-round match against Arsenal. He won a league championship medal the following season (1953–54), although he missed the cup-final leg of the 'Double' against Aberdeen. He was dropped from the replay against Clyde in the next cup final in 1955, the rumour being that Bob Kelly disapproved of a Collins challenge on Hewkins in the 'Bully Wee' goal; and he was unfit for the 1956 cup final against Hearts, when his drive and invention at inside-forward were sadly missed. But it was Collins's goal which put the seal on Celtic's first League Cup final victory, against Partick Thistle a few months after the disappointment of the Hearts match. And though he would not get on the scoresheet in the next League Cup final, he would come mighty close.

This strong and talented little player with the build of a flyweight boxer – and wearing size-four boots, among the smallest in first-class football – had the same ferocious will to win as the man after whom he was later nicknamed 'Lester' by his Celtic team-mates – champion jockey Lester Piggott. Like all competitors who believe the first duty of a professional is to win, Bobby Collins was apparently not averse to letting his colleagues know if they failed to meet his exacting standards of commitment. And who could argue with a player who didn't know the meaning of slackening? Conversely, he was sufficiently self-critical to acknowledge when his personal contribution fell short of his own expectations.

Tom Campbell recalls one particular incident:

Celtic played a Glasgow Cup tie at Cathkin (home of Third Lanark) and won 5–2. I remember one particular incident involving Collins: Celtic produced some good fluid passing play, but Collins – with blatant exaggeration – passed the ball *straight* to John McPhail as if to point out that the centre was not mobile enough to move far for the ball.
[This match was played on 3 September 1951, and McPhail had returned from Celtic's tour of the USA that summer visibly overweight.]

One former team-mate still talks admiringly of the self-confident Collins as a player totally unafraid of any challenge on the pitch ('as hard as iron'), no matter how robust and intimidating the challenger. 'Bobby,' the team-mate adds, 'was a real rubber-ball of a player; he bounced back so quickly from hard tackling.' That determined attitude did not meet with the full approval of the Celtic chairman, Bob Kelly, who once remarked, in rather sniffing tones, that later in his career Collins was 'inclined to become involved physically'. But it is sobering to reflect that the unquenchable drive of the 'Wee Barra', which was so crucial to Celtic reaching the 1957 League Cup final, was almost lost to the club that autumn. At the end of September, Celtic rejected an inquiry from Cardiff City for the player, and Gair Henderson of the *Evening Times* scoffed at the thought that Celtic would allow a player of Collins's talent to go: 'I think that Celtic could reasonably have said "£20,000? We've never been so insulted in our lives." The plain fact is that Collins for the past two years has been the most profitable football player in Scotland, and the Celtic supporters are rightly convinced that he is worth his weight in gold' (30 September 1957). It was not long, however, before a more glamorous destination than South Wales was being suggested for Collins. The Italian club Lazio was reported to be interested in him in the weeks leading up to the League Cup final against Rangers, and this was shortly after Juventus had taken another British player, the Welshman John Charles, from Leeds United to Turin, where he became known as 'The Gentle Giant'. Fortunately for Celtic, Charles never got the chance to pit his considerable footballing wits against 'The Pocket Hercules' from Glasgow in a Roman arena. Instead Bobby was to play an important part in an unforgettable drama on a stage closer to home, before, sadly, he did finally depart the club he had almost been prevented from joining in the first place.

William Provan of Glasgow recalls the era:

In the '50s, Celtic were very much up and down – more down than up. In 1951 they won the Scottish Cup with a team that was not a shadow of the Lisbon Lions. It was their first big trophy since 1938. In 1954 they captured the cup and league 'Double' and among that team was the great Jock Stein, signed from a Welsh non-league club [Llanelly]. But after the 'Double', it was mostly downhill until 1965. It seemed that every good player was transferred. They did get to Scottish Cup finals in 1955 and 1956 and semi-finals in 1957, 1959 and 1960. But the team as a whole was mediocre and often disorganised – although they had a large support, which the directors did not deserve.

Life in the West of Scotland was different then. Officially, there was full employment. I served my time as a joiner in the shipyard and did my National Service which took me to the South of England and to West Germany (including Berlin).

In Glasgow at the time there were numerous dance halls – no discos and no pub entertainment. The Empire Theatre was still with us, with stars like Frank Sinatra, Guy Mitchell and Perry Como.

The bad thing about football then was the bottle fights, and a lot of Celtic supporters got the jail for that. Post-match celebrations in those days were not the same – if you were seen and heard singing Celtic songs in a pub, it was a night in the cells for breach of the peace. The Establishment did not like their team getting beat by a score of 7–1. Today it's different. Although there is no 'cairy oot' to the game itself, you can have singing in the pub without fighting breaking out.

STUMBLE AND RECOVERY

As soon as the draw had been made for the sectional phase of the 1957–58 League Cup, it was widely recognised that Hibernian would present the stiffest challenge to Celtic's hopes of progressing in the competition they had won the previous year. Hibs had opened their campaign with a comfortable 4–0 defeat of East Fife, but had gone down rather surprisingly at Broomfield in the midweek match by 4–1. Despite the Edinburgh side's unexpected loss to Airdrie, Celtic, after two somewhat unsatisfactory albeit winning performances against Airdrie and East Fife, travelled to Easter Road knowing they could not afford to be so slovenly against a Hibs side which, while certainly not up to the standard of the 'Famous Five' sides of the early 1950s when they were Scottish champions in two successive seasons, nevertheless still carried a threat on the wings from Gordon Smith (who would later add league championship medals won with Hearts and Dundee to those he gained with Hibs) and Willie Ormond (who would later manage an impressive Scottish World Cup team). On the other hand, Celtic fans travelling through to the capital on 17 August to make up their portion of a 35,000 crowd could console themselves that Fernie was back. With Sharkey retained at inside-left, this meant no place for Sammy Wilson, who dropped out after his midweek debut.

The Celtic supporters had been murmuring at the shakiness of the defence in the first two matches, with many feeling that right-back Frank Meechan in particular was not at his best, and that Evans was looking a bit uncomfortable in the middle. Within the first 12 minutes of proceedings at Easter Road, that mood of disquiet had turned to one of abject misery. Hibs, attacking fiercely down the famous slope, were two goals up. The first was courtesy of an Ormond effort in five minutes after hesitation on the part of Meechan which allowed the Hibs left-winger to flick the ball knee-high past Beattie, who had raced out from his goalmouth; the second came when Meechan compounded his error by scoring an own goal seven minutes later. In attempting to tap a cross-shot from Smith back to his keeper, he merely succeeded in directing it well to the side of him and into the net. Disaster!

Bobby Collins, beginning to show an appetite for goal that would mark much of Celtic's drive to retain the League Cup, partially retrieved matters only six minutes later when, from a corner kick, his downward header bounced up from the turf and deceived the home defenders to finish in the corner of the net. Fernie now moved forward in an effort to add guile to the Celtic attack as it searched for the equaliser. He was ably assisted by Tully and Collins on the right flank, but Celtic's only shot on target of note was a powerful effort from skipper Bertie Peacock. Meanwhile the younger, less experienced Hibs team competed for every ball and hit the woodwork three times, as well as forcing Beattie into fine saves from several difficult shots. In the final quarter of an hour Celtic upped the tempo and came close to snatching the elusive levelling score more than once. But with time running out, it was the home side which broke away to secure the tie when Fraser exchanged passes with Marshall, assisted by a lucky break of the ball off Celtic's centre-half, Bobby Evans, and then lobbed Beattie.

The Celtic support was understandably downcast in defeat. 'Rex', the famous football correspondent writing in the *Sunday Mail*, adjudged Celtic to be a team going backwards in comparison with the promise shown by the more youthful Hibs and, as John McPhail had done when reporting on the opening match against Airdrie, pointed out that the fact that the veteran Tully was once again Celtic's wiliest forward was 'a warning if ever there was one' (18 August 1957). Celtic fans were also upset by the booking administered by referee G. Mitchell of Falkirk to Billy McPhail. In a 'PS' to his match report, 'Rex' confessed that the caution had him 'beat', since in his view it was Hibs' goalkeeper Leslie who had violently charged McPhail 'without justification', and that McPhail's 'lame effort at retaliation was so obviously a gesture of annoyance rather than malice that the caution seemed grossly unfair'.

> Twenty known Irish nationalists, most of them believed to be members of the IRA, were being held in Northern Ireland cells tonight following the death of an Ulster policeman in a booby-trap explosion. The blast comes only weeks after Eireann leader

> Eamon de Valera's controversial introduction of a state of emergency designed to give his security forces greater freedom to hold those it suspects of IRA membership and responsibility for attacks like today's. (News item, 17 August 1957)

To add to the bad news as far as Celtic supporters were concerned, Rangers had won again, although they had shown defensive frailties in their 4–3 defeat of Raith Rovers at Ibrox. Thus while Rangers topped their section at the halfway stage with maximum points, Celtic lay in third place behind Airdrie, who led on goal average from second-placed Hibs, although all three were level on four points. At this point, the Old Firm took a break from their respective League Cup campaigns to contest the first round of the Glasgow Cup at Ibrox on 19 August, a Monday evening. Following their uncertain start to the season, Celtic supporters did not especially relish the prospect. Rangers, after all, were the reigning Scottish league champions, having secured the title for the second successive season in 1956–57. The sparkling form which had earlier in the year resulted in a fine Scottish Cup win for Celtic on their rivals' own territory had not been sustained in the intervening months. The team had not clicked in the opening matches of the new season, and Ibrox was not a venue which had ever been indulgent of Celtic weaknesses.

> The 1950s were the most democratic era in the history of Scottish football. In the ten seasons from 1949–50 to 1958–59 inclusive, clubs outwith the Old Firm captured 18 of the 30 national trophies up for competition. Of the remaining 12, Rangers won seven, while Celtic took five (plus the St Mungo and Coronation Cups). But Rangers were easily the most consistent team in Scotland during the decade, since five of their haul of honours were league championships. Yet, despite their overall strength, the Ibrox club won no major trophies in seasons 1950–51, 1951–52, 1953–54, 1954–55 or 1957–58. They won no League Cups during the decade and, of their two Scottish Cup wins, the second occurred in 1953. Celtic only managed one league title, while Hibs won two, a feat emulated by Hearts if we extend the period to include the 1959–60 season; the Tynecastle side also won two League Cups and a Scottish Cup between 1954 and 1958. In the Scottish Cup Clyde were twice the victors, in 1955 and 1958, while East Fife and Dundee each won the League Cup twice. Motherwell had triumphs in the Scottish Cup (1952, when they beat Dundee before the astonishing attendance of 136,304) and in the League Cup (1950–51). Aberdeen were champions in

1954–55, and lifted the League Cup the following season. The Dons were unlucky in the premier cup competition, losing in three 'Scottish' finals in the space of seven years. Other provincial teams to gain national honours during the '50s included Falkirk and St Mirren, Scottish Cup winners in 1957 and 1959 respectively.

For the cup-tie against their old rivals, Celtic made one change from the team that had lost on the Saturday to Hibs. Following his nervous display in that match, Meechan was dropped, and his place at right-back was taken by John Donnelly, a 20-year-old making his debut in senior football, although he had played in a couple of matches (both against Spurs) in that summer's tour of America.

Whatever misgivings the Celtic fans heading out to Ibrox had that summer evening, they looked to be about to vanish when, straight from the kick-off, Willie Fernie robbed Rangers' Sammy Baird and laid the ball into the path of Billy McPhail, who in turn, drawing Valentine out of position, chipped the ball back into the space his movement had created, leaving Jim Sharkey with a glorious opportunity from only ten yards to give Celtic a first-minute lead and strike a telling psychological blow. Instead his shot struck the home keeper George Niven, and Rangers survived. Thereafter play was quite entertaining for the sizeable Monday-night crowd (estimated variously at 45,000 or 55,000), with Beattie saving well from Rangers' Alec Scott and Ian McColl, but Celtic playing the more attractive combined football. Unfortunately Celtic's better approach work was not complemented by a willingness to shoot decisively for goal. Instead, it was Baird who gave the home side the lead after 34 minutes and then grabbed a second in the final minute of the match after his first effort had rebounded kindly for him.

The *Glasgow Herald* was forthright in its analysis of Celtic's main failing and cause of their downfall in this match: while granting that the Parkhead men had been 'immeasurably superior' in passing and the finer arts of the game, its correspondent pointedly observed that none of the Celts, 'not even Collins, who played a tremendous game in every other respect, would emulate his opponents' willingness to shoot'. Celtic had been a little unfortunate when for once a shot was forthcoming (from Collins), and Rangers' full-back Bobby Shearer appeared to use an arm to clear it near the goal-line. The referee, Jack Mowat, who would officiate a couple of months later at the League Cup final, was not impressed by the Celtic claims. In the second half Shearer was again instrumental in depriving Celtic of a goal, this time by clearly legitimate means, when he scurried back to clear a shot which Sharkey had driven under Niven's body, following a superb through pass from Tully. Tully, in fact, gave such a fine performance that 'Waverley' (W.G. Gallacher), writing in the *Daily Record*, noted that he was even applauded by the *home* fans after one thrilling 40-yard dribble late in the proceedings.

One consolation for the Celtic support was the display of the debutant Donnelly at right-back. He gave an effective performance and managed to subdue his immediate opponent, the South African Johnny Hubbard, who had often caused Celtic defences severe problems in the past. On the other flank, however, the pace of Alec Scott had troubled Sean Fallon, the Irishman, of course, being well into his thirties by this time. Valentine, although the *Herald* correspondent thought him 'a vulnerable point in Rangers' defence' who did not resemble 'the great Queen's Park centre-half' of the previous season's vintage, was not unduly troubled by Billy McPhail, who seemed 'inordinately reluctant' to try and beat his man on the ground. McPhail's brother, writing in the *Daily Record*, had made an identical criticism of the Celtic striker's performance against Airdrie nine days previously.

The appeal of the Old Firm, even in the 1950s, was pretty much universal. Colm Brogan, writing in the *Evening Citizen* (12 August 1957), told of having recently been in New York, and of how, dropping into a bar to watch baseball on television, he was astounded to hear that the talk around him was not of the Dodgers, Giants or Yankees, but of 'Celtic and Rangers, Rangers and Celtic all the time. The bar was full of New York cops, who listened in a stunned silence. The boss of the bar was a red-hot Celtic man, and his "hauder-on", an elderly exile from Copland Road, was just as strong for Rangers.'

Jim Sharkey, the hero of Celtic's Glasgow Cup success against Rangers on Boxing Day 1955, had not shown the sharpness near goal that was hoped for, and his early miss in this latest encounter with the 'auld enemy' was punished by an immediate demotion, with Eric Smith returning to the line-up for the next match, the return League Cup tie against Airdrie at Broomfield the following Saturday. The Celtic management had also been disappointed that Neil Mochan, fielded in the first few games at outside-left, had not been a more effective performer. Certainly the right-wing partnership of Tully and Collins was outshining the rest of the team, and the left-wing combinations had suffered by comparison. So another young player, Bertie Auld, was selected at outside-left to partner Smith, giving the forward line yet another entirely new look for the visit to the Lanarkshire side who were still topping the section. Auld, like Donnelly, had also made his debut at Ibrox, on Celtic's visit there the previous May in the Charity Cup (a 1–0 win for Rangers).

Airdrie had high hopes of advancing to the quarter-finals, but their preparations for this game took a knock when centre-half Doug Baillie and inside-forward Ian McMillan (both later to play for Rangers) had to call off through injury.[4] The crowd was kept down to 16,000 by the weather, which mimicked the torrential conditions of the first encounter between the clubs at Parkhead on the opening day. On the rainswept pitch, however, both teams gave it their all. Airdrie's newcomer at centre-forward, Caven, caused problems, as he had in the first match, and it was he who opened the scoring after 20 minutes when he latched on to a rebound from the post. Before this Collins had made a hash of an easy chance from three yards, and the visiting supporters must have felt that the old failings in front of goal would prove costly. But just on the half-time whistle, Eric Smith managed to get his head to a Tully corner, and although his contact with the ball was not a firm one, it was enough to give Celtic the equalising goal, with Airdrie keeper Walker apparently thinking that the ball was going wide. After the interval both teams were committed to attack, and both goals had several narrow escapes as the play raged from end to end. With 20 minutes remaining, Celtic decided to push Willie Fernie into the forward line in place of the ineffectual Smith, and this had the effect of turning the match in the visitors' favour, as Fernie 'proceeded to tear the home defence to ribbons' with his superb dribbling runs. He could have had a hat-trick in those final stages, but in the event one goal was enough to give Celtic the points. Fittingly it was Fernie who scored it. Again it came from a Tully corner. McPhail head-flicked the ball on, and Fernie struck it sweetly on the volley to give Walker no chance in the Airdrie goal. Celtic probably deserved the points on the basis of their second-half performance, but they still weren't firing on all cylinders.

On 24 August 1957, the soccer season got under way in England, and Chelsea unveiled a prodigious young talent, aged 17. His name was Jimmy Greaves. Although relatively small and slight, Greaves immediately proved he had all the instincts of a top-class goalscorer. He was lightning fast, and showed a remarkably well-developed positional sense for one so young. It was the start of a career that would see him score 44 times in 57 appearances for England and three times score five goals in club matches. He played in 357 league matches for Chelsea, Tottenham and West Ham before a serious drinking problem forced his retirement. Later, having overcome his problem, he achieved a measure of redemption as a popular television football pundit.

Tully's contribution to the Broomfield match was decisive. In addition to his two corners which led to Celtic's goals, 'nobody else used the crossfield pass so well. Nobody else kept his opponents turning so often on this slippery turf. Yes, Tully all the time and that late Fernie switch were the victory factors' (*Scottish Sunday Express*, 25 August 1957). Donnelly again performed creditably in defence – although he was somewhat fortunate not to concede a penalty for 'hands' – and Auld showed promise, although he was not given enough of the ball. Celtic now moved to the top of the group since, surprisingly, Hibs had been held to a draw against East Fife at Bayview. With two home ties to come against East Fife and Hibs, Celtic had now established themselves as favourites to qualify for the quarter-final stage of the competition. Meanwhile Rangers kept up a 100 per cent record in their section by winning comfortably at Love Street. For Celtic, though, there was still a worry about their finishing, as Harry Andrew noted in the *Sunday Express*: 'I'm sure Celtic feel happier about their side now. Indeed, I would say their only real flaw is still the need of an attack spearhead. Somebody must start to cash in on all that mazy meandering – so nice to watch, but so exasperating when it comes to naught' (25 August 1957). The correspondent of the *Sunday Mail* issue of the same day was more blunt: 'Billy McPhail, right out of touch, took a roasting from the fans . . . '

Perhaps in an effort to address this lack of punch, Sammy Wilson was reintroduced to the line-up for the match with East Fife the following Wednesday at Celtic Park, but this time at inside-left, an unaccustomed position for the player and thus yet another experiment by the Celtic management. This meant Celtic would field their fourth forward-line permutation in six matches. Eric Smith dropped out, while the youngsters Donnelly and Auld kept their places. Significantly, it was the first time that McPhail would have Sammy Wilson as a striking partner in a competitive match (they had played up front together in the second pre-season public trial). The move paid an immediate and handsome dividend, for Celtic easily disposed of the Fifers by six goals to one, with McPhail and Wilson each scoring a brace. The start was a strange one, for East Fife (who had no hope of qualification) pressed eagerly for the first four minutes; but after Bonthrone had a shot saved by Beattie, the latter's clearance downfield was won by Billy McPhail, who then lobbed McCluskey in the visitors' goal to put Celtic into the lead. McPhail should have put the home team further ahead but he shot straight at the keeper from six yards. He soon made amends, however, by rifling home a Tully cross. The sense that Celtic were now in command of the game was shattered when East Fife pulled a goal back through Matthew after Fernie had lost possession in midfield. But shortly afterwards, Auld restored Celtic's two-goal advantage when McCluskey failed to hold a blistering, angled Collins shot from 25 yards – although he did supremely well to parry the ball in the first place. Still East Fife made a fight of it, and a minute from the interval they had the misfortune of hitting a post. But the Celts went to town in the second half. Wilson scored with a superb header from a Peacock cross, and Celtic added two more splendid goals through Collins and Wilson again to make it 6–1.

The loudest cheer of the evening from the 18,000 crowd came at half-time, with the news that Rangers were being beaten by Partick Thistle at Ibrox. The Jags finished that match shock winners by 3–0, and the wheels had started to come off Rangers' early-season bandwagon. It was another indication that John Valentine was having trouble settling into the more demanding environment of Ibrox, and was not providing the defensive solidity to which Rangers' partisans had been accustomed when Woodburn and then Young had occupied the pivot's role. This meant that Rangers had to travel to Kirkcaldy on the Saturday and avoid defeat by two clear goals to be sure of qualifying from their section – and Raith Rovers had managed to score three times themselves at Ibrox in the clubs' earlier meeting. Celtic still had to avoid defeat against Hibs at Parkhead to secure their qualification, an uncertain prospect given that the Easter Road side had beaten Airdrie convincingly by 5–1 on the same night that Celtic were scoring six against East Fife. And, of course, Hibs had already gained a deserved win over Celtic a fortnight previously. The game would undoubtedly be a test of Celtic's character and determination to make the season a successful one.

In time-honoured tradition, the sound of clocks striking midnight marked the moment when Malaya – Britain's last major Asian colony – became a self-governing member of the British Commonwealth, a nation in its own right. The end of 170 years of British rule was signalled by the lowering of the Union Jack in the capital, Kuala Lumpur, the raising in its place of Malaya's new flag, and the undisguised delight of thousands of Malays, Indians, Chinese, Eurasians and Europeans who represented Malaya's rich cultural mix at the official ceremony. (News item, 30 August 1957)

The prospect of witnessing the deciding tie of the section drew 50,000 to Parkhead on the last day of August. Celtic fielded the same team which had defeated East Fife so comprehensively, and hopes were high that the new striking partnership of McPhail and Wilson would continue on the goal trail. Hibs had Eddie Turnbull of the 'Famous Five' forward line back in their side, joining the two other survivors of that justly acclaimed attacking force, Gordon Smith and Willie Ormond. Turnbull was noted for his fierce shooting, and his experience was thought to be a potentially telling factor in a game Hibs had to win.

Billed as a showdown, the match was to prove a little disappointing as a spectacle. Both teams endeavoured to play attractive football in the opening 45 minutes, but they were well matched and neither could provide the goal which might have set the tie alight. Still, at the interval the relatively young Hibs team must have felt that they were in with a good chance of getting the result they wanted. But those wishes were dashed within a minute of the restart when Sammy Wilson headed Celtic into the lead after Collins had flicked on the inevitably well-placed corner from Charlie Tully. Celtic killed the tie in 57 minutes when McPhail's half-hit shot from a Wilson cross doubled the home team's advantage, despite a despairing attempt at a clearance by Hibs' right-back McFarlane, who injured himself by colliding with a goalpost in the process. Although Wilson and McPhail had combined for the goal, its principal architect was once again Charles Patrick Tully, who had released Wilson with a quite glorious pass to start the move. Thereafter, despite switching Smith to centre-forward, Hibs failed to put much pressure on the home defence which, intelligently marshalled by Evans and Peacock, looked more compact than of late. Only in the last five minutes, with Celtic perhaps letting their concentration slip a little, was Beattie tested in earnest. But Celtic held on to their lead and so accomplished the first phase of their attempt to retain their grip on the trophy. The sports editor of the *Daily Record*, James Cameron, had no doubt whom Celtic had most to thank for their victory: 'Parkhead praise be to that bonnie, balding prince of footballers from over the water, Charlie Tully . . . The anti-Tully fans had better shed that anti. Without Charlie Bhoy, Celtic might quite well not have won this tie.' (2 September 1957)

Meanwhile, at a packed Starks Park, Rangers came perilously close to being eliminated from the competition. With their defence again giving an uncertain performance, they lost to Raith Rovers 4–3. Had the home team scored one more goal, the Ibrox men would have failed ignominiously to qualify for the later stages. Instead, although both clubs finished on eight points, Rangers squeezed through on goal average (1.8 to Raith's 1.6 – both conceded ten goals, but Rangers had scored 18 to the Kirkcaldy side's 16). Indeed, it is one of the great ironies of the League Cup final of 1957 – a match which has entered the folklore of Scottish football – that Rangers might easily have not been involved in it, so troubled was their passage of entry to the final tie. Of course the same could be said of Celtic. But certainly the supporters of the latter club must be grateful that the men from Kirkcaldy did not manage a fifth goal against their opponents on that last day of August, 1957.

Those same supporters, reflecting on Celtic's form in the sectional ties, must have been delighted by the brilliant early-season form of Charlie

Tully. Now fielded at outside-right, and supported by the free-running Fernie at right-half and the industrious Collins at inside-right, the Irishman had proved his close-season critics wrong. At a time when Celtic were struggling to 'click' up front, it was Tully, time and again, who provided the inspiration to win the crucial games with telling corners, astute passes and crosses, and a fine sense of the weak spots in the opposition defences. Charlie was once again the darling of the fans.

John Eadie recalls:

> One song we used to sing about Tully went like this:
> 'I'll sing a hymn to Charlie,
> The daddy of them all,
> The greatest inside-forward that ever kicked a ball
> Oh teach them, Charlie Tully, how to play the game;
> When Orangemen blaspheme thee,
> I'll love and bless thy name.'[5]

BERTIE PEACOCK

Celtic had begun their defence of the League Cup in August 1957 with a new skipper, left-half Bertie Peacock. He had been appointed team captain on board the SS *Mauretania* as the Celtic party sailed westwards from Southampton to begin their close-season tour of the USA. It was a richly deserved and popular honour for this Northern Irishman (and a Protestant to boot), albeit a mishandled one, judging by the unpleasant shock which the decision came as to the incumbent (and another great club servant), Bobby Evans. Evans later claimed he learned of it in a conversation with a journalist at Prestwick Airport during a stop-over en route from Spain (where he had played for Scotland) prior to meeting up with the Celtic party in America. The matter clearly still rankled with Evans when he gave his version of events in a *Scottish Daily Express* series three years later, just as he was leaving Celtic for Chelsea: 'I had not been asked to relinquish the job. I had not been told I was being relieved of it. And I certainly had not asked to be relieved. Although I said nothing at the time, I was bitterly disappointed. Particularly when it turned out that Bertie's appointment was a permanency' (27 May 1960).

Genial and quiet-spoken, Coleraine-born Bertie Peacock had joined Celtic in 1949, when the club's fortunes were at a low ebb. Andrew Smith of the (Glasgow) *Evening News*, writing in the year of Peacock's arrival in the city, noted that while Rangers were 'going stronger than ever', Celtic 'have slipped back quite a bit in recent years ... Celtic fans suggest that there has been a steady decline in Parkhead standards since the retiral, several years ago, of the former "boss", Willie Maley ... They can still rise to the occasion, but much of their time-honoured skill and ability has been blunted by the passing of the years.'

It is typical of the supporters' low expectations at the time that in an article previewing season 1950–51 in the official handbook of the Celtic Supporters Association, only rather cautious optimism was expressed about the much-needed punch at inside-forward being acquired. This was deemed an absolute necessity if the team was to 'go places'. The handbook continued: 'Youngsters Fernie and Peacock were played in these positions in the last few months of the season with the intention of being given the opportunity to settle in and make the positions their own. Whether they shall turn out to be the answer to the supporters' prayers, time alone will tell. Both are still very young, and may, with experience, meet requirements. End-of-season indications, however, were that we may wait a while yet before fulfilment is achieved.'

In Peacock's case, at least, there had been clear signs, notably in the Charity Cup final victory over Rangers at Hampden in May 1950, that he was about to make the inside-left position his own, so profitable already was his left-wing partnership with the inimitable Charlie Tully. The balance the pair brought to Celtic's left flank was just about perfect – the hardworking, unselfish, 'unshowy' Peacock complementing the tricky, flamboyant exhibitionist that was Tully. If Tully could set the presses rolling by simply stepping off the boat from Larne, Bertie had to wander around Glasgow for two hours when he first arrived before he finally summoned up enough courage to ask for directions to his new landlady's flat. He was, he recalled in later years, 'just a young lad lost in the big city'. It was Peacock whose youthful enthusiasm provided just the kind of 'straight-man' foil to his fellow Ulsterman's 'comic' genius, both on and off the field. Surprisingly, but perhaps typically, Peacock still singles out that 1950 Charity Cup triumph – an early glimmer of promise that Celtic could emerge from Rangers' shadow at the start of the new decade – as his favourite match, rather than the 7–1 'spectacular' seven years later, even though he was captain on the latter occasion. In 1950, by contrast, he was still a 'rookie', but he had made the all-important breakthrough. His combination with his fellow countryman Tully flourished in the early years of the decade and gave Celtic renewed hope after the dark days of the late 1940s, with the result that trophies duly found their way to Celtic Park once again. Indeed, such was the understanding developed between the two players that they frequently swapped positions in those early years of their partnership.

While the Supporters' Handbook had been tentative in its praise for the young newcomer, Peacock cast aside all doubt about his capabilities by being the only ever-present in the Celtic side of season 1950–51, a record of consistency and application which earned its reward when the club secured its first major trophy since 1938 by beating Motherwell in the Scottish Cup final in April. Two years later, Peacock underlined his growing reputation as a goalscorer by cracking home a terrific shot against the much-fancied Manchester United in the Coronation Cup semi-final (with Tully providing the cross), so rattling the Old Trafford side and giving substance to Celtic's early onslaught in that match.

Edmund Burns (Glasgow) recalls:

I first saw Celtic before the war in a match at Parkhead against Albion Rovers. The only thing I remember about it was that Albion Rovers had blue jerseys. It might have been Boxing Day 1936, and I was taken by an uncle and was 'lifted over'. But I started going more regularly from about 1944 onwards – I can remember going to games at Cathkin and Hampden about then.

I was a founder member of the Busby and Eaglesham Celtic Supporters Club, round about 1950 or 1951. We paid dues of £5 per annum, plus extra for games at Aberdeen and Queen of the South. One problem was that I and quite a few others worked most Saturday mornings, so I generally missed the Aberdeen trip. During the '50s, Celtic went up and down like waves – results were very unpredictable. But we were always enthusiastic. If we got a good result on the Saturday, we would walk into work on the Monday elated, straight shoulders, head up.

I was at Brockville when Charlie Tully scored with the two corner kicks, the first disallowed, then scoring with the retake. I remember another game when Delaney was playing for Falkirk – anyway, Sean Fallon's arm was broken by Delaney's hip. [This match took place at Brockville on 20 December 1952, a few months before the Scottish Cup tie of Tully's twin corners fame. Fallon finished the match, and even cleared one shot off the line late on.]

I liked Bertie Peacock as a player, a great workhorse for the team. I'll always remember the goal he scored against Manchester United in the Coronation Cup – he just came running in like a train and hit it first time from Tully's chip-back. That was some goal, just about the best I ever saw.

The following season saw a positional change for Bertie that would, with rare exceptions, develop into a fixture. Injury had forced both Joe Baillie and John McPhail (the latter reverting to a midfield role after his time as spearhead of the Celtic attack) to give up the left-half berth, a position each had otherwise threatened to secure permanently. In stepped Bertie Peacock, whose versatility made him a natural choice as replacement. Alongside Bobby Evans and Jock Stein, he helped to form one of the most formidable half-back lines in the club's history with his keen tackling, uncanny sense of anticipation, and sheer hard graft. He and Evans were like two 'human dynamos' beside the commanding presence of Stein in the middle. It was in this role that Peacock became a bulwark of the side which in 1953–54 earned the club's first League and Scottish Cup 'Double' in 40 years. Promotion to captaincy was thus a natural progression soon after Jock Stein's injury put an end to his playing days. Peacock accepted the pinnacle of his Celtic career modestly, describing it simply as 'a great honour'. He demonstrated what it meant for him by scoring Celtic's winning goal in the first match of the 1957–58 season at a time when the side was struggling to strike form, thus playing the captain's part according to script, and setting the team on the road which would lead to Hampden glory in October.

Bertie Peacock was also – a fact often unjustly forgotten – an integral member of the excellent Northern Ireland team which acquitted itself so well in the 1958 World Cup in Sweden (where a young Pele came to international prominence). The Swedish journalists nicknamed Peacock 'The Little Black Ant' because his jet-black mop of hair was so much in evidence all over the pitch in matches against Czechoslovakia, Argentina, West Germany and Czechoslovakia again (when Bertie was unlucky to have a 'goal' chalked off, an effort contributed despite his carrying an injury at the time). The experience gained in Sweden was soon put to good use at Parkhead. As his own service to Celtic was drawing to a close towards the end of the decade, this great club man was helping to bring on the next generation of Celts. During that decade, he and others such as Jock Stein, Neil Mochan, Sean Fallon and Alec Boden would often have conversations in Ferrari's restaurant about the new style of play that was coming into the game – a style most consummately given expression by the great Hungarian team which, witnessed in person by these Celtic players, thrashed England at Wembley in 1953. By the end of the 1950s, Bertie was passing on his knowledge of the game in that same restaurant to up-and-coming youngsters such as Billy McNeill, Bertie Auld and Pat Crerand. Crerand remained so impressed by Peacock's contribution to his development as a player that when interviewed by one of the authors years later, he commented: 'In those days you learned about the game by watching and listening and playing beside players like Bertie Peacock. He was always helpful, always there with a word or two of advice. A smashing guy, Bertie . . . ' Peacock's advice and encouragement would have been much appreciated in the Scottish Cup final replay of 1961 when, though fit to play, Bertie was not selected and told he could turn out for Northern Ireland in Rome instead. His experience was sadly missed as Celtic went down to Jock Stein's Dunfermline. Happily, though, it was still very much available to the Celtic team in the autumn of 1957.

*   *   *

Celtic were drawn to play Third Lanark over two legs in the League Cup quarter-final, while Rangers were paired with Kilmarnock, who had been beaten finalists in the previous season's Scottish Cup after a replay with Falkirk. But before the next round of League Cup action, the league programme had to get under way, with the Old Firm due to meet at Ibrox on league business on 21 September – a match in which Celtic would exact full revenge for their Glasgow Cup defeat at the same venue a month earlier.

'50S MEMORIES
Gerry Heaney (now resident in Vancouver, Canada) remembers the '50s well:

> Billy McNeill, Bobby Murdoch and I played for the successful school team of Our Lady's High, Motherwell in the mid to late '50s.[6] I also played alongside John Cushley in the school team when he captained it – he later became McNeill's understudy at Celtic Park. And I played for Scotland v. England Schools with Andy Roxburgh [later manager of the national team] in 1961. Andy and I both carried on together to Jordanhill College to become teachers.
>
> I have fond memories of the late 1950s – football, friends and rock 'n' roll music! Because I played a lot (for both school and boys' club teams) I did not get to see many league games at Celtic Park, but I well recall the glorious games I did attend, especially the 1951 and 1954 cup finals, and the Coronation Cup victory against Hibs – what a thunderbolt by Neilly Mochan! Every time I see one of those 'Best 100 Goals Ever' videos I keep thinking of that rocket shot which was the equal of any of today's goals. He really could hit them, as he showed again in the 7–1 game.
>
> The 7–1 game was around the time that rock 'n' roll hit Glasgow. I remember going to see Bill Haley in *Rock around the Clock* at the Gaumont picture house in King's Park, a suburb near where I lived and only a stone's throw from Hampden Park. The sites of two of my most outstanding memories as a teenager, Bill Haley and The 7–1 were so close together in time and so similar in several ways. I recall having to queue up for both events with such nervous anticipation. People who had seen Bill Haley before were singing and dancing in the queue. After the show we gathered outside to discuss it. We were all infected by the music and could not wait to buy the records. We were hooked on rock,

91

big-time. The next movie was *The Girl Can't Help It*, starring such legends of the future as Little Richard, Fats Domino and my favourite, Gene Vincent. I later saw him together with Eddie Cochrane at the 'Land [Barrowland Dance Hall]. It was pandemonium and chaos as the crowd surged to the stage time and time again. Girls were fainting from the heat and excitement and their bodies were passed up to the stage to avoid the crush. An event and a half! Other concerts and movies followed and it was exciting to be a teenager then.

My dad was a college teacher. My mum did not work, so with five kids to feed, a car was not on. We did not get a TV until 1960 – also a phone. We lived in a council house and were well provided for. We rented a house at the coast every year, I remember, for our summer holiday at Girvan or Millport. That provided a lot of very happy memories. Our folks sacrificed a lot personally to make sure we were educated and had opportunities to do the best we could.

My dad had played for Partick Thistle, but when a serious injury in a game against Aberdeen cut short his career, he resumed his support for Celtic. He saw the game in which John Thomson died (1931), and his recollections of John and other Celtic legends, games and team histories will stay with me forever. I am trying to pass the torch on to my own boys. It is harder, living in Canada, but they have been to Parkhead and loved it.

Seamus Murphy, now resident in Milton Keynes, has vivid memories of those late summer/early autumn days of 1957, as well as of the '50s generally:

I was in the merchant navy at the time, and was home on leave for about a month. I saw the two Hibs games. They beat us 3–1 at Easter Road, but we got revenge at 'Paradise'. I also saw the thrashing of East Fife (6–1) and the two quarter-final games against the 'Hi-Hi's' (Third Lanark). But I had to sign on again two days after the second of those games. On 16 September I joined the MV *Egyptian*, which was bound for the Mediterranean. Most of the crew was from the Glasgow area. And as I recall, the 'Huns' outnumbered us 'Tims' aboard ship. About a week into the trip we beat Rangers 3–2 in the league game at Ibrox. As you can imagine, the Rangers lads were going mental. Mind you, on board ship you have to get along with each other, so things didn't get out of hand *too* much. Then, when both Celtic and Rangers got through to the League Cup final, you couldn't shut the 'Bluenoses' up – what they were going to do to us when they got us at Hampden, the last result had been a fluke, etc. Their arrogance was unbearable.

What was life like in the '50s in Glasgow and the West of Scotland? Well, for me it was pretty drab and miserable most of the time. Mind you, I was lucky enough to sail around the world to exotic and interesting places: Rio, Buenos Aires, New Orleans, New York, Los Angeles, 'Frisco, Sydney, Cape Town, to name just a few. Having said that, I was always happy to get home, especially to see the Celts play. Most afternoons I would go to the pictures, then, two or three times a week, I would either go to Barrowland, the Locarno, or the F and F in Partick [dance halls]. Sundays after Mass and dinner were spent at 'the Barras', or walking around the art galleries. And in the evening, I'd hop on a number 21 tram to Paisley Road Toll to see if any shipmates were home. We'd spend the evening in the café drinking coffee (the café at the Toll was the Europa Café; it was just off Paisley Road West). There wasn't much else to do on a Sunday. In the summer I'd get a red bus to Helensburgh – 2s 6d [12½ pence] return. I'd walk up and down the promenade and feast on fish and chips before heading home.

Usually by the end of the first week ashore I was 'skint'. I remember taking a girl home from the Locarno one night. She lived in Knightswood – a long bus ride. Being the gentleman, I paid her fare, which left me penniless after seeing her to the door. After the usual 'snog' and arranging another date, I asked if I could borrow my bus fare back into town. I never saw her again!

Another time – I can't remember what year it was – it was a midweek game and Celtic were playing Rangers at home. I don't know if I was broke or couldn't get a ticket. I had the price of a pint and was in Grant's Bar on the corner of Robertson Street and Argyle Street. In comes my mate Harry. 'Come on, Shamie, we're off to the match.' So we jumps on a number 9 tram instead of the usual number 15 which would have taken us up the Gallowgate and into 'The Jungle'. The number 9 went along the London Road. When we arrived, the game was in progress. Harry makes for the Rangers end – I've stuck my scarf deep into my coat pocket, wondering what he's playing at. He gets halfway round the Rangers end, and says, 'This will do us.' 'Keep going!' says I. The steward let us into 'The Jungle' – what a relief! Anyway, at half-time the 'Gers were leading 3–0. Then in the second half, Fernie and Tully and co. really turned it on and with ten minutes to go it was 3–3. Then Rangers got a late winner. That's the way it was; we were used to it. The thing is, to this day I can't remember if that game was a League Cup or a Charity Cup game – nobody seems to remember it.[7]

That day was the one and only time I had been round the *front* of Celtic Park. My usual route was to walk down the High Street, along the Gallowgate, and into Janefield Street to 'The Jungle' or the Celtic end. At half-time, if Celtic were attacking the Rangers end, I'd walk round through 'The Jungle' and stand behind the opposition's goal – except during Rangers games, of course!

Back to Sundays. Mass was compulsory and my parish church was St Mungo's in Parson Street, Townhead. I lived with an Irish family, as did my pal Harry and a couple of other ex-orphanage boys. Harry and I would enter the chapel and head straight for the entrance behind the altar, and come out on to McAslin Street. We'd then buy the *News of the World* (which was 'banned' by the Church), and have a good read and a coffee in the café on the Parliamentary Road until it was time for Mass coming out. We'd then mingle with the congregation as they exited the chapel, and then go home to a lovely big fry-up.

Oh, by the way, going back to that 4–3 game – I don't know if Harry had lost his bearings on account of entering a strange turnstile. Maybe he thought we were at the Celtic end. I forgot to mention – Harry was colour-blind!

If it wasn't for Celtic, I most probably would have had a better life. An example: I docked into South Shields, Tyneside, and was paid off from a tanker, the MV *Lucerna*, on a trip from Houston and Galveston, Texas. That was on 12 December 1955. Blowing most of my money in the pubs, I went along to the 'pool' in North Shields to sign on. I was offered a maiden voyager, a grain carrier called *The Sept Isles*. It was built, I believe, for a Canadian company on the Saint Lawrence river, and after years of service on her I could have stayed on in Canada. But it was only two weeks to Hogmanay. I refused her and signed on a collier, which took coal down to London. I signed off on 23 December 1955, and took the train home to Glasgow. I met the lads and was at Easter Road the next day to see the Celts beat Hibs 3–2 (Mochan got two goals). After the game we managed to get to Leith Docks, to the pubs there, which was a feat in itself, because the police in Edinburgh always herded us back to the trains, and made sure every last Celtic supporter was aboard them. Anyway, we were all in high spirits: Celtic were going great guns and were sitting on top of the league. So, as you can imagine, we couldn't wait for the Ne'erday game. But, as usual, Celtic managed to disappoint us. Beattie was left stranded yards from his goal and the Rangers centre-forward [Kichenbrand] lobbed it over his head into the net. Final score, Celts 0 'Gers 1 [2 January 1956]. After that, it was downhill for Celtic, and I was relieved to sign on a ship bound for Australia.

But getting back to the beginning of the story, if it wasn't for my love of Celtic I most probably would have been in Canada now – after all, there was nothing in Glasgow for me. I was only living in digs, with no family of my own, except a much younger brother who was adopted by a family in Blantyre, and didn't even know who I was. If I had gone to Canada, who knows what possibilities would have been in store for me?

Another experience of Glasgow in those days: I took a couple of months ashore, so I went to the 'Buroo' for a job to tide me over. I kept coming back from each interview still without a job, so finally the man behind the counter says to me, 'The next job I send you to, take your scarf off, and tell them you're Episcopalian or C of E.' I must have stood out like a sore thumb – school: St Peter's, Partick and Castlebay School in the Isle of Barra (which is 95 per cent Catholic); and my name didn't help: Seamus Patrick Bernard Murphy. Anyway, Harry finally got me in with him at McGavin's Whisky Bond in Robertson Lane.

I often wonder what kept us so loyal to the Celts in the '50s. Always being let down before the season's end. Mind you, 'The Jungle' wasn't always packed like it was in recent years before its demise. Often it was less than half full, and the rain came through the corrugated roof, and your feet got soaked from standing in the wet ash. A few gates were under 10,000. My last game in '58 was a boring 2–2 draw against Motherwell [21 April 1958]. I reckon there must only have been 5,000 at that game. And that in a season when we had thrashed Rangers 7–1! But there was always the thrill of seeing the hoops running out of the tunnel – that was enough on its own.

Going back to my orphanage days, all the lads were Celtic fans, and we played football every minute possible each day. I was always Willie Miller in goal – he was my hero.[8] And when we weren't playing, we were singing the Celtic songs: 'Delaney was in the centre'; 'Three goals in three minutes was McGrory's delight'; 'Johnny Thomson'; and 'After the ball was centred', to name but a few. Can you imagine a couple of dozen boys singing at the top of their voices:

'As I was passing Celtic Park, I heard a mighty roar
The mugs in blue were beat six-two
By the Bhoys in green and white.
Delaney was in the centre, the ball was in the net,
And poor old Jerry Dawson, he was lying in the wet.' [9]

I can't remember the rest. Happy memories!

Peter Sweeney of Glasgow is another with clear memories of the early and middle 1950s:

I was a member of the Gorbals-based Sarsfield Celtic Supporters Club in those days. No one knew where the name came from, but it had been around since the 1920s when the fans were going to 'Paradise' on horse-drawn carts.

At this time (the early '50s) there was a great deal of controversy about the flying of the (Irish) tricolour at Celtic Park, and there was a lot of back-biting regarding bigotry, i.e. the names of some Rangers clubs being linked to the Orange Order, etc. Out of the 'blue' appeared a letter in the press saying, 'How can Celtic fans claim there's bigotry in [Rangers] clubs' names, when *they* have a club named after Patrick Sarsfield, that notorious butcher of Protestants in the seventeenth century?'

To say we were 'gobsmacked' is putting it mildly, and it sent us searching in the library to find out about 'our' Patrick. Sure enough, he was there in the history book, although there was no mention of him being a 'butcher'. [Sarsfield was the titular Earl of Lucan.] The book claimed he was one of King James's best commanders up to and including the Battle of the Boyne. He was credited with spotting William of Orange's tactics on the day – to divide his army, sending the largest part to cross the river further south and outflank James's forces. Sarsfield pleaded with the King to counter this move, but the King chose not to, saying it was just a decoy. Too late he saw the danger and the rest is history. Just think what a different result there might have been that day if James had taken Sarsfield's advice. I seem to remember reading that his last words were 'I die, Ireland, but it is all in vain'. When we read this, we were – for all the wrong reasons – even more proud of our name![10]

As always, there was great rivalry between supporters clubs over who had the best banner or board to place at the rear of the bus for away games. We in the Sarsfield had a beautiful, handmade, hand-painted board with letters of the club individually made and stuck on to the board. On one trip to Dundee we realised we were causing some amusement as we drove along. At the bus park, there was more hilarity – only then did we realise we had come all that way with the letter 'S' missing from our name! We never discovered if it was by accident or intent.

The Sarsfield Club had chosen to make an annual visit to the grave of John Millsopp, a young Celtic player who had died tragically in 1952.[11] We usually managed to fill a coach with 30 to 40 'mourners'. The reason for this good turnout will become apparent later. It was usual to contact Celtic Park and ask for a couple of players to join us. On the occasion I went, it was a bitterly cold and wet Sunday afternoon and already starting to get dark. As we approached the cemetery gates, we could see two figures huddled against the wall sheltering from the elements. To our surprise, they turned out to be Bertie Peacock and Jock Stein. We got them on to the bus before they froze to death. That's right – they had come by public transport!

We made our way to the graveside, laid our wreath and said a few prayers, then made our way back to the coach. Bertie and Jock came back to the clubrooms with us, where a dram or two plus a hot meal

The Real 7–1 Team

The Celtic team which beat Rangers in the 1957 League Cup final in sensational fashion. Top row (left to right): Donnelly, Evans, Fallon, Beattie, McPhail, Fernie. Bottom row (left to right): McGrory (manager), Tully, Collins, Peacock (captain), Wilson, Mochan, Johnstone (trainer).

[The 7–1 poster reproduced in miniature on the front cover has been selected as a representative of the commemorative items of memorabilia of famous victories which have been on sale outside Celtic Park on match days down through the years. However, this poster – which may have been on sale shortly after the 7–1 match (there is no indication anywhere of the publication date) – has a captioning error, since it is Peter Goldie, not John Donnelly, who appears in the top left-hand corner of the poster. Donnelly was absent from the team at the time due to a bout of influenza.]

DICK BEATTIE—Goalkeeper. 5 ft. 11 in., 11 st. 2 lb. Was taken to Parkhead from Duntocher Hibs in 1954. A 'keeper of outstanding ability.

JOHN DONNELLY—Right-back. 5 ft. 9 in., 11 st. Arrived from Armadale in 1955 as a centre-half, but has taken over Mike Haughney's berth and made it his own by his consistency and resource. Reveals commendable positional sense and endeavours to keep in touch with his colleagues immediately in front of him.

SEAN FALLON—Left-back. 5 ft. 8 in., 12 st. 6 lb. From Glenavon to Parkhead, March, 1950. Was centre-forward with Sligo Rovers before joining Glenavon, for whom his excellent form at back impressed Manager McGrory. Played for the Irish League against the League of Ireland.

WILLIAM FERNIE—Right-half. 5 ft. 7 in., 10 st. 10 lb. Brought from Kinglassie Colliery to Parkhead in 1949, his promise as a junior came to fruition and is now well established. Artistic ball worker who can go in and take a goal on his own. Honours—England 1957; Wales and Ireland 1955, 57; English League 1953, 54, 57; Finland 1954; Yugoslavia 1957.

ROBERT EVANS—Centre-half. Born Glasgow. 5 ft. 6 in., 10 st. 10 lb. Sir John Stirling Maxwell School, Thornliebank Methodist, St. Anthony's, Celtic, 1944. One of the 1949 Wembley heroes. Got all the honours in 1949 and was never on the losing side. Helped to beat France at Hampden and toured America and Canda with the S.F.A. Honours—England 1949, 51, 54, 56; Wales 1949, 50, 54, 56; Ireland 1949, 50, 52, 54, 56, 58; English League 1950, 51, 52, 53, 54, 55, 56; Irish League 1949, 50 51, 54, 55, 56, 57; League of Ireland 1950, 53, 55, 56, 57, 58; France 1949, 50; Switzerland 1950; Portugal 1950, 55; Austria 1950, 55, 56; Sweden 1953; Norway 1954; Finland 1954; Gugoslavia 1955; Hungary 1955; South Africa 1956; Germany 1957; Spain 1957.

ROBERT PEACOCK—Left-half. 5 ft. 8 in., 10 st. 10 lb. Came from the Irish club Coleraine in 1949. Fast-moving, astute schemer, who knows the passes his forwards like to take on the run. Has been " capped " for Ireland against England and Scotland and for Great Britain against the Rest of Europe. Gave a brilliant display for Ireland against Scotland, in Belfast, this month. Is the Celtic captain.

CHARLES TULLY—Outside-right. Born Belfast. 5 ft 8 in., 10½ st. From Belfast Celtic to Parkhead June, 1948. Can hold the ball to advantage. An Irish League honour before joining Celtic, he has since collected six full "caps" for Ireland against Scotland, England and France.

ROBERT COLLINS—Inside-right. Born Glasgow. 5 ft. 3 in., 10 st. Arrived at Parkhead from Pollok in 1949 and was straightaway brought into the first team against Rangers to prove himself as a lad who knows the value of getting the ball across when his colleagues are placed to meet it. Honours—Wales 1950, 56, 57; Ireland 1950, 56, 58; English League 1953, 55, 57; Irish League 1950, 52, 55, 56, 57; League of Ireland 1950, 52, 55, 56, 57, 58; Austria 1955; Yugoslavia 1955; Hungary 1955; South Africa 1956; Spain 1957; Germany 1957.

BILLY McPHAIL—Centre-forward. 5 ft. 9½ in., 10 st. 7 lb. Was transferred from Clyde and became

LEAGUE CUP DUELS
Rangers won 9, Celtic won 5.

SOUTHERN LEAGUE CUP
1941–42—Rangers 2–0 (Semi-final, Hampden).
1942–43—Rangers 3–0 (Ibrox), Rangers 2–0 (Parkhead).
1943–4—Rangers 4–2 (Semi-final, Hampden).

SCOTTISH LEAGUE CUP
1947–48—Rangers 2–0 (Ibrox), Celtic 2–0 (Parkhead).
1948–49—Rangers 2–1 (Ibr9x), Celtic 3–1 (Parkhead).
1949–50—Rangers 2–0 (Ibrox), Celtic 3–2 (Parkhead).
1951–52—Rangers 3–0 (Semi-final, Hampden).
1955–56—Celtic 4–1 (Ibrox). Rangers 4–0 (Parkhead).
1956–57—Celtic (Parkhead 2–1, Draw 0–0 (Ibrox).

the recognised leader. Has scored more than one vital goal against Rangers.

SAMMY WILSON—Inside-left. 5 ft. 8 in., 10 st. 10 lb. Was taken on a free transfer at the end of the season from St. Mirren, as a wing-half, and on getting his chance up front, accepted it with such alacrity and success that he has not only held it, but has brought praiseworthy command and punch to the line.

NEIL MOCHAN—Outside-left. 5 ft. 7 in., 12 st. Comes in on the wing after being out of the first team more than once this season. This former Morton and Middlesbrough forward carries a powerful shot which has won more than one game.

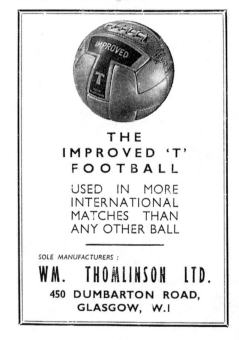

Player profiles in the 1957 League Cup final match programme. (Courtesy of the Scottish Football League)

GEORGE NIVEN—Goalkeeper. Born Blairhall. 5 ft. 9½ in., 11 st. 5 lb. Signed in December, 1947. Had to wait some time before getting his "first-team" place. When the opportunity did come, however, he made the position his own by his consistency. Can rise to heights of brilliance. Honours—English League 1955; Irish League 1954. 55; League of Ireland 1954.

BOBBY SHEARER—Right-back. Born Hamilton. 5 ft. 7 in., 11 st. Was transferred from Hamilton Academicals in 1955 and played his part last season in winning the League Championship for the 30th time. A lion-hearted, determined defender who never gives up.

ERIC CALDOW—Left-back. Born Cumnock. 5 ft. 8 in., 10 st. 5 lb. Was signed from Muirkirk Juniors in July, 1952. The Ayrshire lad was groomed in the Reserve team and when the chance came to step up, accepted it with conspicuous success. A restless, eager defender who uses the ball with foresight once he has cleared his perimeter of danger. Honours—England 1957; Ireland 1958; English League 1957; Spain 1957 (twice); Switzerland 1957; Germany 1957; League of Ireland 1958.

IAN McCOLL—Right-half and captain. Born Alexandria. 5 ft. 10½ in., 11 st. 6 lb. Arrived at Ibrox from Queen's Park, turning professional in June, 1945. "Capped" against England 1950, 1957; Wales 1951 and 1957 and Ireland 1951, 1957 and 1958; played against France 1950, and Belgium 1951; and honoured against Irish League in 1953 and League of Ireland 1952. One of the most effective half-backs in the country. Strong in the tackle and thoughtful in the pass, virtues which saw him "capped" against Spain and Switzerland in the World Cup series last season and also against Germany.

JOHN VALENTINE—Centre-half. Born Buckie. 5 ft 11½ in., 11 st. 10 lb. Turned professional from Queen's Park at the end of last season, but was unlucky to suffer an injury which kept him out of the game for a few weeks. A resolute pivot who misses few balls in the air.

HAROLD DAVIS—Left-half. Born Cupar. 6 ft., 12 st. 7 lb. Was with Newburgh Juniors when signed for East Fife by Manager Scot Symon. Was brought to The Stadium last season from Methil and took over the pivotal berth during George Young's injury. Then moved to left-half in which position he has excelled.

ALEX. SCOTT—Outside-right. Born Falkirk. 5 ft. 10 in., 11 st. On being called up from Bo'ness, Alex. made a memorable debut by recording the hat-trick against Falkirk at Ibrox, in 1955. He also thrilled the London Scots by scoring two of Rangers' three goals against Arsenal at Highbury. Was a Junior Internationalist. Played against the Eire League, Ireland, Yugoslavia and Germany last season and also against the League of Ireland this season. Had to withdraw from the match against Ireland this month because of flu.

BILLY SIMPSON—Inside-right. Born Belfast. 5 ft. 11 in., 11 st. 6 lb. Was transferred from Linfield in October, 1950. Came in to lead the line as a regular first-team player before switching to inside-right. Scored the goal that won Rangers the Scottish Cup in season 1952–53 final replay against Aberdeen. "Capped" for Ireland against Scotland and England.

MAX MURRAY—Centre-forward. Born Falkirk. 5 ft. 9½ in., 11 st. Another Queen's Parker to take the professional ticket with Rangers, moving from Hampden to Ibrox in 1955. Fast moving, artistic forward who keeps in close touch with his colleagues in line with him.

SAM BAIRD—Inside-left. Born Denny. 6 ft. 1 in., 12 st. 4 lb. Went from Clyde to Preston North End and then transferred from Deepdale to Rangers in 1955. A strong assertive player with a powerful shot. Honours—League of Ireland 1954, 58; Ireland 1958; Yugoslavia 1957; Spain 1957 (twice); Switzerland 1957; Germany 1957.

JOHN HUBBARD—Outside-left. Born Pretoria. 5 ft. 5½ in., 8 st. 10 lb. Arrived at Ibrox from South Africa in July, 1949, and emphasised his control and subtlety on the wing. Balances his lack of weight by his cleverness. An expert header of the ball. Played for the Scottish League against the Irish League at Ibrox, the League of Ireland in Dublin and the English League at Hillsborough in 1956.

TOP: Willie Fernie has everything under control in a match at Celtic Park in the mid-1950s. Note the youngsters taken down to the front of the terracing to get a better view. (Courtesy of D.C. Thomson)

CENTRE: Bertie Peacock lets fly during a match at Brockville (v. Falkirk) in the 1950s. (Courtesy of D.C. Thomson)

BOTTOM: Bobby Evans in the thick of things, as usual, during an Old Firm match at Ibrox in the 1950s. (Courtesy of D.C. Thomson)

'Cheeky Charlie'
(Alphie Woods wrote this poem about Charlie Tully
in 1952)

He tips it here and he taps it there,
As on his way he gaily goes,
Wherever the ball is on the field,
It's seldom far from Tully's toes.

He feints, he swerves and meanders on,
The defence left standing in his tracks,
The goal net shudders, the thousands roar,
A natural climax to Charlie's attacks.

Now who's to tell where those feet will rove,
A thankless task for half or back,
The capers he cuts as he juggles along
Simply can't be put in check.

His crosses invite the finishing touch,
His passes stop at his colleague's toe,
The ball is ever at his command,
And rolls along where he wills it to go.

No limit there is to his tricks and traps,
His schemes all come to a happy end,
The combination of head and feet,
For the cheeky chap makes a perfect blend.

The 'Cheeky Chappie', the one and only Charlie Tully, shows his nifty footwork to admirers in the enclosure below the stand at Celtic Park in a 1950s match. (Courtesy of D.C. Thomson)

WEEK-END RADIO AND TELEVISION

TO-DAY

TELEVISION

B.B.C.

3.0 —Swimming, from Newport.
4.0 —Movie Museum.
4.15—I Married Joan.
4.45—Children's TV.
5.45—Scottish Sport.
6.0 —News Headlines, Weather.
6.5 —Six-Five Special.
7.0 —News Summary.
7.5 —Wells Fargo.
7.30—Dixon of Dock Green.
8.0 —Tommy Steele in The Golden Year.
9.10—What's My Line?
9.35—Phil Silvers Show.
10.0 —Sports Special.
10.20—Scottish Sport.
10.30—News.
10.45—Sky at Night, Weather.

STV

5.15—Abbott and Costello.
5.40—News and Sports Results.
6.0 —Sports Desk.
6.30—The Scarlet Pimpernel.
7.0 —Wyatt Earp.
7.30—Office of Strategic Services.
8.0 —64,000 Question.
8.30—Val Parnell's Saturday Spectacular.
9.30—Five Names for Johnny
10.0 —National News.
10.5 —The Great Pictures of Alexander Korda.
12.0 —Close Down.

RADIO

SCOTTISH (371m.)

2.0—No Hero: Saturday Matinee.
3.0—Scottish Dance Music. 3.30—Association Football. 4.30—Recital: Matthew Nisbet (baritone). 4.45—Sportsreel. 5.0 — Children's Hour. 5.55—Weather. 6.15—News and Sports Results. 6.28 — Sportsreel. 6.50 —Scottish Dance Music. 7.25 —The Glens of Glendale. 7.45—Scots Songs. 8.0—Variety Playhouse. 9.0—News. 9.15—While the Sun Shines. 10.45—Family Prayers. 11.0-11.8—News and Weather.

LIGHT (1500m., 247m.)

2.0 p.m.—Come Into the Parlour. 2.45—Watch Your Step. 3.0—Bandstand. 3.45—Wales v England (foot-

LAST NIGHT ON RADIO

IN "Scope," Edward Boyd told a story very reminiscent of his Country Cameo series in the "Evening Times." It was one of the best he has told in this series.

♦ ♦ ♦

"MY Word" has returned to the air again, and on last night's hearing it has improved. Frank Muir, Denis Norden, and Nancy Spain were back, and with them was E. Arnott Robertson. However, this is a case where time will tell, for after a few sessions in the last series I found interest waned considerably, and the show became rather flat.

"One Minute Please" is still the best game on the air at present, and the cleverest idea for some time. A. M. K.

ball). 4.45 — Sandy Macpherson (organ). 5.0—Sports report. 6.0—Guitar Club. 6.30—Just Jazz. 7.0—News, Radio-Newsreel, and Football Summary. 7.30—Sing It Again. 8.0 —The State Visit to the U.S.A. 8.10 —Melody on the Line. 9.0—Saturday Popular Concert. 10.0—B.B.C. Studio Choir. 10.30—News. 10.40—Richard Attenborough (records). 11.15—Take Your Partners. 11.55-12.0—News and Shipping Forecast.

THIRD (464m., 194m.)

NETWORK THREE—6.30 p.m.—The World of Books. 7.0-7.45—Record Review. THIRD — 8.0 — Orchestral Concert: B.B.C. Symphony Orchestra. 8.45—The State of the Parties (talk). 9.5 — Orchestral Concert: Part II. 9.40 — Richard Tauber (talk). 10.10 — Poems by Baudelaire. 10.35-10.50 — Fernando Valenti (harpsichord).

LUXEMBOURG (208m.)

6.0 — Requests Records. 7.0 — Rythem on the Range. 7.30—Intrigue. 8.0 — Jamboree. 10.0 — Remembering Glenn Miller. 10.30—Spin with the Stars. 11.0—Bringing Christ to the Nations. 11.30—Record Round-up. 12.0—Close Down.

TO-MORROW

TELEVISION

B.B.C.

11 a.m. - 12.30 p.m. — High Mass, from Buckfast Abbey.
2.30—Gardening Club.
3.0 —News Review.
3.30—Concert Hour.
4.15—Brains Trust.
4.55—Lifeboat, from Dover.

5.0 —Children's TV.
6.12—Weather.
7.0 —Meeting Point.
7.25—News Summary.
7.30—Water Rats.
8.0 —Play, "The Mulberry Bush."
9.30—The Borneo Story.
10.0 —Max Jaffa, Music at Ten.
10.30—News.
10.45—The Epilogue.

STV

2.15—Armand and Michaela Denis.
2.30—Free Speech.
3.0 —The Rosemary Clooney Show.
3.30—Film Festival.
the Mohicans.
4.50—Hawkeye and the Last of
5.20—Robin Hood.
5.50—The Passing Scene.
6.5 —National News.
6.15—Sign Off.
7.0 —About Religion.
7.25—National News.
7.30—I Love Lucy.
8.0 —Sunday Night at the London Palladium.
9.0 —Highway Patrol.
9.30—Armchair Theatre.
10.30—National News.
10.35—The Jack Jackson Show.
11.5 —Theatre Royal.
11.30—Close Down.

RADIO

SCOTTISH (371m.)

7.50 a.m. — Reading. 7.55—Weather. 8.0—News. 8.10—Programme Parade. 8.18—Morning Melody. 8.55—Weather. 9.0—News. 9.10—Home for the Day. 9.45—

Service. 10.30—Music Magazine. 11.20—International Concert Hall. 12.10—The Critics. 12.55—Weather. 1.0—News. 1.10—Portrait of Washington. 1.40—Opera by Radio. 2.0—The Scottish Garden. 2.15—Recital. 2.30—Symphony Concert. 3.15—By-ways of Biography. 3.30—Symphony Concert (Part 2). 4.15—Can I Help You? 4.30—Talking About Music. 5.0—Children's Hour. 5.50—Money Matters. 5.55—Weather. 6.0—News. 6.15—Radio Newsreel. 6.45—Grand Hotel. 7.30—Letter From America. 7.45—Service. 8.25—Appeal. 8.30—The Claverings (Part 8). 9.0—News. 9.15—Strike Back (Nato Exercise). 10.0 —Music Making. 10.50—The Epilogue. 11.0-11.8—News and Weather

LIGHT (1500m., 247m.)

9.0 — Silver Chords. 9.30 — Good Morning Music. 10.30—Top of the Form. 11.0—Men About Music. 11.30 — Service. 12.0 — Family Favourites. 1.15—Billy Cotton Band Show. 1.45—Educating Archie. 2.15 Ray's A Laugh. 2.45—Movie-Go-Round. 3.30—Melody Hour 4.30—Ambrose in London (Part 4) 5.0—Mr Bentley and Mr Braden. 5.30—The Hit Parade. 6.0—Sing It Again. 6.30—Round the Bend. 7.0—Semprini Serenade. 7.30—News 7.35—Transatlantic Spotlight. 7.45—Confidentially They're Off. 8.15—Just For You (records) 9.15—Does the Team Think? 9.45—Ian Stewart (piano). 10.0 — Community Hymn-singing. 10.30—News. 10.40 — Rendezvous (piano music). 11.0-11.55—Pick of the Pops (records). 11.55-12.0—News and Weather

THIRD (464m., 194m.)

5.0—La Vida Breve (opera) on gramophone records) Act 1 5.45—The German Occupation of Russia. 6.5—La Vida Breve (Act 2) 6.40—Irene (play). 8.55—Orchestral Concert 10.0—Orchestra (Poem for Dancing). 10.45-11.10 — Hindemith and Bloch.

LUXEMBOURG (208m.)

6.0—Beaver Club. 6.15—You Lucky People. 6.45 — Accordion Time. 7.0—The David Whitfield Show. 7.30—The Winifred Atwell Show. 8.0—Opportunity Knocks. 8.30—Take Your Pick. 9.0—This I Believe. 9.30—Your Sunday Valentine. 10.0—Record Rendezvous. 10.30—Bing Sings. 10.45—Ted Heath and His Music. 11.0—Top Twenty. 12.0—Close Down.

League Cup Final
Celtic
v
Rangers
To-morrow (Sat)
Hampden Park. Kick-off 2.45 p.m.
Stands Fully Booked
Enclosure 3/-, Ground 2/-,
Boys 9d.
30 mins. Extra Time if necessary

TOP: The radio and television programmes for the weekend of the League Cup final, 19 October 1957. The second half of the match was broadcast on Scottish radio between 3.30 and 4.30 p.m. (Courtesy of the Glasgow *Evening Times*)

BOTTOM: The match advertisement in the *Evening Times*, 18 October 1957. (Courtesy of the Glasgow *Evening Times*)

LEFT: What was on in Glasgow's cinemas, theatres and dance halls on the day of the League Cup final. (Courtesy of the Glasgow *Evening Times*)

BOTTOM: The singles charts with best-selling pop records in the UK on 19 October 1957 (from *40 Years of NME Charts*). (Courtesy of Boxtree Ltd)

October – November 1957

TOP: Three famous Celts – Bertie Peacock, Charlie Tully and Bobby Evans – pictured during a break from training at Celtic Park, 1957.

CENTRE: Jimmy McGrory, the epitome of the genial, pipe-smoking manager (as per the press cliché of the time), photographed at Celtic Park circa 1960. (Courtesy of Scottish Media Newspapers Ltd)

RIGHT: Sean Fallon, the 'Iron Man', gets in some heading practice at Celtic Park during a training session, 1957–58. Note the cantilever cover at the Celtic end which came into use that season. (Courtesy of D.C. Thomson)

would be waiting. (Hence the good turnout, as a dram on a Sunday in those days, when pubs were closed, was liquid gold!) After the refreshments, several of us were talking to Jock about football in general when the subject of Celtic's recent signing, Billy McPhail, came up. His injury problems were well known. The joke going around Glasgow at the time went like this: Clyde's manager Haddow to Jimmy McGrory at the completion of the signing: 'Now, where do you want me to send the crutches?'

To our surprise, Jock blurted out, 'They've signed the wrong man. McPhail's days are over. He has two dodgy knees and will never finish a game again.' How wrong could Jock have been? Billy went on to finish many games and who will ever forget his hat-trick in the 7–1 game?

When it was time for Bertie and Jock to leave, several of us walked with them to the tram stop. No flash cars for Celtic players in those days. On average a first-team player was earning £12 per week, not much more than the average fan.

Next year when the subject of a visit to John Millsopp's grave was raised, I opposed it as club treasurer on grounds of cost, adding, 'When did any of us last visit the grave of a loved one?' There was a stony silence all round and that was the end of the visits. I was very unpopular for a while.

At one of the Sarsfield meetings in the mid-'50s, some members suggested that we have a visit to Celtic Park. Our first surprise came with the reply agreeing to our visit. It was written on a piece of ordinary notepaper by Jimmy McGrory. There were more surprises to come. About 20 of us met outside the main entrance to Celtic Park and were then invited through by an official. Most of us were going through that door for the first time. We were left in a dismal and poorly lit entrance hall for a few minutes. On the walls were several portraits of people like Brother Walfrid and some giants who had worn the hoops. They all looked very sad. Eventually Jimmy McGrory appeared to welcome us. Most wanted to see the trophy room. Here the disappointment started.

Celtic had done the 'Double' the year before, so these trophies were there, along with the Empire Exhibition Trophy, etc. But the presentation was very bad – there was a hole in the carpet and you could have written your name in the dust on some of the cabinets. All the trophies were needing some attention. One member asked where the Coronation Cup was. Jimmy didn't know but said we could help him look for it in the cabinets and drawers! We found it on the floor behind the door we had just come through. It was a sorry sight, tarnished and still bearing the green and white ribbons from the day it was won, but they were faded and wrinkled.

As the tour continued, things didn't improve. The chairman's office looked like a scene from *Steptoe and Son* [a '60s comedy show whose main characters were rag-and-bone men]. The manager's office was tiny and bare. The directors' room was a joke – odd chairs, maybe they were antiques! The treatment room was so small that the trainer, who had a young player on the table, had to step aside so that we, one by one, could 'peek' round the door. The dressing-rooms were so impoverished it prompted one of our members to say, 'I've seen better facilities at a junior club.'

Our tour ended with a cup of tea, then Jimmy said training would soon be over and we could get some autographs. Personally, I had seen enough and made my excuses, as did several others. Outside the ground we were saying to each other, 'What did they do with the money?' Someone made the excuse of the war, but the war had been over for ten years. Thankfully, the present set-up is a vast improvement.

Still on the '50s, most members of our club would tell you that the real highlight of the season was the visit to Aberdeen, even though it usually fell in January. It entailed an overnight stay in a local boarding house, 17s 6d [87½ pence] for dinner, bed and breakfast. After the game, no matter the outcome, we would all be signed into the local British Legion Club by our host and his friends. They were always great nights, with no hint of trouble. Our members would provide at least half the entertainment. The highspot of the evening would come from a local Celtic fan, who would sing 'The Ballad of John Thomson'. When he finished there would not be a dry eye in the hall. At closing time it was back to the boarding house where the 'cairy oot' was already laid in. No matter how badly we felt the next morning, most of us still managed to make it to Mass at the Cathedral.

Soon it became time to say farewell to our Aberdeen friends, with a cheery 'See you next year!'. Time and weather permitting, we would make a detour on the way home to visit the grave of John Thomson in Fife.

ENDNOTES

1 Valentine had made his debut against his old club in the Charity Cup final the previous May, and so the League Cup match with St Mirren was only his second appearance for Rangers.

2 Jim Sharkey was transferred in November 1957 to Airdrie, where he was highly popular. He became known as 'The Tully of Broomfield', both for his excellent on-field contribution and for his warm and engaging personality in the dressing-room.

3 This match was played on 31 March 1962, and was the scene of a field invasion by Celtic fans frustrated at their team's losing performance against St Mirren in the semi-final of the Scottish Cup.

4 McMillan was predictably nicknamed 'The Wee Prime Minister'. One of Airdrie's better players on the day was Billy Price, who later joined Celtic, for whom he gave fine service for a couple of seasons, starting in 1961. Unusually, Price had been suspended *sine die* in June 1953 while a provisional signing with Airdrie, but had the suspension lifted a year later. Unlike Willie Woodburn of Rangers, whose *sine die* suspension was lifted after three years, Price elected to take the opportunity to continue playing professional football. Of course, Woodburn was already in his late thirties when his suspension was lifted, while Price was nearly 20 at the time of his reprieve.

5 This ditty was, of course, adapted from a popular Catholic hymn of the time sung in honour of Mary, the mother of Christ.

6 Our Lady's High School (Motherwell), with McNeill as captain, reached the final of the 1957 Scottish Secondary Schools Shield. The first match was drawn and, as Billy McNeill confirmed to one of the authors, the replay never took place due to a dispute over the venue (the ground of junior club Blantyre Victoria, described by one of the headmasters as 'a dump-heap'). Billy also remembers Mr Heaney as being a good player on the school team.

7 The match was in fact a Glasgow Cup first-round tie, played on 21 August 1956. During this game, Rangers' Sammy Baird came off second best in his physical jousts with Sean Fallon, damaging his shoulder after one clash between what the *Daily Record* described as 'types who will not give an inch'.

8 Willie Miller was an exceptionally fine goalkeeper for Celtic during the 1940s who often won the hearts of both Celtic and opposing fans with daring displays of bravery.

9 This is a version of a song commemorating a famous Celtic victory over Rangers at Celtic Park by six goals to two on 10 September 1938. Jimmy Delaney was indeed a scorer against Rangers' famous keeper Jerry Dawson, although the star man in the hoops that day was Malky MacDonald with a hat-trick.

10 In Mr Sweeney's original recollection, Patrick Sarsfield was killed at the Battle of the Boyne and the dying words attributed to him in the text were supposedly

uttered on that occasion. In fact, however, according to his entry in the *Concise Dictionary of National Biography*, Sarsfield survived that battle and was active as a military cómmander of Irish soldiers on James II's behalf for a further three years, and was in 1692 in command of Irish troops intended for an invasion of England, before being mortally wounded at Landen in 1693 while in the French service. Whether he ever spoke the dying words quoted is thus a matter for conjecture, although the attribution is understandable in view of his leading role in James's Irish soldiery. 'The Battle of the Boyne is celebrated in Northern Ireland as a victory for the Protestant cause on 12 July, which is actually the "old style" date of the more decisive Battle of Aughrim in the following year [1691]' [*Encyclopedia Britannica*]. Sarsfield, acknowledged as a superb cavalry commander, was in charge of the reserve at Aughrim. The Battle of the Boyne actually took place on 1 July 1690.

11 Millsopp, a versatile young utility player who had been with the club since 1947, was taken ill after training on 9 September 1952 and operated on for appendicitis. Complications set in, and he died just over a week later in the Glasgow Royal Infirmary. Rangers were visitors to Celtic Park on 20 September, and both sets of players wore black armbands, having attended the funeral that morning. The mood of the Celtic players was hardened during the minute's silence when at least one shout of 'F*** the Pope' echoed over the ground, followed by a growing growl of disapproval from the home support. The referee cut the silence short (at about 45 seconds), and within ten minutes of the start, Celtic led 2–0. They finished 2–1 winners.

CHAPTER FOUR

The Eve of Triumph

Over comes a very high ball;
Up goes McPhail above them all.
The ball and Billy's head have met.
A lovely sight, the ball is in the net.

THE SEASON CONTINUES
Having qualified for the League Cup quarter-finals, Celtic opened their 1957–58 league campaign with an away match on 7 September 1957 against the Scottish Cup holders Falkirk at Brockville. The Parkhead club's league form had declined considerably during the previous two seasons (1955–56 and 1956–57), when they finished fifth twice running, compared to the top and runners-up spots achieved in the two seasons before that. After the tailspin in form in the spring of 1957, few supporters could muster much optimism that Celtic were ready to mount a serious challenge for the league flag in the new season. Although they had come out on top in their League Cup section in August, winning it eventually by a margin of three points, they had shown too many signs of the old frailties for the fans to think they could sustain a real effort to capture the championship. The previous season, Falkirk, despite their cup win, had finished in the lower half of the league table, and had started the new season without showing to advantage, finishing a distant second behind Aberdeen in their League Cup group.

Celtic introduced yet another debutant for the game, 17-year-old Jim Conway taking over from an unfit McPhail. The Parkhead side came away with both points thanks to a tremendous strike from 25 yards by Fernie after delightful play by Tully and Collins just before the interval; but it was a match they were very fortunate to win. Donnelly had to make two

101

desperate goal-line clearances, while Beattie pulled off a couple of superb stops from Falkirk's wingers, Murray and O'Hara. The home side pressed for long periods and Celtic's attack rarely got going, with the inexperienced Conway frequently being caught offside. The only shots of note from Celtic apart from the goal were a terrific 30-yarder from that man Collins again, and a fine effort from Tully. It was clear that, the Fernie–Tully–Collins triangle on the right apart, Celtic were still a mediocre combination. Even the normally reliable Bobby Evans was faulted for being too often and too easily drawn out of position in this match (although his aerial work was still good), while young Bertie Auld showed a flash of temper – a character trait which would later see him depart from Celtic for Birmingham at Bob Kelly's insistence – when he was booked for a foul on Falkirk's Scottish international full-back, Parker. Meanwhile, Rangers, despite losing another two goals at home, defeated Queen of the South, while Hearts handed out a statement of intent by humbling Dundee 6–0 at Tynecastle. Three days earlier, Rangers, representing Scotland in the European Cup, had given a highly creditable performance against St Etienne, winning 3–1 after conceding an early goal before an Ibrox crowd of 85,000.

On the Wednesday following the start of the league programme (11 September), the first legs of the League Cup quarter-final ties were played, with Celtic at home to Third Lanark and Rangers away to Kilmarnock. At Rugby Park, just under 27,000 saw Rangers go down by two goals to one. The following Saturday, a massive crowd of 78,000 – an attendance only exceeded in that season's competition at the final itself – turned out at Ibrox to see if Rangers could overcome the deficit. It was a tie dogged by controversy over Rangers' centre-forward Don Kichenbrand. The rumbustious South African, dubbed 'The Rhino' (and the hero of a young Rangers supporter called Kenny Dalglish), was dropped from the return leg at Ibrox after press criticism of his 'tough-tactics display' in the first match at Rugby Park, where he had been barracked by the home fans for 'charging' at Willie Toner (who had been on Celtic's books at the start of the decade) and Jimmy Brown, the Ayrshire club's centre-half and goalkeeper respectively. Kichenbrand's rather crude, cumbersome, 'bulldozing' style apart, he had also been singled out as the chief culprit in squandering opportunities to kill off the tie in that first leg instead of ending up, in the event, on the losing side. Although he had netted Rangers' goal, his finishing was described as 'atrocious' by at least one reporter. But the Light Blues, with Max Murray in Kichenbrand's place for the return match in Glasgow, did make it to the semi-finals, albeit only by the narrowest of margins, needing a Johnny Hubbard penalty and two goals in the final 15 minutes to take them through on a 4–3 aggregate scoreline. Kilmarnock were, in 1957, just beginning to produce the strong sides which would, after a series of near misses, culminate in their capture of the league championship immediately prior to the start of Celtic's nine-in-a-row run of titles under Jock Stein.

By comparison with Rangers, Celtic qualified for the semi-finals at a canter. For the first leg at Parkhead, Billy McPhail was restored at centre-forward. With Celtic playing their ninth match in under five weeks, only 20,000 were on hand to see Bobby Collins – in tremendous early-season form – open the scoring in 12 minutes when he hustled a 'Hi-Hi' defender into an error and fired home the resulting loose ball from close range. Thereafter Celtic cruised, going in at the interval four goals to the good and finishing up victors by 6–1. But, most significantly as regards the destiny of the 1957–58 League Cup, this was the game when Billy McPhail really struck form for the first time since the start of the season. His erstwhile most severe judge – his brother John – noted that Billy, 'with a glorious exhibition of head and foot work, silenced his critics and with a bit of luck might have notched four goals instead of only two'. McPhail's first, coming only eight minutes after Collins's opener, was a beauty, and somewhat reminiscent of the goal his brother John had scored against Motherwell to win the Scottish Cup in 1951. He head-flicked the ball past his immediate opponent Lewis, sped past a full-back, and crashed the ball home from about ten yards. Sammy Wilson, described in John McPhail's match report for the *Daily Record* (12 September 1957) as 'a revelation in this Celtic forward line', added the third after a combined move with Collins, while McPhail's heading ability was decisive in the fourth. The *Record's* man on the scene praised Wilson in particular for 'his snappy ground passes and positional intelligence' which, he noted, blended perfectly with 'the dash of Collins and the subtlety of Tully'. Collins and Auld completed the scoring for the home side. John McPhail at last expressed satisfaction with the Celtic forward line and predicted, 'They will score many goals.' He undoubtedly had no inkling of just how many in one particular match a little over a month away! The new goalscoring partnership of McPhail and Wilson was now added to the trickery and invention of Tully and Collins. And it was good to see the youngster Auld redeem himself somewhat from his indiscretion at Brockville with a refreshing display and a fine solo goal.

The five-goal margin of victory made the return leg at Cathkin on the Saturday a formality. Fielding an unchanged team, Celtic added another three goals without reply to extend the aggregate score to 9–1. Once again, Bobby Collins was first off the mark with a powerful free-kick from outside the penalty area. Then McPhail headed home after a Tully–Fernie move at a set-piece. And from a Tully cut-back from the byline, Wilson notched the third. In addition to the fine play and goalscoring form of the forwards, Willie Fernie, who had been rather subdued in the first leg, gave a sparkling display of ball-artistry, spreading the play with great accuracy and showing all his tricks against the forlorn Thirds defence. In the other quarter-final ties, Clyde beat Aberdeen home and away, while in an all-Second Division clash, Brechin City disposed of Hamilton by an aggregate score of 5–2.

The following Wednesday saw a break from club action, but Evans and Collins were on duty for the Scottish League against the League of Ireland in Dublin. The Scots won easily by 5–1, and the highlight was the hat-trick scored by Bobby Collins. Here was one Celt at least who had started the season in absolutely top form.

With the forward line beginning to gel, Celtic supporters headed to Ibrox for the league clash with their old rivals on 21 September with renewed optimism. The problems which had marred earlier displays were now being ironed out, while Rangers had shown a growing uncertainty, particularly in defence, in their recent displays. Against that, Celtic had not won a league match at Ibrox since the war. Indeed, discounting three wartime victories there, in Ne'erday Southern League matches (1941 and 1945 and in September 1943), Celtic had not won in the Scottish League on Rangers' home turf since 1935, 22 years previously. The long wait was about to end for the green and white contingent in the large crowd.

The Celtic supporters must have experienced a moment of disquiet, however, when the forward line was announced. Celtic rested the inexperienced Auld for this match (perhaps fearing that his temperament might be suspect in the cauldron of an Old Firm clash), and Jim Sharkey returned – an understandable switch in favour of the more mature player. But Sharkey was fielded at outside-right, while Tully was moved over to the left wing in Auld's place. This seemed to indicate that the Fernie–Tully–Collins triangle on the right flank, which had been the highlight of Celtic's recent play, would be broken up in a vital match. Was this just a tactical ploy aimed at confusing the Rangers rearguard? Would this upset Celtic's new-found attacking rhythm?

That night's sports edition of the *Evening Times* described the atmosphere on the terraces as kick-off time approached: 'The air above Ibrox was damp and clammy, but the terracing atmosphere was tinder dry 20 minutes before the start when a full half-dozen Eire tricolours were brandished at the Celtic end of the ground. Immediately a like number of Union Jacks came up in "retaliation" at the other end of the ground, and a 70,000 crowd was at simmering point when Rangers made the sensational announcement that Alan Austin, the old Kilmarnock Amateur boy, was to be thrown in at the deep end at left-half.' If the news that Rangers would be fielding an inexperienced half-back gave Celtic ranks a fillip, it didn't look that way in the opening quarter of an hour. Rangers, with the aid of a significant breeze, pressed from the kick-off and Celtic 'just weren't at the races' in the initial phase of the match. The home side claimed a penalty for 'hands' against Celtic skipper Peacock, but their appeals were brusquely dismissed by referee Hugh Phillips of Wishaw.

Then, with 19 minutes of the match gone, and rather against the run of play, Celtic struck in the diminutive shape of Bobby Collins. The build-up to the goal provided an indication of things to come in the clubs' next meeting. McPhail beat Valentine to a well-directed clearance from Sean Fallon, and, with the deftest of head-flicks, guided it perfectly into the path of the 'Wee Barra'. Taking the ball in his stride, Collins cut into the penalty area, drew Rangers' keeper Ritchie, and smacked the ball past him for a glorious leading goal, one which Gair Henderson, reporting for the *Evening Times*, claimed 'had no equal for pure spectacle at Ibrox this season'. It was a beautifully worked and timed move, and it had sliced open the Rangers rearguard with surprising ease. Shortly afterwards, Tully and Shearer got involved in a confrontation and had to be spoken to by referee Phillips, though neither was officially cautioned. The home side were clearly stung by the unexpected reverse, but it was Celtic who began to exert greater control in midfield, with Fernie striding forward to good purpose. And the Celts could have gone further ahead when Tully, swerving past several challenges, juggled the ball at the byline and then centred for Sharkey in an excellent position. His shot was blocked by Baird, although some Celts thought he had made illegal use of the arm to do so. But it should have been a goal and Tully 'looked appealingly to the sky' after the chance was lost. As in the Glasgow Cup match a month before, Sharkey had failed to reproduce the deadliness of his Boxing Day 1955 finishing.

But just as Celtic's goal was scored against the run of play, so was the equaliser. Six minutes from the interval, Scott, for once getting the better of Fallon, sent over a cross which was met brilliantly by Billy Simpson, Rangers' Northern Irish inside-right, and as Gair Henderson described it, the Copland Road end of the ground was instantly transformed, 'fluttering from top to bottom in one hysterical blue mass'. Beattie in the Celtic goal seemed somewhat at fault for not trying to cut out the cross. The teams went in level after 45 minutes, and despite the loss of an equalising goal, Celtic could feel satisfied with their first half's work. Playing against the wind, they had weathered successfully the early Rangers storm and scored a fine goal themselves, and their attacking forays, if less frequent than those of their opponents, had carried more menace.

Oddly, Rangers, first out of the tunnel for the restart, were kept waiting a full two minutes before they were joined by their opponents on the pitch. But it was Celtic who created the first opportunity to score, Wilson mistiming his attempt to connect with a McPhail cross, and Shearer having to look sharp to scramble the ball clear. Celtic continued to attack, and nine minutes into the second half Wilson was stopped illegally 25 yards from goal – just the kind of range favoured by Bobby Collins for a direct shot. While the Ibrox defenders were still forming their 'wall' in expectation of such a goal-attempt by Collins, the Celtic inside-right quickly lobbed the ball in the direction of McPhail, who was standing wide of the still-forming Light Blue barrier. With a marvellous header he propelled it goalwards, and the ball sailed just under the crossbar with Ritchie beaten all ends up. Once again, questions would be asked of Valentine – for McPhail had been given plenty of room in which to launch the ball in the direction he wished. Celtic almost added a third soon after through Wilson, who sent the ball just past the upright. But a two-goal lead was not long in coming. Ten minutes after McPhail's counter, he became provider. Moving out to the left to take advantage of a penetrating passing movement involving Tully and Collins, he drew Valentine from the middle and then sent over a perfectly placed cross for Sammy Wilson to bullet a header past a motionless Ritchie. It was another piercing move which had completely bamboozled the home defence. At this point Rangers looked certain losers, but although they had been outplayed by the visitors, they refused to be outfought. They launched themselves into attack, and got a reward almost immediately. Only four minutes had elapsed since Wilson's goal when Simpson got his second of the match, after Beattie had failed to intercept a Murray back-header into the goalmouth. Rangers pressed for most of the remainder of the match, and struck a post, but they lacked sufficient guile to open up a Celtic defence in which Bobby Evans had a magnificent game, dispelling all doubts over whether he would win another cap in the upcoming Home International match against Northern Ireland in Belfast.

Reviewing the contest, commentators were virtually unanimous in judging that Celtic deserved their 3–2 win. Most felt that the turning point was the brilliant opening goal scored by Collins, for up until that point Rangers had dominated proceedings, although without turning the wind to their advantage in scoring terms. After the interval, with the wind growing stronger, it was always going to be more difficult for the Ibrox side. As in the Glasgow Cup tie, Celtic had shown greater poise and a superior ability to play cohesive, controlled football, but this time they had added the all-important ingredient of decisive finishing. The Celtic supporters were jubilant, the panic evident at the heart of Rangers' defence causing one of them to chortle on his way out of the ground, 'It's no a Valentine the Rangers want – it's a get-well card!'

Once again Collins had shown he was in fine goalscoring mood. Once again the McPhail–Wilson striking combination had done what it was paid to do. Once again Charlie Tully ('some veteran this!' commented one report) had caused havoc with his skilful dribbling and clever distribution of the ball. And Fernie had shown that his mastery of the ball in windy conditions was second to no one's. But with Rangers doing much of the attacking, it was also vital that the Celtic rearguard, so shaky at times in the League Cup sectional matches, stood firm, and this too was accomplished. Peacock had a fine game, as did Donnelly, who easily mastered the veteran Johnny Hubbard. More surprising was the control Sean Fallon had exerted over Alec Scott on the opposite flank. The Irishman, now in his 36th year, had been troubled by the Ranger's speed in the Glasgow Cup match, but this time he had stuck to his task, using all his experience to counter the winger's attempts at deception. Only Beattie's hesitancy at the Rangers goals gave cause for concern. But chief among the reasons he hadn't been more troubled, despite Rangers' considerable possession of the ball, was the almost flawless display given by Celtic's red-headed centre-half.

BOBBY EVANS
Patsy Keane (now resident in Yorktown Heights, New York, USA) recalls the player he loved watching then:

> My favourite Celtic player of the '50s was always Bobby Evans. He was a tremendous player. He had great anticipation, and he was a marvellous tackler – the amazing thing was that his tackling was also so clean. He always played the ball fairly. He was a great, great player, was Bobby Evans.

An ironic feature of Rangers' catastrophic defeat in the 1957 League Cup final is the little-known fact that one of the chief agents of their downfall might have been lining up that day on their side. In a 1959 profile of Scotland's captain, the sportswriter Alec Fraser recalled that before he signed for Celtic in 1944 (during wartime), Bobby Evans might well have joined Rangers had not two famous players of the latter club, namely Willie Waddell and Willie Woodburn, felt at the time neither sufficiently qualified nor senior enough in status to recommend Evans to their then manager, Bill Struth, after spotting the player's talent in the colours of the junior club St Anthony's, whose ground was close to Ibrox. Nor would Evans have been lining up in Celtic's colours at Hampden that day had he accepted an approach by a representative of the Millionarios club of Bogota after several Colombian football clubs broke away from their national association and formed their own league. This was at a time (1950) when British footballers were not being paid sums commensurate with their drawing power at the gate during the post-war attendance boom. The rebel Colombian clubs, being then outwith FIFA's jurisdiction, were able to pay levels of remuneration of their own choosing, rather than those laid down by the game's official legislators. One of those who succumbed to temptation, Charlie Mitten of Manchester United, claimed he had signed up for more money than he had earned in his 14 years as a professional footballer. But despite such financial inducements – and a package which guaranteed a house, complete with servants, and a car –

Evans opted to remain in Scotland, mainly in view of the reluctance of his fiancée (later his wife) to leave for South America. (Had he gone, he would have lined up alongside the fabulous Alfredo di Stefano, who was later to become arguably the game's first modern 'superstar' with Real Madrid.) Another factor was the time-limit imposed on the decision – Evans was given only one hour to make up his mind!

Just how much both Rangers and Millionarios lost out on became clear as the red-headed dynamo – once described as 'a team in himself' – developed into the accomplished player he was for Celtic in the ensuing decade. His early years with Celtic were, of course, unsuccessful ones for the club, causing one observer to comment after another tireless but fruitless display by Evans, 'It must be shattering to put so much into a game and get nothing out of it.'

Evans was a tenacious tackler and resolute defender who also bounded into attack at every opportunity, perhaps not surprisingly for a player who in his early days was fielded in every position in the forward line, and whose best position, as late as 1948, was thought to be at inside-left. Indeed, his first appearance in the right-half berth which he was to make his own for most of the 1950s came in the Dens Park 'relegation' clash with Dundee on 17 April 1948, when Celtic needed – and got – a victory to secure their Division 'A' status.[1] Evans was initially reluctant to persevere in his new role as a half-back and hankered for a return to the forward line. But soon he was playing in his new position for Scotland, winning the first of his 48 full caps in October 1948. The following year he helped Scotland dump the English at Wembley by 3–1, and was again on the winning side at Wembley two years later. In 1955 he took over the centre-half spot in the national team from Rangers' George Young (and gave near-perfect performances in Vienna and Budapest in a position which he later made his own). And by the end of the decade he was leading the national side out on to the hallowed turf of Wembley as Scotland's captain, opposite the great Billy Wright.

As a Celt, Bobby Evans's most brilliant form was reserved for the Coronation Cup. It was his interception and sudden, penetrating pass in the opening minutes which rocked Arsenal back on their heels. And after another excellent performance against Manchester United, he played the game of his life against Hibs' Lawrie Reilly in the final. Bobby was, of course, a pillar of the 'Double'-winning side the following year, and in 1956 he became the first Celtic captain ever to lift the League Cup aloft after the replayed final tie against Partick Thistle, temporarily taking the armband while Jock Stein struggled in vain to recover from injury.

A Celtic team-mate, Billy McPhail, describes Evans as 'the cleanest player I've ever seen, and the most immaculate "taker-away" of the ball in a tackle I've ever seen'. Such, too, was his appetite for the fray that even the most casual of observers at a Celtic match could not fail to be struck by a man who seemed to cover every blade of grass, no matter the circumstances. Some said he carried the team. This, after all (as the aforesaid Alec Fraser revealed), was 'the young carpenter who used to race to Parkhead in his overalls, covered with sawdust. Not a minute of the light nights, the training, were to be missed.' Evans never lost that zest for training and match-play, which caused one commentator to remark that he was 'the nearest thing to perpetual motion I've ever seen' and another team-mate, Willie Fernie, to recall that 'Bobby always wanted to be a winner'.

Evans's retention of a seemingly boundless energy and a boyish enthusiasm for the game made him an idol to the mass of Celtic supporters and facilitated his transformation from a right-half, his standard berth through most of the 1950s, into a centre-half at the start of the 1957–58 season. John Jack, the previous season's incumbent, had failed to convince the Celtic management as a 'stopper' (being 'a pivot lacking anticipation', in the words of one writer of the time). Some Celtic fans had reservations about Evans filling a position he had already graced in the national side, preferring a taller and more robust figure at the heart of the defence. But Evans himself, ultra-professional in his approach and never afraid of a challenge, insisted that it was a player's timing in the jump and in the tackle that mattered. In addition to which, there was no greater reader of a game in Scotland at the time, nor any superior as an interceptor. Not that Evans had much time for the critics. Interviewed by Arthur Montford of the newly formed Scottish Television on the *Scotsport* programme after taking part in a 7–0 victory for the Scottish League over the Irish League at Ibrox (9 October 1957), Evans bristled at the unflattering comments in the press regarding recent performances by representative Scottish sides, and signed off with the following response to the interviewer's request for advice to young, up-and-coming players: 'I'd advise them not to read the papers – the Scottish press particularly.' For Bobby Evans, the joy in football was always in the playing.

SEMI-FINAL

One week after beating Rangers, Celtic returned to Ibrox, this time to face Clyde, promoted as Second Division champions the previous season, in the League Cup semi-final. The Shawfield club, buoyed by their success in returning to the top flight after an absence of only one season, had been in brilliant form at the start of the new campaign. They had won their League Cup section with maximum points, and had followed that up by winning both their opening league matches. In the quarter-finals they had scored six goals against Aberdeen over two legs, and with their forwards in free-scoring mood, 'Bully Wee' supporters were confident their team could reach the League Cup final for the first time. (Clyde, in fact, were destined for an impressive season. Not only did they win the Scottish Cup that term, they also finished a highly creditable fourth in the league placings – an excellent showing after their spell in the lower division.)

Previewing the match for the *Evening Times*, Gair Henderson relished the prospect of a high-scoring game: 'So what happens now when an attack which has run up the fantastic total of 52 goals in 11 games meets a Celtic team riding high on the crest of a wave? Well may you ask! But I do know this – the proceedings at Ibrox on Saturday should be the most exciting of the season, and there will surely be an 80,000 crowd to see if the Celtic defence can succeed where others have failed so miserably' (23 September 1957). Henderson's guess at the attendance was far too optimistic, and little more than half the number he suggested actually paid their way into Ibrox on the day. It should be recalled that many Celtic fans at that time – and later – made a point of not attending matches at Rangers' stadium, some for fear of trouble at Old Firm encounters; but even when that was not a factor, many objected on principle to contributing to the coffers of a club whose discriminatory employment policies were known to all, if rarely the subject of public debate in the media. Even so, the 42,000 attendance was over 5,000 higher than when Celtic had beaten Clyde at Hampden at the same stage of the competition the previous season (although Clyde were a Second Division team on that occasion).

On the eve of the match, Clyde were dealt a potentially fatal blow. They were handicapped by the absence of three key players who had been struck down by the virulent brand of influenza then sweeping the central belt of Scotland. Despite this setback the Shawfield side greatly contributed to a classic contest, one which in every respect bar the attendance justified Gair Henderson's positive expectations of it.

Once again Celtic made changes in the forward line. Tully was not fully fit, and his place was taken by Eric Smith, with Sharkey, again a sinner in front of goal against Rangers a week earlier, being overlooked. Bertie Auld was fielded at outside-left. The loss of the in-form Tully was surely a blow. With two youngsters on the wing, it was going to take all the match-winning genius of Bobby Collins, the dribbling flair of Willie Fernie and the thrust of McPhail and Wilson to secure a place in the Hampden final for the cup-holders. Fortunately for Celtic, that's precisely what these four men provided.

Harry Andrew, writing in the *Scottish Sunday Express* the following day, had no doubt as to who had been his man of the match: 'Bobby [Collins] didn't just have one inspired moment. He had a dozen. And four of them produced goals. He was outstandingly THE man of this League Cup semi-final . . . the one forward of all ten who combined energy, subtlety, ball control, accuracy in the pass and a finishing punch' (29 September 1957). The last of these assets exploded into view in the tenth minute of the second half. Clyde had fought back gloriously to equalise after being two goals down and had Celtic in trouble when Collins suddenly transformed the tie. He took possession of a loose ball 30 yards from goal. 'Not a man on the field, not a spectator in the stand or on the terracing expected what followed,' reported Monday's *Daily Record*. In a split second, Collins, with the Clyde defence funnelling back into position expecting a pass, sent a stupendous drive swerving into the roof of the net behind goalkeeper McCulloch (making his debut in senior football), who had no time even to move towards the ball. It was one of the greatest goals of Collins's career, one to match the marvellous counter he had scored at the same venue six years previously against Rangers. The Celtic players and fans went berserk, while Collins himself showed unabashed delight as he was mobbed by his ecstatic team-mates. The goal stopped Clyde in their hitherto venturesome tracks and put the Parkhead team back on the rails in a match which had just minutes before looked like slipping from their grasp.

Clyde had in fact started the match the better of the two teams, but Celtic, just as they had against Rangers the previous week, scored against the run of play when Collins sent an inch-perfect pass through the middle to Wilson, who eluded one defender before lobbing home. It was Collins again, with another beautifully timed and weighted pass, who sent McPhail clear four minutes from the interval, seemingly to put Celtic in a commanding lead. But just on the half-time whistle, Archie Robertson, the inside-forward whose late corner had broken Celtic hearts just over a couple of years before at Hampden, hit a shot which took fortuitous deflections off first his own centre-forward and then Evans to trickle past Beattie and put Clyde back in the match. Five minutes after the restart they were indeed back with a bang. Tommy Ring, scorer of the winning goal in the replay of that 1955 final, produced a dazzling dribble which took him to the byline. Just when he seemed to have lost the advantage, he passed the ball inside to McInnes, who struck a precise finish high into the net, despite the presence of several hooped defenders in the vicinity. Then came Collins's wonder goal. Four minutes later, Collins – who else? – sent Smith clear down the right, and from his centre, Willie Fernie waltzed the ball past his marker and the goalkeeper before coolly piloting it into the unguarded net with his left foot. That ended the scoring (4–2), although Clyde fought gamely to the end. Celtic, who had experienced the greatest difficulty in the League Cup during its first ten years in operation, were now through to their second successive final!

Edmund Burns recalls:

I can remember a game at Shawfield between Clyde and Celtic some time in the 1950s. In those days, there was no segregation of the supporters, and I found myself standing in an area with quite a few home supporters. Tommy Ring, Clyde's winger, got a great chance to score but he missed it. A Clyde fan standing nearby, in an effort to console the player, shouted out, 'Never mind, Tommy, your heart's in the Clyde!' Immediately, another Clyde supporter retorted, 'Yer whole effing body should be in the Clyde!'

Journalistic comment in the aftermath of the game naturally centred on the marvellous display of Bobby Collins. He was 'That Pint-Sized Genius' and a 'Mighty Atom' (the nickname originally belonging to that other legendary match-winning genius, Patsy Gallacher), while Gair Henderson was of the opinion that Celtic would be crazy to sell Collins to any of the clubs beginning to show interest in him. But while Collins certainly stole the show, there was another man in the team that day who could also take great satisfaction both from his personal performance and from the fact that after an uncertain beginning to his Parkhead career, he now seemed established as a fixture in the first team. His goal after 12 minutes had put Celtic on the road to Hampden, and it was his seventh in only eight competitive games for the club – a happy omen!

SAMMY WILSON

There is such a fairy-tale element about the Celtic career of Sammy Wilson, a man who won his only major honour in football within six months of joining the club on a free transfer, that it tends to obscure an often overlooked fact: namely, that a scrutiny of his early background (which received little press coverage) leads to the conclusion, admittedly in hindsight, that he was destined to be a Celt sooner or later. Indeed, he might have been Parkhead-bound a year or so earlier, since Wilson recalls being linked in an exchange deal with the out-of-favour Jimmy Walsh, who, however, jibbed at signing for St Mirren (and later joined Leicester City).

A cousin of Joe McLaughlin, a Celtic forward of the 1940s, Sammy was also a friend of the Bogan family – whose most famous member, Tommy, was another Celt of '40s vintage. In addition, Wilson played in the same Boys' Guild side, Uddingston St John's, as that vastly talented but unlucky player John Higgins, a winger in the Jimmy Delaney mould, whose career at Parkhead was truncated by injury – a fate shared, unhappily, by too many of his Celtic contemporaries. Delaney himself was a boyhood hero of Wilson, who still cherishes the memory of being congratulated on his performance by the great man after a Falkirk v. St Mirren match at Brockville in the early 1950s, when Delaney lined up for the Bairns in opposition to Wilson's 'Buddies'.

Wilson joined Celtic as a wing-half, the position in which he made his debut at Methil in the League Cup sectional tie. Sammy's adherence to Charlie Tully's pre-match request that he be given the ball as early and as often as possible earned the plaudits of the Irish winger afterwards – 'I've never had so much of the ball in my life!' – although it was expressed in rather more colourful and typical fashion. Sammy had owed that start in the first team to the absence of Willie Fernie due to an injury sustained in the first match of the season against Airdrie. And he had to wait another fortnight for an opportunity to really stake a claim for a place in the side, in the return match with East Fife at Parkhead. Wilson relates that he had never played at inside-left before that game, at least in a competitive match, although he had played there in Celtic's second pre-season public trial (a young Billy McNeill was in the opposing 'Whites' team). He had previously been fielded in senior football at inside-right, right-half and left-half. Inside-left had been something of a problem position for Celtic in recent times, with no fewer than seven players having been tried in that role the previous season, none of them filling the berth to the total satisfaction of the club's management. With one of them, Willie Fernie, being moved back to right-half at the start of the 1957–58 season, the position was up for grabs. But two of the candidates for it were out of favour with chairman Bob Kelly, who everyone inside Celtic Park knew – and most people outside Celtic Park strongly suspected – possessed the final say on team selection. The two were Jim Sharkey, who would make only four appearances in this season before being transferred in November, and Eric Smith, who would later claim that his Celtic career in the mid-1950s had suffered as a result of National Service, stating that before he was demobbed in September 1957 he managed to get weekend passes fairly regularly to travel to Scotland from Worcester and then Farnborough to turn out for Celtic, 'but the travelling was no joke. I was faced with a 12-hour train journey, and it didn't do me a lot of good.' (*Charles Buchan's Football Monthly*, May 1960)

Sammy Wilson credits his switch to the inside-left spot to Jimmy Gribben, a veteran trainer-cum-scout who passed on invaluable advice to many a youngster at Parkhead and who was a figure held in such esteem that he had the ear of Bob Kelly. He was, after all, the man who suggested that Celtic acquire the services of an obscure figure called Jock Stein from Welsh non-leaguers Llanelly in December 1951 . . . [2]

Wilson, a naturally two-footed player, recalls how easy he found it to score goals with an attacking team like Celtic's in 1957, a welcome contrast to the defensive outlook he was used to at St Mirren. His partnership with Billy McPhail was to become almost telepathic, producing a rich harvest en route to the League Cup final (with a combined total of 13 goals in five matches up to and including the semi-final). And Wilson was quick to pay tribute to the other half of one of the most prolific and productive combinations in the club's history. Writing in a magazine article, he lavished praise on his partner: 'Billy is the perfect leader. He has the height, the heading power to make goals with his head, and a phenomenal burst of speed to take him through on his own. If you're in an open space, and Billy has the ball . . . it's yours! I make no claims to being a great goalscorer, but playing alongside Billy makes goalscoring easy.' However, as the old saying goes, it takes two to tango, and Sammy was the perfect foil for the admittedly more debonair McPhail. Jimmy Delaney, no mean scorer himself, would have been proud of 'Slammin' Sammy', as the Celtic fans dubbed the man who arrived at Parkhead unheralded and departed a hero.

'THE OTHER LOT'

Rangers, and John Valentine in particular, answered their critics following the league defeat by Celtic by travelling to France just a few days later and producing a 'backs-to-the-wall' performance to gain victory over St Etienne in the European Cup. Although the Frenchmen won the match with a late goal, Rangers defended stoutly throughout, and deservedly went through to the draw for the next round on a 4–3 aggregate score. Valentine, castigated for a weak display on the Saturday against Billy McPhail, was hailed as a stand-out and commended for his bravery when he had to play the whole of the second half holding a pad to a split eyebrow. He had been thus confirmed as a 'true Ranger', or so it seemed. But, typical of his rollercoaster career at Ibrox, by the end of the same week his suitability was once again being called into question after yet another unimpressive display, this time against Brechin City in the League Cup semi-final, watched by 28,000 at Hampden Park – 50,000 fewer than had seen Rangers' home tie with Kilmarnock in the previous round. (Of course, Brechin were not so attractive a proposition, while Rangers fielded several reserves and a virtually unrecognisable forward line.) Sandy Adamson, writing in the *Daily Record*, memorably characterised Valentine's performance in this match by describing him as 'the man with the disobedient legs'. The Ibrox club's decision to field a much-changed line-up for this match was forced upon it – the missing players, like Clyde's in the other semi, had fallen victim to the flu bug then raging in Scotland.[3]

Rangers' eventual 4–0 victory over the lower-division Angus side was not especially convincing. It had taken the Light Blues 25 minutes to break down a stuffy rearguard, and Brechin always looked dangerous in the breakaway. With the score only 2–0 in favour of the Ibrox side, Valentine brought down a Brechin forward for what seemed a certain penalty, but the claim was waved away. Rangers themselves had needed a penalty to establish the two-goal advantage they held at that stage, and their second two goals came very late in the match, one of them an own goal. The ex-Dundee captain, Alfie Boyd, reporting on the match for the *Sunday Post*, described the win as one carved out by effort and industry, rather than poise or classy football. Nearly a week later, in a D.C. Thomson stablemate, the *Glasgow Weekly News*, Boyd (himself a distinguished defender in his day) put his finger on the source of Rangers' vulnerability: the centre-half position which had been troubling Rangers since the retiral at the end of the previous season of the formidable veteran George Young, who himself had taken over from the highly capable Willie Woodburn after the latter's *sine die* suspension three years before, following his fourth ordering-off (the sentence reflecting the standards of behaviour expected in the 1950s). Commenting on Young's successor, Boyd said that 'unless Valentine becomes surer in the tackle and improves his kicking, then Rangers will surely lose unnecessary goals. Also, until Valentine becomes a commanding figure, the other defenders, McColl especially, will have to be ready to do a lot of covering up. And this must reduce, to a certain degree, the efficiency of the defence as a whole' (5 October 1957). It was a measure of the respect in which George Young had been held by his fellow professionals in Scotland that Jock Stein, sitting as captain of Celtic on a sports panel organised by the *Scottish Sunday Express* in the winter of 1954–55, confessed that his favourite player was his opposite number at Ibrox. Young had helped to weld together a defensive set-up at Ibrox which retained a substantial measure of the authority once wielded by Rangers' post-war 'Iron Curtain' defence, whose heyday lasted several years from the 1940s into the early 1950s. Young himself had earlier been a mainstay of that famous rearguard, but at right-back. His transfer to centre-half when Woodburn was sidelined resulted in Rangers recapturing and retaining the Scottish league title in the two seasons prior to 1957–58, and thus restoring some of the old sense of invulnerability to the Govan club – a sense that was, however, soon to be shattered.

The league programme took a break at the start of October, to allow for the Home International match between Scotland and Northern Ireland in Belfast (5 October), which resulted in a 1–1 draw (and heavy criticism of the Scots in the football press, much to Bobby Evans's chagrin), and the game between the Scottish League and the Irish League at Ibrox four days later, which the home team won easily by 7–0. Bobby Evans and Bobby Collins won full caps in the former match, as did Bertie Peacock on the opposing side, while Evans and Collins also turned out in the League international, Collins scoring one of the goals from the penalty spot.

Three days later domestic league action resumed. Rangers players had already been criticised that season for rough play, particularly in their League Cup tie with Kilmarnock, and further cause for concern on this score was given on the occasion of their visit to Love Street on league business on 12 October. The visitors came away with both points following a 3–1 win, but they had not won any friends by the manner in which they had done so. A week later, on the day of the League Cup final, an interview appeared in the *Glasgow Weekly News* with the St Mirren manager Willie Reid, who was still nursing his wrath over the rough treatment meted out to his classy inside-forward Tommy Gemmell in the match with Rangers. Condemning the lack of protection from officialdom which saw his player going about with a stud scar that stretched from his knees to his hips and with legs that were a mass of bruises, the 'Buddies" boss angrily made his feelings plain: 'I rarely complain about referees – except when we play Rangers. To me it seems they habitually gloss over rough play when it comes from Rangers players, in direct contrast to their attitude when the opposition are the culprits. I always thought so when I was a player. As a manager the feeling is, if anything, stronger. Mind you, I don't think they [referees] are aware of this weakness. But I do think a great many of them have the feeling deep down that they are inviting trouble if they do anything to offend the most powerful club in the country. I don't know what the solution is. I only wish I did.'

Commenting on this explosive statement, the interviewer remarked, 'In the old days, of course, the allegation that referees were biased in Rangers' favour was greatly bandied about. But it's long enough since anyone in managerial circles – except in the privacy of the boardroom – has come right out and said it' (19 October 1957).

But despite their troubles in terms of discipline and defensive form, Rangers could have had no inkling of what lay in store for them when they faced Celtic in the League Cup final, a sense of security that must have been reinforced when the lack of conviction with which the Parkhead club had opened the 1957–58 season reappeared only a week before their date with destiny at Hampden. In the league match at Celtic Park versus Raith Rovers on the Saturday preceding the final, the home team could only manage a 1–1 draw and a performance described by one critic as 'one long yawn'. Jimmy Dunbar's view of this disappointing show was a trenchant one: 'Celtic will have to do much better at Hampden next Saturday if they mean to retain the League Cup. Against Raith Rovers at Parkhead today they were suspect in defence and scrappy in attack' (*Evening Times* 'Sports Final', 12 October 1957).

In a match which unfortunately foreshadowed much of Celtic's later home form that season, Celtic lacked ideas and accuracy up front and allowed the visitors too much leeway for comfort at the back. Having gone ahead early in the match, Celtic just couldn't find top gear despite Collins's strenuous efforts, and after the interval it was Raith Rovers, a team which had made a bright start to their season, who looked the more dangerous outfit. Indeed, they hit the bar in that period, and then deservedly, if somewhat fortunately, grabbed an equaliser 20 minutes from time when Beattie hesitated in coming for a ball and Evans, confused by his keeper's indecision, made a poor attempt at a pass back which was duly intercepted by Rovers' Copland. Despite his part in the loss of the goal, Evans was one of the few Celtic players to play to anything like form on the day. Once again the team formation had been upset, although this time it was due to an injury to Billy McPhail. With Smith replacing Auld on the left, Neil Mochan was recalled at centre-forward, and his goal was one of the few consolations for the 20,000 crowd. It came in the ninth minute. He beat Raith's Scottish international Willie McNaught to a high ball some 20 yards out from goal, before swivelling on to his own header and lashing the ball high into the net. After his absence from the team for several weeks, it was a welcome sign of a return to sharpness from Mochan. But although he showed flashes of his old form, few observers could have anticipated the mighty deeds he would perform for Celtic a week later.

NEIL MOCHAN
John McKechnie recalls:

> Neilly could certainly hit a ball, as Rangers found to their cost. The ball in those days was far removed from today's lightweight footballs. And to *head* a wet ball in the '50s required some forethought! I knew a few players who would rather slip or fall than head for glory – myself included!

Seamus Murphy wrote a poem commemorating the Coronation Cup victory, the opening two verses of which read:

> *I was in the Merchant Navy*
> *Way back in '53,*
> *Serving on a BP tanker*
> *In the Mediterranean Sea.*
> *We were homeward-bound for Scotland*
> *And my heart was full of joy,*
> *For I was heading home to Parkhead*
> *Just to see the Timalloys.*
>
> *Just to see dear Charlie Tully,*
> *Bobby Evans and Jock Stein;*
> *Bobby Collins, Alex Rollo,*
> *Sure the best there's ever been;*
> *Bonnar, Haughney, Walsh and Peacock,*
> *McPhail, and Fernie best of all,*
> *And the new Bhoy Neilly Mochan*
> *Who could really whack the ball.*

Neil Mochan made an explosive start to his Celtic career in May 1953 when he won two cup-winner's medals (Charity and Coronation) immediately following his transfer from Middlesbrough and before he had even played his first match in the hoops at Celtic Park. The following season, which saw Celtic land a long-missing 'Double', proved that his Hampden triumphs – the most spectacular expression of which was his 'goal in a century from 30 yards' (as the BBC radio commentator put it) in the Coronation final – were no fluke and owed nothing to beginner's luck (even though his screamer in the final was scored with his 'wrong' foot – his right).[4] In that title-winning season of 1953–54, Mochan was Celtic's top scorer with 25 goals, 20 of them scored in the championship, which was clinched on 17 April when Neilly got a brace at Easter Road, one at the start of each half. A week later it was his fierce cross-shot, deflected into goal by Aberdeen's centre-half Young six minutes into the second half, which put Celtic on the way to the added glory of a Scottish Cup victory in the frenzied atmosphere generated by a 130,000 Hampden crowd. Mochan was a man for whom the bigger the occasion, the better it was. Having done so well with Celtic in his first full season, Mochan was selected for the first (ridiculously undersized, and ill-fated) Scottish squad to compete in the final stages of the World Cup (Switzerland 1954).[5]

Despite his zest, pace and shooting power, Mochan was frequently the victim of chairman Bob Kelly's selection whims. He sat out both the first game and the replay of the 1955 Scottish Cup final against Clyde, even though poor shooting by Celtic was a notable feature of the first 90 minutes. The forward line was, however, fully 'Mochanical' in the 1956 League Cup final replay which was won against Partick Thistle.

Although he was widely regarded at the time as the hardest striker of a ball in Scottish football (the press predictably dubbing him 'The man with the cannonball shot'), Neil Mochan's future at Parkhead looked pretty bleak in the early weeks of season 1957–58. For all his determination not to be discarded from the first team, he returned from the close-season American tour worried about his loss of form there, and about his weight (which was half a stone more than it should have been). Far from taking the post-tour break prescribed by the management, he turned up daily at Parkhead to work hard at recovering his sharpness and fitness, in furtherance of which aim he volunteered to play in just about every five-a-side team fielded by Celtic in the late summer tournaments of that type. (These were, along with public trial matches, a common feature of Scottish football at the time.) If anything, he seems to have tried too hard, judging by the several indifferent performances he put up at the start of the season, which soon saw him relegated to the reserves. In the second XI, as manager Jimmy McGrory was quoted as saying at the time, Neil 'didn't show up too well even in the slower pace there'. He was so out of favour, in fact, that in late September 1957, the ex-Ranger Willie

Thornton, then manager of a Dundee side who were propping up the table after losing all three of their opening league games (having failed to score a single goal in any of them), visited Celtic Park to take in an Old Firm reserve match and to inquire about Mochan's availability for transfer. No business was concluded, although it was believed that this was down to two obstacles – the player's known reluctance to leave Celtic and disagreement about the transfer fee. (Although Celtic's avowed policy was that no senior player would be transferred if it was against his wishes, no one seriously believed that this would in practice prove a decisive block to any contemplated transaction.) Thornton, desperately in need of a proven goalscorer and convinced that Mochan fitted the bill, left disappointed. But had Mochan himself been watching from the stand, he must have had reason to feel gloomy about his prospects at Celtic, particularly in the centre-forward position where he had made his name. For the reserve side won the match against the Ibrox 'Colts' 2–1, 'brilliantly led' (according to the *Daily Record* reporter) by the precocious 17-year-old Jim Conway. Mochan's nickname, 'Smiler', could rarely have been less apt.

But fortunately his 'commando training' began to pay off, and restoration to his ideal weight was rewarded by a return to first-team duty, albeit as a result of yet another injury to centre-forward Billy McPhail. Taking McPhail's place in the league match against Raith Rovers, only a week prior to the League Cup final, Mochan hinted that he was approaching his best form and did enough to justify his selection for the big occasion the following Saturday at Hampden (although it was at outside-left, rather than leading the attack). However, the feeling that it was not a vote of confidence on the management's part in the 'forgotten man of Scottish football' (as Mochan was described by one writer on the eve of the final) would be found to have some justification a few days after the cup final. News would leak out that Mochan's display, which proved devastating to Rangers, had effectively scuppered a bid by Watford, then an English Third Division (South) club, to take him to England – a move backed by £2,000 provided by the Watford fans as a contribution to the transfer fee. When word of the mooted transaction emerged in the aftermath of his personal Hampden triumph, it may have struck some as an insult – but by then, 'Smiler' had had the last laugh.

BUILD-UP TO THE FINAL

It was widely noted in the press that this would be the first national cup final between Celtic and Rangers since 1928, an interval of almost 30 years. On that occasion, Rangers had won the Scottish Cup for the first time in a quarter-century, and so Celtic had every incentive to seek revenge. But it was also the first meeting of the clubs in the final tie of the League Cup, a competition which had had a previous incarnation as the

Southern League Cup, inaugurated in the spring of 1941, and which was later placed – and given its new title – under the auspices of the Scottish League when that body recommenced operations after the war. The original idea for a competition along these lines had in fact been suggested as early as 1939 by a Rangers director, James Bowie (a man later deposed in an Ibrox boardroom coup in 1947).

Transportation for the fans to Hampden for the 1957 final came in various forms. British Rail (Scottish Region) had arranged for a frequent service of 20 'specials' from Glasgow Central to Mount Florida. Special trains were also running from Gourock to pick up supporters in places like Greenock and Port Glasgow; from Paisley; from Law Junction to transport fans from places such as Wishaw, Motherwell, Hamilton and Blantyre; and from Coatbridge Central, collecting those from Whifflet, Bellshill, Uddingston and Burnside. Glasgow Corporation laid on a fleet of special buses from the city centre, and with car ownership on the increase – albeit the majority of fans still relied on public transport or supporters' buses – the police introduced for this final a new, experimental 'get tough' parking policy around the ground, which involved reorganising the traffic routes to banish 'jam-ups' and eliminate 'careless and indiscriminate parking' in quiet streets near the stadium. To cope with an expected crowd of over 100,000, 500 police officers were on duty for the occasion in and around Hampden. The kick-off was scheduled for 2.45 p.m. Since Hampden would not have floodlighting for another four years, the slightly advanced start was necessary – in view of the earlier autumn sunset – to allow for the possibility of extra time.

It was decided not to make the match an all-ticket one, although this prospect had been mooted after the semi-finals. In the event only the stands were bookable, and in fact the attendance was significantly less than anticipated, although still very large at 82,293 (with gate receipts of approximately £11,000). The somewhat-lower-than-expected crowd may have been due in part to the influenza which was rife at the time, and which had already affected the personnel of both Rangers and Clyde at the semi-final stage (and had also caused the postponement of a recent Partick Thistle v. Hearts match due to the Tynecastle club losing five first-team regulars to the virus). But although attendances at Scottish football matches could still be massive in the later 1950s – witness the 78,000 who turned out for the second leg of the Rangers v. Kilmarnock quarter-final or the 108,000 who would watch the 1959 Scottish Cup final between St Mirren and Aberdeen – it is clear in retrospect that a decline had begun. The previous season (1956–57) had seen Celtic's lowest average home league attendance since the war (around the 18,500 mark) and poor crowds at both the League Cup final and replay; while Rangers' average league gate, although fluctuating with results, had also begun to decline somewhat from the peak years of the late '40s and early '50s.[6]

Despite their poor showing in the league match with Raith Rovers the weekend before the final, the Celtic players were quietly confident about the outcome. They had, after all, recently beaten Rangers in a closely contested league match at Ibrox, and although they had lost there in the Glasgow Cup, they had shown greater skill on the ball even in that match. Having found a profitable twin strike-force in McPhail and Wilson, and with Collins and Tully in splendid form, they must have felt they had a good chance against a Rangers defence showing uncharacteristic weaknesses in the weeks leading up to the final. The Ibrox club, of course, prided itself on always being ready for the big occasion. Theirs was a team with a heritage defined by one of its historians, Willie Allison, as one of 'grim, no-team-is-our-equal conviction'. Moreover, Celtic had often failed in crunch matches against Rangers in the competition since the war, losing out on qualification on four out of the five occasions the sides had met at the sectional stage, and once in the semi-final. On the other hand, Celtic had gone to Ibrox the previous February in a Scottish Cup replay and completely outplayed the home team to win 2–0. In that match and others, Celtic players were made all too aware of Rangers' capacity for intimidation – euphemistically described in the press as 'power-play' – but they had triumphed nonetheless. The same crudely physical approach to the game had been on display in Rangers' recent matches against Kilmarnock and St Mirren, and while the Celtic squad must have retained considerable self-belief, there was always the worry that they could be thrown off their stride in the fast and furious atmosphere in immediate prospect.

But the mood in the Celtic camp took a distinct turn for the worse only 48 hours before the match. An outburst of internal strife revealed at least a touch of edginess just prior to the big showdown. It involved two of the club's most famous personalities and finest players who, however, represented rather differing philosophies about the way the game should be played: the happy-go-lucky Charlie Tully, and the more puritanical and ultra-professional Bobby Evans. The two men, by the former's own admission, 'could hardly be called chums'. Shortly before training on that Thursday, the two men had to be separated by team-mates in the dressing-room after indulging in a fist-fight which was provoked by a remark of Tully's made the previous weekend in his regular Saturday newspaper column entitled 'Tullyvision' in the *Evening Citizen*: 'Whether you people over here like it or not, only two Scots would have a chance of a place in any Great Britain team. These two are Younger and Parker. The rest lack class' (12 October 1957). Younger was the Liverpool goalkeeper, formerly of Hibernian, and Parker was a full-back with Falkirk. Ironically, the backdrop to the article was an idea proposed by Bob Kelly, not only the Celtic chairman but a leading football legislator, that an all-Britain team be fielded in the World Cup competition, a suggestion which provoked debate in all the countries represented by the four home football associations. It drew criticism, for example, in a Wolverhampton Wanderers match programme for the resultant loss of voting power at FIFA level: 'If you are one country on the field of play, you are one country off the field.' There is no reason to doubt that Tully's views on football were as sincerely held as Kelly's, but no prouder player ever donned a jersey for club and country than Bobby Evans – whom Tully, even more ironically, had acknowledged as 'the perfect professional' – and the fiery-haired half-back may have detected a calculated insult in Tully's frankness. In the event it was a piece of journalism (albeit ghost-written) that Tully was quick to retract, or at least back-pedal upon, in the following week's column, after he received strongly worded letters from Celtic supporters objecting to the omission from the category of 'British-class' not only of Bobby Evans but also of Bobby Collins. Rather disingenuously, Tully reacted by claiming, 'Well, of course, I was referring only to the form of that game,' a reference to a recent international match in which Scotland barely salvaged a draw with Northern Ireland in Belfast.[7] Whether the fracas was also a sign of pre-match nerves or not, as an unintentional piece of psychology the offending article worked a treat, releasing pent-up tensions in a manner which directed Celtic's energy and fire – not least those of Evans – in the direction of the 'auld enemy'. In retrospect, the 'timing' could not have been more perfect!

A popular Jungle ditty of the 1950s ran as follows (to the tune of 'The Lambeth Walk'):

Put another Celtic player in,
Seven Rangers cannae win,
What we want in Scotland's team
Is Evans, Evans, Evans.

Reflecting the general uncertainty and division in the press about the outcome of the final, the *Glasgow Weekly News* writer predicted a win for Celtic on the grounds that 'the science of Fernie and Tully, the punch of Collins, and the brilliance of a better-than-ever McPhail' would be too much for an Ibrox combination noted more for its industry and determination than skilful ball-play; but his counterpart in *The Scotsman* thought that the predicted heavy ground conditions caused by rain which had hit Glasgow the day before the match would favour Rangers: 'The inside trio of Simpson, Murray and Baird will not be dismayed by the miry prospects. Previous matches this season indicated that they take to it like buffaloes . . . Football strategy and surer passing may take Celtic to the presentation dais, but their finer arts tend to be spasmodic in their occurrence.' The writer fancied Rangers to lift the cup after wearing down the lighter Celtic outfit in the second half.

Both teams would be at full strength, Billy McPhail having passed a fitness test a few days beforehand, after missing the Raith Rovers league match. He had injured his ankle at training. Intriguingly, in his report of McPhail's return to duty, Gair Henderson noted that Celtic's one-and-a-half-hour training session that day consisted of 'lapping, PT, scaling up and down the terracing steps and ball practice . . . with the players working flat out but obviously happy at their work'; but he added in a footnote that Rangers were that day 'enjoying themselves at Kilmacolm golf course' (*Evening Times*, 16 October 1957). Did this casual outing bespeak an air of cocky over-confidence on the part of the Ibrox club? Perhaps.

On the eve of the final, Hugh Taylor in his *Evening Citizen* column viewed the contest as one between evenly matched teams, whose outcome would revolve around two individual duels: would John Valentine contain the lethal heading power of Billy McPhail, a player who 'when rising to hawk height' could flick the ball venomously for goal or to a well-placed colleague; and would Bobby Evans snuff out the rapier thrusts of Max Murray, Rangers' centre-forward, who had been restored to the line-up in place of the more cumbersome Kichenbrand? In the rival Glasgow newspaper, the *Evening Times*, its chief football writer Gair Henderson thought that the match would require extra time to sort out the winner, but believed that Celtic would eventually triumph, being 'the boys who have the football craft and the ability to turn midfield play into goals when the pinch is on'. He expressed surprise at the outlook of the bookmaking fraternity (or 'commission agents' as they styled themselves then): 'For some utterly fantastic reason,' he wrote, 'the bookies are prepared to lay you 7–4 against Celtic [as holders] keeping firm tabs on the League Cup when they go out tomorrow against Rangers in the League Cup final at Hampden. The same boys who lay the odds and who usually are very well versed in the time of the day will lay you no more than even money against a Rangers victory!'

Joe Connelly (Glasgow) recalls his emotional and financial investment in the outcome:

> When I woke that Saturday morning my first thoughts were, 'This is the big one.' It was a beautiful autumn morning, the skies were clear and blue and it promised to be a lovely day. But the weather was secondary – it was the day of the cup final, Celtic v. Rangers at Hampden. The butterflies were starting in my stomach, not least because of my bet of £40 on Celtic to win at 7–4 against. I had had a good night at the Carntyne dogs [greyhound racing] on the previous

Tuesday night, and had decided to reinvest the winnings in a Celtic victory. Don't forget – this was 1957 and wages were an average of £6 per week! I had felt a little apprehensive that morning, but after all, we were the greatest cup fighters in Scottish football history, and I felt more confident as we walked from Haghill down through Glasgow Cross and up past the Gorbals to Hampden, surrounded by green and white, as these were all great Celtic districts.

In his match preview, 'Waverley' of the *Daily Record*, writing on the morning of the game, refused to make a definite prediction, but thought that 'one late goal' could decide the issue. He praised Celtic's half-back line of Fernie, Evans and Peacock, noting that Fernie had steadily improved in his new-found role as a wing-half. But he was more sceptical of Celtic's attack – printed in bold capital letters were the following words: 'But here is where I question the Celtic make-up. I have doubts about the Celtic front line, and it has been made obvious that those in control at Parkhead share my qualms.' The phrase 'those in control at Parkhead' was a clear indication that the writer did not regard manager Jimmy McGrory as the man in true charge of team matters. 'Waverley' continued, mostly in lowercase, 'To date they have called on TEN different forwards to make up EIGHT different attacks.' He specifically mentioned the outside-left berth as being a problem spot for Celtic. Unlike Rangers' players, who all knew they were the first-choice representatives of their club, Neil Mochan was now being asked to show, after previously being dropped, that he was 'an improvement on the other left wingers . . . like Smith, Tully and Auld' (19 October 1957). The knowledge that Rangers would be fielding a clearly settled XI in their preferred formation would perhaps, he suggested, give the Ibrox side a slight psychological advantage. Like Hugh Taylor, 'Waverley' concluded that the game would turn on the personal duels between the opposing centre-halves and centre-forwards: Evans versus Murray, Valentine versus McPhail.

SETTING OFF FOR HAMPDEN
David Potter recalls the day of the final:

One day I went up to the 'Gaffie' (The Pavilion cinema in Forfar) to the matinée – *Rob Roy* was showing, if memory serves me correctly, and I remember making jokes about who would win the League Cup final that day, for Celtic were playing Rangers. I had seen supporters going away that morning, and was all fired up about the big game. I nevertheless watched the picture, then the serial which was always on at the end, before coming home, blinking to accustom my eyes to the daylight . . .

Peter Sweeney recalls this extra-special day in his life:

A day to remember for all Celtic fans, yet I nearly missed the game because our first child was due to be born any time that day. As the morning wore on, then early afternoon, my mother-in-law and mother both said, 'Go to the final, and go to the hospital in the evening.' No fathers present at births in those days! I set off for Hampden with my friend John Martin (now sadly deceased). We, like most Celtic fans, were not too optimistic. I said to John that I would want to leave early to go to the Maternity. He replied dejectedly, 'If we're three or four down, you won't be the only one leaving early.' [to be continued!]

Gerard O'Donnell (now resident in London) relates an amusing tale about his father's journey to the game:

On the day of the final, my father and his friend 'Bunny' Fearon were going to the game. They then met their friend Henry McIver whom, after a few drinks of the old Eldorado [wine], they talked into going to the match with them. What was really funny was that Henry had a brand new pair of white trousers on which he thought looked really smart.

As they were walking from Clydebank towards Partick, a friend of theirs called Rab Toner, who was a driver for McGinlay's Coal, stopped his lorry and asked them if they wanted a lift. He told them to jump on the back of the lorry. This they did. After a few minutes, McIver's new white trousers were getting really dirty and he did not stop moaning about it. He wanted to get off after a while. After picking up more fans on the way, the back of the lorry was quite full. Most of the fans were having a laugh, especially as McIver wouldn't stop moaning, going on and on about his trousers. Then they were stopped by the police, who were no doubt 'Bluenoses'. They then nicked Rab Toner for allowing all the people to ride on the back of his coal lorry. While they were asking the rest of them their names etc., they came to Henry McIver and started to laugh at his trousers! McIver then 'lost the heid', and began calling the coppers all the 'f's and b's' in the world. So he was nicked for breach of the peace!

McIver and Rab Toner were kept in the cells, and my father says there was a 'Tim' copper on duty that day, and every time Celtic scored, the copper came in and told Toner and McIver. Toner said he was jumping around mad, but that McIver was *still* moaning about his trousers. My dad and 'Bunny' Fearon reckon that even to this day, McIver won't laugh about it. You just can't please some people, can you?

125

Father Lawrence Byrne CP (now resident in Tsabong, Botswana) recalls his trip to Hampden:

It was a bright sunny morning when myself and my old schoolfriend Albert Trainer departed by steam train from Irvine station on our way to see Celtic v. Rangers in the League Cup final at Hampden Park. Not only was it our first visit to Hampden, but it was our first big game of any description; and for two 16-year-olds from darkest Ayrshire – where Celtic fans in those days were few and far between – it was a day full of excitement and adventure. Little did we realise that it was a day that would be recalled forever in Celtic history books, and that both of us could proudly say in the years ahead: 'We were there . . .'

Charlie Harvey presents a vivid recollection of how he made his way to the game:

On to a number 50 bus, Pollok's link to the outside world – when you can get on to one, that is. If you can't, then you're stuck in Glasgow Corporation's version of Siberia. B*******! Fare into town, 8d. When we came here five years ago it was 6d [2½ pence]. Scandalous. Must be this inflation thing the papers have started on about. The *Sunday Post* keeps warning the workers that if they don't slave for peanuts a pint will cost 31 shillings [£1.55] by the end of the century. Newspapers will be five bob [25 pence]. Bye-bye *Sunday Post!* Crivvens Jings Michty Me!

Down to Bellahouston, past the White City with the Albion just beside it. There must have been greyhound meetings last night, for the punters' discarded lines are ankle-deep on the pavements. Over to the left, Ibrox – a place of many unhappy memories. A place which is a magnet for those who would gloat at their fellow man's misfortune. A place which will be empty if the 'Gers ever encounter serious misfortune. A dread place where Auld Nick sits enthroned and is worshipped (or so we imagined). God doesn't seem to care that we're going to get gubbed again today, badly. Me and my mates have to hide the giggles when we hear the words 'Five Sorrowful Mysteries'. They remind us of Celtic's forward line.

Into dockland, which is choked with ships from every corner of the globe. There'll be a queue of boats a mile long down at the Tail o' the Bank, all waiting for a berth. Just downstream you can see the cranes in half a dozen shipyards. You should be in this part of Glasgow at half seven in the morning. It's like watching a great army on the move when the blokes are heading for the docks and the yards. I went to St Gerard's school, which is next door to Harland & Wolff. The clang of the steam hammers was non-stop and it became a part of your existence. Sometimes the boys in the shipyards would down tools and

126

the silence was deafening. It was a total distraction. Everyone who stays near the yards says the noise is easier to live with than the occasional creepy silence.

Last lap into town. It would be a really great day if thoughts about Rangers didn't intrude. They're so contemptuous of Celts' chances that you can't get a decent argument with a 'Bluenose'. They've got that big b****** from Clyde, Sammy Baird. He'll cripple Fernie and the ref will look the other way. He's taken his nickname with him to Rangers 'The Hun'. Wonder if it will catch on?

Pubs and cinemas at almost every corner. No queues at the picture houses now, though. Never thought I'd see that happen! The owners say that TV is driving them out of business. Could be, quite a few lucky sods have got them. It's more likely the owners are greetin the face aff us so they can put the prices up. I won't pay any more. Two and sixpence [12½ pence] is all I'd give to watch any movie.

That's us in town. A bonny-looking wee clippie with a voice as menacing as a Hollywood gangster has just yelled, 'TERMINUS, BROOMIELAW, EVRYBUDY AFF . . .'

I mentioned elsewhere this unusual weather. On the bus into town the Kilpatricks and the Campsies looked very close. Along Eglinton Street. I can see the hill in Queen's Park, and beyond that the Cathkin Braes. A very rare sight. The smoke pall usually restricts vision to a mile or so. This is the first time I realised I stay in 'the Hielans'!

A wee bit of time to kill, so a walk through St Enoch's Square will be nice. The Railway Station and Hotel are up there on stilts. I like railways but I've got mixed feelings about this place. It's great seeing all the happy groups setting off in summer for the Ayrshire coast, especially at 'The Fair'. On the other hand it's harrowing to have watched families about to break up forever when the emigrants head for the special trains to Greenock. Ten pounds only and they're off to Princes Pier for passage to Australia on the 'Captain Cook'. No visits home from that distance. Emigration is cruel. The parting scenes remind me of an old Glasgow ballad:

> 'Twas early in the morning, just at the break o' day,
> We were wakened by the turnkey, who unto us did say,
> Arise ye Calton weavers, arise ye ane an' a'
> This is the day ye are tae gae frae Caledonia.

Time to face the music at Hampden. Just a short stroll along to Central Station . . .

Tommy Lanigan gives his recollections:

The build-up to the game was indescribable and the atmosphere in Glasgow was electric. Celts had won the League Cup the previous year, beating Thistle, but this match with Rangers was a different ball game. For us Celts it truly was a matter of life or death. That's how important it was to us. Celtic, as always, were an attractive team to watch, geared to attacking football. Rangers, however, dominated Scottish football and had done so for many years. Their defence had for long been known as the 'Iron Curtain'. They didn't lose many goals. We still dreaded the names of the original 'Iron Curtain': Brown, Young and Shaw; McColl, Woodburn and Cox. You see? I still remember them when I'd have to think about the Celtic defence of the time.

Anyway, I'd jumped on the back of a lorry and was on my way to Hampden. This could be a dangerous pastime and it wasn't unknown for blokes to be spilled on to the road. The obliging driver would be a Celtic fan and he could get carried away with the merriment going on behind him. If this happened the driving became rather cavalier, especially on bends and at traffic lights. I was experienced, though, and always stood behind the cab where I had something to hold on to. Although the lorry drivers genuinely did it from kindness alone, we always passed a bunnet round for them to give them an extra pay-day.

Gerard Campbell recalls:

I confess . . . On the day in question one of my uncles offered to take me to the game . . . He had a spare ticket . . . As a very young lad, I turned him down, as I had already arranged to go up to the park to play football with my wee cronies. No doubt the Big Yin immediately withdrew my entry pass tae Purgatory because of this!

Robert McAulay (of Johnstone) relates:

On the day of the 1957 League Cup final my old man, Christopher, or 'Jock' as he is known, who was then living in Norman Street, Bridgeton, set off around 11.30 a.m. to walk the two and a half miles or so to Hampden Park. Dad had a programme-selling pitch at the Mount Florida (Rangers) end of the ground where the 'caurs' turned, and after collecting his programmes from the main stand he walked up the wee hill past Lesser Hampden [Queen's Park's training ground] and took up his stance. For selling his 120 programmes over a period of two hours or so he would receive ten shillings [50 pence] and a complimentary ticket. This ten shillings would supplement his meagre £9 a week wages from his job as a railway worker at Polmadie rail depot.

TOP: 31 August 1957 at Parkhead – Sammy Wilson's close-in header sets Celtic on the road to the quarter-finals of the League Cup. Billy McPhail (left) looks on as goalkeeper Leslie and right-back MacFarlane of Hibs are left helpless.

LEFT: 'Smiler' (Neil Mochan) pictured during 'shooting-in' before a match at Celtic Park in 1955. A ball boy looks on. (Courtesy of D.C. Thomson)

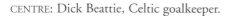

CENTRE: Dick Beattie, Celtic goalkeeper.

RIGHT: 'The Wee Barra' (Bobby Collins) in typically determined mood at Parkhead, 1956. (Courtesy of D.C. Thomson)

BELOW LEFT: Sammy Wilson turns to celebrate after his opener has hit the back of the net in the 1957 League Cup final. Goalkeeper Niven is left stranded as Caldow wheels around in dismay. Bertie Peacock (the Celt in the middle) looks on, whilst in the background (on left) Bobby Evans jumps for joy. (Courtesy of D.C. Thomson)

BELOW RIGHT: Arms aloft, Wilson celebrates his goal, while Shearer and goalkeeper Niven are left standing on the goal-line and Caldow turns round in despair. Other Celts in the picture are McPhail (to left of Wilson) and Tully, who has a close-up view of the goal. (Courtesy of the *Daily Record* and *Sunday Mail*)

BOTTOM: Goalkeeper Niven is beaten at his near post by Neil Mochan's shot from an acute angle. Caldow, Valentine and Shearer (left to right) are the other Rangers players looking on as Celtic go 2–0 up. (Courtesy of D.C. Thomson)

TOP RIGHT: 'The case of the missing film' – telerecording equipment of the type in use at the BBC in the 1950s. (Courtesy of BBC Photograph)

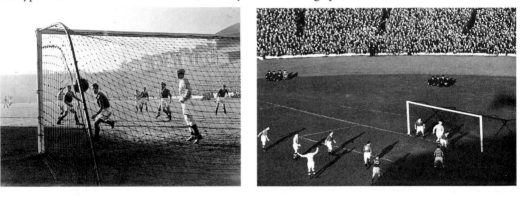

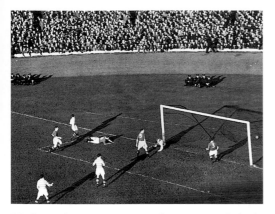

Neil Mochan turns away after netting Celtic's second goal. Shearer, McColl (no. 4, on ground), Valentine (5) and Caldow (3) can do nothing about it as goalkeeper Niven is beaten. (Courtesy of the *Daily Record* and *Sunday Mail*)

Billy McPhail (centre of photo) heads Celtic's third goal, with Rangers' Shearer (no. 2, on goal-line) about to make a vain attempt to clear. McPhail's partner, Sammy Wilson, looks on. (Courtesy of Scottish Media Newspapers Ltd)

BOTTOM: Billy McPhail celebrates netting Celtic's third goal as Shearer (2) tries to kick clear. Sammy Wilson (rushing in) and Neil Mochan (arms aloft in the foreground) are about to congratulate the scorer. (Courtesy of the *Daily Record* and *Sunday Mail*)

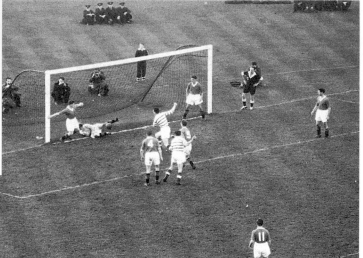

TOP LEFT: The net bulges as McPhail makes it 4–1. Niven is left helpless as Valentine and McColl (behind McPhail) look on.

CENTRE: Number two for Billy McPhail (and number four for Celtic) coming up. He dashes in to score after Wilson's effort is blocked on the goal-line. (Courtesy of the *Daily Record* and *Sunday Mail*)

BOTTOM: All goalkeeper Niven sees is a blur as Mochan's shot enters the net for Celtic's fifth goal. Billy McPhail is suitably impressed, but it looks as if Valentine and Shearer of Rangers have that sinking feeling . . . (Courtesy of Scottish Media Newspapers Ltd)

TOP RIGHT: Billy Simpson nets what turned out to be Rangers' consolation goal. Dick Beattie is rooted to the goal-line.

CENTRE: Celtic's Neil Mochan (on left) watches his shot fly in to the net for his side's fifth goal. It's becoming all too familiar for McColl (No. 4) and Shearer (No. 2) of Rangers. (Courtesy of the *Daily Record* and *Sunday Mail*)

BOTTOM: Billy McPhail leaves Caldow trailing as he clips the ball past Niven for Celtic's sixth goal. (Courtesy D.C. Thomson)

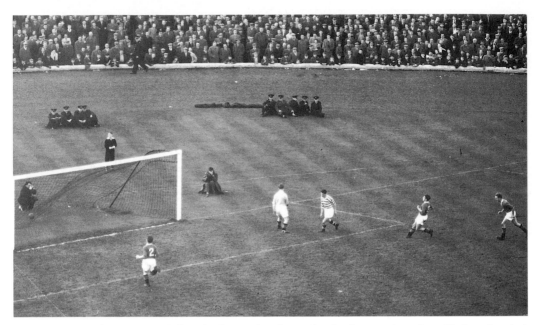

TOP: 6–1 to Celtic. Rangers' fans look on glumly as the final turns into humiliation for their favourites. Billy McPhail completes his hat-trick after outstripping the opposing defence. (Courtesy of the *Daily Record* and *Sunday Mail*)

BOTTOM: The final curtain for Rangers: Fernie makes it seven with a last-minute penalty. (Courtesy of the *Daily Record* and *Sunday Mail*)

BOTTOM LEFT INSET: Willie Fernie makes the penalty kick look easy as he makes it 7–1. Celts looking on at the edge of the penalty box are (left to right): Tully, McPhail, Collins and Mochan. (Courtesy of D.C. Thomson)

TOP LEFT: The goalscorers – Fernie, McPhail, Mochan and Wilson – pose with the League Cup trophy at the after-match celebrations in Ferrari's restaurant in Glasgow's city centre. (Courtesy of the *Daily Record* and *Sunday Mail*)

TOP RIGHT: A proud Bertie Peacock, the Celtic captain, stands to attention during a training break at Celtic Park during the 1957–58 season. Note the Rangers End terracing in the background. (Courtesy of D.C. Thomson)

BOTTOM: Celtic FC 1957–58. This photo was taken at the first home match after the League Cup final triumph. The only player missing from the 7–1 line up is John Donnelly, a flu victim. Peter Goldie took his place at right back. Pictured with the League Cup trophy are: top row (left to right) Goldie, Fallon, Beattie, McPhail, Fernie, Evans. Front row (left to right) Johnstone (trainer), Tully, Collins, Peacock (captain), Wilson, Mochan, McGrory (manager). Note the alternative strip used to avoid a clash with their opponents, Kilmarnock. The 'Shamrock jersey' would be used as an alternative one until the mid-1960s. The strip – a white jersey with green sleeves and collar and a shamrock emblem on the breast (plus green and white stockings) – reflects the club's associations through its founders and supporters with Ireland. (Courtesy of the *Daily Record* and *Sunday Mail*)

'GERS WERE LUCKY NOT TO LOSE TEN

What a Celtic joy day

ALL HAIL, McPHAIL

7-goal Celts humble Light Blues

By GAIR HENDERSON

PARTICK TWO UP IN 19 MINS.

By JAYMAK

ENGLAND'S BIG WIN AT CARDIFF

CENTRE: Dick Beattie lets the Celtic fans know the score after Fernie's penalty brings his team's total to seven.

SURROUND: Newspaper headlines following the match.

CELTIC - - - 7

It was as difficult to pick out a star Celt as to pick out a star Ranger—Celts had eleven Rangers none —Rex Kingsley.

RANGERS - - 1

The most disgraceful exhibition I have seen from a Rangers team—especially one playing as League champions and carrying our hopes in the European Cup —Rex Kingsley.

"Spacemen" Celts In Seventh Heaven!

A RECORD WIN

CELTIC 7, RANGERS 1

MARK this day well. In future years we may look back on it as the "October Revolution" in Scottish football.

This was the day all Scotland rose and acknowledged that pure football, played in the traditional Scottish manner, can smash the mightiest of opposition.

WIZARD OF DRIBBLE

Once he had got all his programmes sold, his free ticket gained him access to the King's Park (Celtic) end of the ground and he and his brothers eagerly climbed the terracing stairs in anticipation of the big game . . .

Gerry Heaney recalls the unusual location from which he ended up watching the match:

I remember going to the 7–1 game with the same feeling of anticipation with which I attended rock 'n' roll concerts, but in addition there was some apprehension and fear that we might not be good enough to win. The large crowd moving towards the stadium meant there would be a good atmosphere, but as we drew closer to the ground we saw huge lines of 'Tic fans. We naively decided to try the other end – for the first and last time! Soon we were into the terracing and surrounded by The Forces of Darkness. We had wisely stuffed our scarves in our jackets on the way in, otherwise we might have been molecated immediately! My companion John, who was 15, a year older than me, led us deep into the belly of the beast . . .

Patsy Keane relates a similar experience:

At that time I was living in Edinburgh, in digs with my brother John [now a director of Celtic FC]. We were a bit undecided as to whether to go to the game or not. But I was keen, and as the morning wore on, I said, 'Come on, John – let's go!' So we took a train from Haymarket station. Unfortunately the train was taking its time in getting to Glasgow; it kept on stopping and not moving. I was getting more and more panicky that we'd miss the game. Eventually we got to Queen Street Station, and I just leapt off the train and ran out to look for a taxi. John was behind me, but I wasn't paying any attention to him, I was just intent on getting to the game. The first taxi I spotted, I jumped in, leaving my brother behind. There were other guys in it going to the game too – I just said 'Hampden'. But the others were Rangers fans, and so the taxi deposited me at the Mount Florida end of the ground. The game had already started and I could hear the roar of the crowd, so being eager not to miss any more action I just got into the Rangers end and watched the game from there. I had my scarf on and was shouting and everything, but I didn't care. I was told later I was lucky to get out alive. John, it turned out, made it to the Celtic end, and saw the game from there . . .

Others 'swelled' the Celtic-supporting contingent at the Mount Florida end that day, as Edmund Burns recalls:

129

I had been working that morning at the office, and didn't get away until quite late. When I got to the ground the match had already started, and I could hear the crowd. I was anxious to see the game, and as I was approaching Hampden from the Mount Florida direction, I just decided to go into the Rangers end, and see if I could get a transfer to the North Enclosure from there. But when I got in, it was chock-a-block, so I stayed where I was and watched the whole match from the Rangers end . . .

Paul Byron relates:

My dad Tom Byron was there – he's in a hospice in Clydebank right now and can't contribute at the moment, but his story tells of how he and a very short 'Tim' friend managed to see the game. Unfortunately, from the Rangers end! My dad was able to keep his emotions under control but ugly scenes ensued when the wee man could no longer contain himself. I'm not sure they saw the end of the game! If my dad regains consciousness maybe he can tell me. Afterwards he always went on about [most of] the BBC film of the match being lost. [Sadly, Tom Byron passed away not long after his son contributed this story. RIP.]

Roy McGuinness remembers the pessimism which affected many among the Celtic support:

It was well accepted that Celtic had no chance of winning that day. I had to coax my pals into going to the game and to assure them it was not a waste of time. By the time I talked them round, getting to the game was a problem. We got the subway to Bridge Street and walked to Hampden from there. Celtic were up 1–0 when we entered the Park, and we heard a rumour that Evans and Tully had had a fight before the game. To our amazement, Celtic turned it on and gave one of the greatest displays of soccer we have seen from the hoops.

Paul Cantley (now resident in London) relates a moving family tale which centred around the events of 19 October 1957:

The story commences with the arrival of my eldest sister Anne in March 1957, the first-born of Jim and Norma Cantley. Naturally, they were elated at this and planned a future for their new family. Ten days later, however, their whole life was turned upside-down when Anne suffered a massive brain haemorrhage and was committed to hospital. The distress and the ordeal, with such a young infant, of the will she/won't she recover scenario, thinking about what caused the haemorrhage and could there be a repetition? – it was unbearable to think about. So the summer months of 1957 were a long and painful struggle for my parents, the guilt never too far from their collective conscience, as to whether there was anything that they could have done to avoid what had happened. It was only to get worse. In September 1957, after months of examination, the news was broken to my parents that their daughter had been diagnosed as suffering from hydrocephalus (i.e. water on the brain). She was permanently and severely brain damaged and would never progress mentally. Physically, her life expectancy was put at no better than five years.

Naturally, the strain had taken its toll on my parents' life, marriage, their religious beliefs – everything! They questioned whether they would risk having any more children, with the possibility, however much dismissed by the medical profession, of a recurrence. Life was not worth living and my father, who was a fanatical Celtic/football man, quite naturally, had somewhat lost his appetite for the game.

It was my mother who convinced him to go to Hampden that October day – she said he would regret not going if they won – although I think Rangers were firm favourites for the final. She said he left for the game enduring a complex of emotions – a 25-year-old going to see his team in a cup final against their greatest rivals versus the guilt of not staying at home in his family's hour of need. The match details are well documented elsewhere and I won't dwell on them here except to say that it was the most exceptional scoreline that is ever likely to occur in the history of this fixture.

After the game, Mum opened the door to Dad (who'd come straight home, being a teetotaller!) and said that he had a grin from ear to ear – the first she had seen for months. Although they had spent the previous six and a half months in a living nightmare, they knew at that defining moment that there was life and joy beyond their misery, and that everything, although not perfect, was not as bleak as they had imagined before. 'The ways of the Lord are mysterious, but wise!'

The outcome was a rethink on the children front. My eldest brother was born in July 1958 (work it out if you have to!), the second of what were to be seven children (I'm number five) in the next ten years.

The rest? Anne never did recover and was institutionalised from the age of five, unable to communicate with the outside world, but she did live to the ripe old age of 27. Dad, my inspiration, passed away in 1989, after a stroke. My last cup final with him was the 'Centenary' cup final in 1988 – a day our family will never forget and one which we constantly hark back to with fond memories.

I suppose you could say that the League Cup final victory of 1957 had a profound effect on all those who witnessed it for a variety of reasons. Life, such as the tragedy of Dunblane, is a great leveller in putting sporting rivalry such as the Old Firm's into perspective. But the opposite, as in this instance, can also be true . . .

ENDNOTES

1 The Scottish League's top two divisions were known as 'A' and 'B' from 1946–47 to 1955–56. Thereafter, until league reorganisation in the mid-1970s the names were changed to Divisons One and Two, as was the case prior to World War II.

2 'Llanelly' was the spelling in 1951, before it was changed to 'Llanelli' at the insistence of Welsh nationalists.

3 Two of the replacements that day, Jimmy Millar and Davie Wilson, were to star in the successful Rangers teams of the early 1960s.

4 The goal was more fully described by the commentator, George Davidson, thus: 'Mochan beat Combe very nicely, Mochan shooting from 20 yards, WWWHHAAAATAGOOALLL!!!! [spoken to the background of an almighty roar] OOOHH, A GOAL IN A CENTURY FROM 30 YARDS!!! He slipped that ball past Combe, and with his right foot sent a screeeaaaammer into the corner of the net. Younger diiiivvved across, but no goalkeeper could have stopped that ball, no goalkeeper would have expected a shot from that distance. And that goal deserves to win a cup in itself.'

5 In that World Cup, Scotland lost disastrously in Basle to Uruguay by the score of 7–0. Twenty years later, Mochan reacalled that 'The competition was treated almost as an end-of-season tour', a verdict endorsed by his team-mate Willie Fernie, who recalls the Scottish players turning up for training in their own gear ('We looked like liquorice allsorts'). Perhaps speaking tongue-in-cheek, the Uruguayan coach amazed Scottish pressmen with his observation that 'The result was satisfactory, but the team performance was not'.

6 In the nine seasons from 1948–49 to 1956–57, Rangers' home league average only twice dipped below 35,000. In the following nine seasons (1957–58 to 1965–66), it was only three times above that same figure.

7 In his book *Passed to You*, published the following year, Tully entitled one chapter 'Bobby Evans – Best of the Lot'. Perhaps he wished simply to put the episode behind him once and for all, and underline that he bore no grudges over it, by paying a fulsome tribute to Evans's qualities as a player – although he also wrote candidly of the incident and of the differences in temperament between himself and his team-mate which contributed to the flare-up.

CHAPTER FIVE

Sheer Bliss!

Young Sam Wilson has them rocked.
But unluckily his shot was blocked.
Then Big Bill with a lovely lob
Makes it look such an easy job.

THE MATCH
Gair Henderson, reporting on the final for the sports edition of the *Evening Times* as the match unravelled, described the perfect weather, while also making oblique reference to the tribal passions on display as the teams prepared for battle: 'Hampden in technicolour. That was the setting for the League Cup final. From a sky of Mediterranean blue the sun splashed down on turf as green as emerald, but there were other colours on parade.' (19 October 1957) The *Sporting Post* (Dundee) – seemingly uniquely among newspapers – used the present tense for match reports, and it too set the scene for the first-ever Old Firm meeting in a League Cup final and, like the *Evening Times*'s correspondent, noted the mood manifested by the more partisan elements among the 82,000 spectators: 'This is it. The day the faithful have been waiting 30 years for. The first meeting of Rangers and Celtic in a major cup final since season 1927–28. Then it was the Scottish Cup and Rangers won 4–0. This time it's the League Cup, with Celtic the holders and Rangers slight favourites in pre-match betting. The banners are waving, the party songs being sung long before the 2.45 p.m. start. A snell wind, the kind that is usually followed by reports of snow on the hills, is not having the slightest effect on the excitement.'

The teams lined up as follows:[1]

CELTIC: Beattie, Donnelly, Fallon; Fernie, Evans, Peacock; Tully, Collins; McPhail; Wilson, Mochan.

RANGERS: Niven, Shearer, Caldow; McColl, Valentine, Davis; Scott, Simpson; Murray; Baird, Hubbard.[2]

Celtic won the toss and captain Bertie Peacock booked the assistance of the sun and the wind for the opening 45 minutes as his team – playing together for the first time as a unit – got down to the business of retaining the trophy won just under a year earlier. After a brisk opening ten minutes or so, with both sides engaged in probing raids designed to test the respective defences, Celtic were the first to settle. But there was already an ominous sign for the bookmakers' favourites of the potential havoc that could be wreaked by one player who was showing clear indications of being on song – Willie Fernie. He was to have practically the first and last word in this final, albeit he had entered it, reportedly, unhappy in his deeper role. The first portent of Fernie's intentions that afternoon was a 50-yard dribble that took him deep into Rangers' penalty area, where only with difficulty was he crowded out. No opponent relished playing Fernie in this mood, when his weaving feints, with the ball seemingly tied to his bootlaces, enabled him to glide with ease past would-be tacklers. One opponent in particular, Rangers' inside-left Sammy Baird, had in the past suffered at the hands – or rather the feet – of this supremely gifted ball-player, and had vented his frustrations at previous bouts of Fernie wizardry through coarse challenges. But Baird, like his wing-half colleagues Ian McColl and Harold Davis, was destined for more grief on this occasion – and to a scarcely believable extent – as Fernie punished Rangers time and time again with electrifying runs from deep, and in so doing extracted satisfying revenge for the mistreatment he had been subjected to in previous encounters. A team-mate, Sean Fallon, describes Fernie as a player whose intentions were difficult for opponents to fathom – 'He had this great balance, able to sway this way and that as he juggled the ball, keeping defenders guessing as to which side he would attempt to bypass them on.' This early in the proceedings, Fernie the 'master craftsman' (as the *Sporting Post* described him) was setting out his stall and causing panic with his forays into enemy territory; as that newspaper put it, 'Every time he goes for a dander, Valentine and his pals are in trouble.' Also menacing to Rangers in the opening minutes was Neil Mochan, who was soon giving Shearer a great deal of trouble – including a strong shoulder-charge which sent the full-back sprawling over the touchline after the Ibrox player had tried to test out Mochan's physical mettle.

John Valentine in the centre of Rangers' back-line would soon have to undergo a form of torture from another opponent who had generally come off second best in their previous jousts. Billy McPhail had found the new Rangers pivot an awkward customer in previous clashes, which had included encounters when the pair had met in the colours of two of Glasgow's lesser clubs, Queen's Park and Clyde. A noted historian of the

'Spiders', Bob Crampsey, gives a generally favourable assessment of Valentine's abilities prior to his ill-fated departure for Rangers in his excellent book, *The Game for the Game's Sake*: 'It was not that Valentine was flaw-free. He was never a particularly outstanding passer of a ball, and against real pace down the middle he could occasionally be suspect. But in the essential qualities of belief in himself and determination in the tackle, he was unparalleled.' But those qualities deserted the tall man from Buckie in this, the most important match of his Rangers career to date, as McPhail scented when the match was barely under way. The *Sporting Post* reporter seemed to be quite taken by the Celt's subtle early touches ('Billy McPhail turns on a bit of the Ritz with a perfect back-heeler that leaves Valentine sprawling'). But this was no mere exhibitionism on the part of the leader of Celtic's attack, for all the rather quaint commentary it elicited – for McPhail was in a mood to parlay his tricks into a handsome profit near goal. Billy believed that even this early in the match Valentine was feeling the pressure of the occasion. The latter had been the focus of intense press scrutiny and the subject of much unfavourable comment in recent matches on the part of the Ibrox club's demanding, hypercritical support. Those fans had been reared on the rock-like qualities of Geordie Young and Willie Woodburn at the heart of the Light Blue back division, and had reserved judgement on the hitherto less commanding figure of the newcomer. To add to his troubles, Valentine was early in the match sent reeling 'for a full five seconds' when he got his head in the way of a powerfully driven cross from Mochan as Celtic went in search of the opening goal.

Whatever anxieties Valentine may have had, they were not eased by the knowledge that the referee, J.A. Mowat of Burnside, was generally considered to be among the most scrupulous in Scotland. Although inclined to let the play flow and to avoid over-zealousness, he was noted for keeping a tight rein on proceedings (qualities which enabled him to make the proud boast that he had never sent off a player in his lengthy career as a top match official). And keen-eyed Mowat could not overlook Valentine's blatant nudge on McPhail some 30 yards from goal with little more than ten minutes played. The centre-half came uncomfortably close to being much more severely punished for this indiscretion since, from the resultant free-kick, Celtic's right-wing pair of Tully and Collins indulged in some wiles of deception before the latter drove the ball against the crossbar, with goalkeeper Niven merely 'a desperate flurry of arms and legs as he attempted to save'. The inrushing Mochan was too startled by the power of the rebound to take advantage. Valentine's increasing nervousness was evident shortly afterwards when he almost headed past his own keeper. And moments later he, along with McColl and Caldow, was outfoxed by a cunning Charlie Tully dribble which the Irishman rounded off with a shot that struck Niven's near post, flew across the face of the goal, and then away to safety. It was an indication that Tully was in the mood to try anything, since the angle had not been one which would customarily have invited a direct attempt at goal. 'Rex', covering the match for the *Sunday Mail*, described some Rangers defenders at this stage as shaking 'as if they were operating pneumatic drills' (20 October 1957).

Having seen their team hit the woodwork twice, thoughts of looming misfortune must naturally have occurred to the mass of Celtic supporters standing behind the goal which had been under siege for most of the match so far, especially when a shot from Murray at the other end looked to be on target before being blocked. But with Rangers fans sighing with relief at their twin let-offs and urging their team to get more into the match, Celtic swept forward again and took a 23rd-minute lead – and, in the words of Gair Henderson, 'the terracings became a huge sea of green and white waves'. The powerful running of Neil Mochan, recalled to the team only a week before, had forced McColl into conceding a corner after the outside-left had brushed past Shearer. Mochan took the kick himself, and from a poor headed clearance Tully fired in a shot which was blocked by Caldow. The ball rebounded out to the right where Collins regained possession for Celtic. Deciding to try a less direct route to goal, he floated over a cross in the direction of McPhail, lurking near the penalty spot. McPhail outjumped Valentine and McColl, and astutely nodded the ball down and a yard or two backwards to the unmarked Wilson, who promptly despatched it past three startled Rangers defenders – Niven, Shearer and Caldow – stationed on the goal-line. Seconds after the restart, Tully had a chance to double Celtic's advantage after McColl completely missed a Mochan cross, but the Irishman was penalised for using a hand to control the unexpected ball.

But the goal had come at a vital time. Sammy Wilson's perfectly placed shot, struck before the ball had even touched the ground and aimed toward Niven's left-hand stanchion, had given Celtic a deserved if overdue lead. The *Sporting Post* commented, 'Celtic are playing the better football, Rangers are relying too much on the speculative punt.' The climax to the scoring move had been manufactured by a duet which was now becoming so prolific that, in the view of Sean Fallon, Rangers' manager Scot Symon paid an indirect tribute to the twin strike-force of McPhail and Wilson by deciding, in the aftermath of the débâcle about to unfold, to model the Rangers attack along similar lines (with Jimmy Millar and Ralph Brand employed in the striking roles) – a tactic which was to be rewarded with considerable success for the Ibrox club in the coming years.[3]

Rangers were to find the going tough for the remainder of the first half, despite posing the odd threat to Celtic's goal, including a free-kick plucked out of the air in brilliant fashion by Dick Beattie and a shot from

Baird that rose a couple of feet over the crossbar. But the Light Blues were indebted to their own goalkeeper when he prevented Celtic going further ahead by palming a 30-yard free-kick from Collins on to the bar. As half-time approached, Celtic could have been forgiven for thinking that, having come so close to scoring on several occasions – including three efforts against the woodwork – a one-goal lead was meagre reward for their fine attacking play. They would have to face the sun and the breeze in the second period, and Rangers would make a determined fight of it with only a single-goal deficit to overcome. Or so it seemed. But then, with a minute left of play in the first half, McPhail and Wilson combined in a heading movement in the centre of the Rangers half and the ex-Clyde man used the resulting possession intelligently, spreading the play out to Mochan on the left touchline. Neilly set off on an exhilarating run which took him well inside the Rangers' penalty box, and then, having swept past Shearer and eluded a hesitant McColl, he hit a blistering drive from a narrow, 'nigh-impossible' angle. The ball rocketed in between Niven and his right-hand post – a gap of only two feet – and was still rising as it bulged the net at the far corner of the goal. Although the swerve on the ball may have taken Niven unawares, the sheer power and accuracy of the shot would have had any goalkeeper in trouble.

Mochan's explosive finish was as timely as it was brilliant. Just how crucial a strike this was can be judged by Billy McPhail's recollection of its impact on the Celtic team – 'We went into the dressing-room at half-time knowing it just had to be our day now, but nobody could have guessed just how sensationally it all turned out . . .'

The goal was a shattering blow to Rangers' hopes of turning things around after the interval, and they would face the added problem of having to adjust their line-up due to a knock sustained by Murray, although it had been self-inflicted when he tried to tackle Evans. The half-time interval was marked by jubilant scenes among a Celtic following still buzzing over the superlative quality of Mochan's goal, and the excellent showing of their team as a whole. But the celebrations were short-lived for some overly demonstrative individuals: 'At half-time a posse of police moved in on the scene of general rejoicing at the Celtic end of the terracing, and they came down with two pieces of "human evidence" to show for their raid.' At the other end of the stadium, trouble was brewing: 'At the same time a youth dressed in Rangers blue was frog-marched from the terracing at the west end' (*Evening Times*, sports edition, 19 October 1957).

Rangers emerged for the restart with a recast forward line. Murray, with his leg now bandaged, was moved to outside-left, and Simpson took over at centre-forward. The Light Blues' attack now read: Scott, Hubbard, Simpson, Baird, Murray. Predictably, and despite the change to their attacking formation, Rangers swung into immediate action in a bid to retrieve the situation. But their frantic efforts were tinged with an obvious desperation ('Simpson smashes one shot wild and high'). Their attempts at pressing forward also left them vulnerable to counter-attacks, and from the first of these Celtic almost grabbed a third goal, Niven having to snatch at a Collins header before it crossed the line. The opportunity had been provided by Mochan, now enjoying a field-day against a bewildered Bobby Shearer.

But a third goal was only slightly delayed. In the 53rd minute, Fernie set off on a marauding gallop from midfield which carried him several yards into the Rangers penalty area. After engaging in a moment or two of his customary dalliance in front of a defender who was left spinning round in obvious confusion, Fernie chipped over a dangerous cross which Shearer, positioned near Niven's right-hand post, was obliged to head behind for a corner. Mochan took the kick, and the ball was only partially cleared out to Collins who, having retrieved possession, swivelled and approached the junction of the 18-yard line and side-line of the Rangers penalty area (on Celtic's right). From there he lofted the ball into the goalmouth and, despite the attentions of Valentine, who was attempting to mark him, Niven, who had advanced prematurely to intercept the cross, and Shearer, who was guarding the goal-line, Billy McPhail nodded cleanly into the net with an almost contemptuous flick of his dark head. Only twice before since the war had Celtic enjoyed a three-goal lead over Rangers (the Charity Cup final in 1950 when they were 3–0 ahead at one stage before Rangers pulled two goals back, and a League Cup tie at Ibrox which finished 4–1 for the visitors in 1955).

Rangers were now in deep trouble. But they refused to concede defeat, especially the ever-combative Sammy Baird. A couple of minutes after McPhail's goal, he brought down Bobby Evans in a rash challenge after the Celtic centre-half had taken the ball past him. The Celtic players seemed to stop playing for a moment, expecting to hear the sound of referee Mowat's whistle. It didn't come, and Hubbard and Scott combined to set up Murray for a strong shot which Beattie had to tip over the bar. Beattie was alert then, but a couple of minutes later, with Evans off the field receiving attention, he was easily beaten by the bullet-like speed of a Simpson header following a well-placed cross from McColl, up in support of his right-winger Scott (3–1). Then McColl himself came close to reducing the deficit further with a free-kick. Soon after, in the 62nd minute, Baird, who had been spoken to by the referee for a foul on Fernie in the first half, was booked for an offence which was not apparent to many of the spectators or match correspondents, but which seems to have been a foul on Wilson, one born of frustration.

Despite their reducing the deficit, any thoughts of a Rangers fightback were shortly to vanish. Simpson's fine goal would constitute the sole mitigation of a thoroughly miserable afternoon for the Ibrox club and their supporters. The dam was about to burst, as McPhail increased his mastery over a hapless John Valentine. As *The Scotsman*'s correspondent put it, 'The adroit distribution and positional sense of McPhail made him [Valentine] look as uncomfortable as if the damp was seeping into his boots.' (21 October 1957. The Hampden turf, although drying rapidly in the wind and sun, was perhaps still moist from the previous day's rain.)

With McPhail's elegant moves causing havoc through the middle, and Mochan and Tully keeping the Rangers full-backs fully occupied, the Ibrox side's wing-halves McColl and Davis were now having to cover a lot of ground to shore up the gaps. But as they darted and scuttled across a porous defensive line in a vain attempt to stop the flow of Celtic's dangerous advances, the Parkhead side's wingers now had more options, attacking down the flanks or cutting inside as they chose. And with Collins and Wilson also roving in search of a killer goal, Willie Fernie enjoyed increasing space in which to impress upon the match the stamp of his genius, his influence such that George Aitken, reporting the final for that evening's sports edition of the local *Evening Citizen*, was awe-struck by the player's contribution: 'Fernie's acceleration and thrusts into the Ibrox defence were magnificent.'

Rangers' defence was now on the rack. 'Caldow's tongue was hanging out trying to catch Charlie,' recalls one of Tully's team-mates with a chuckle reminiscent of the Belfast Bhoy himself. Tully had once remarked that the trouble with Rangers players was that they didn't smile often enough, but now the ebullient Irishman was intent on taking even the remembrance of a smile away from the Ibrox men. Shedding his happy-go-lucky image ('laugh-a-minute Charlie', as John Donnelly remembers him), he tormented his opponents with an exhibition of thoughtful manoeuvring and passing, as if to give a two-fingered salute to critics who had dismissed him as entertaining but ineffective. 'Waverley' was impressed by a Tully performance which 'had the Rangers from first to last in state of puzzlement. The Irishman may be a bit of a kidder, but here he was in deadly earnest, almost serious-minded and purposeful, never the jester.' (*Daily Record*, 21 October 1957)

As the second half wore on, Rangers defence came to resemble a house of cards, so beleaguered that it eventually panicked itself into a state of collapse. It became, said one critic, 'as wide open as a barn door'. As Sean Fallon even more graphically remarks, 'You could have driven a bus through that Rangers defence.'

With the Ibrox side's defenders being pulled this way and that, it was no surprise when Celtic increased their lead in the 68th minute. Neil Mochan, having once again discomfited his immediate opponent, ventured inside and let loose a low shot which Niven scrambled round the post. 'Smiler' took the resulting corner himself, and his high centre from the left was met by Sammy Wilson, whose downward header from six or seven yards was blocked on the goal-line by the combined efforts of Niven and Shearer. But the ball spun out only as far as McPhail who, from almost point-blank range, whipped a venomous shot high above the grounded goalkeeper and into the net. 4–1 – there was no way back now for Rangers, and they knew it.

A little over six minutes later, Sammy Wilson, who had nearly scored the fourth himself, had a hand in the fifth. He raced down the right and, from a position near the intersection of the penalty area sideline and the byline, swung over a testing cross which was too high for the smallish Niven and was angled slightly back across the goalmouth. It dropped invitingly at the feet of Neil Mochan, poised to strike at the corner of the six-yard box, and although his first-time cross-shot was not as cleanly or as powerfully hit as the one which had resulted in his first goal just before the interval, the ball sailed head-high across Niven before landing a couple of feet inside the far upright. 5–1 – it was rapidly becoming a rout.

If the finish to Celtic's fifth goal did not reach the acme of perfection, the sixth, scored with ten minutes to go, came close. All five of Celtic's goals so far had resulted from raids on either flank. But this one had a touch of directness about it which contrasted vividly with the short passing, precise crossing and clever individual runs which were tearing Rangers' defence to shreds. Not for the first time that season, the goal stemmed from a long downfield punt from goalkeeper Dick Beattie. His kicking had improved markedly from the previous season's campaign, so much so that informal discussions among the players had led to it being deliberately harnessed as an attacking ploy, as Beattie was cheerfully to admit shortly after the final. The idea behind it was to exploit Billy McPhail's exceptional ability in the air. On this occasion, both the latter and Valentine challenged for Beattie's lengthy clearance into the Rangers half. Once again, Valentine came off second best in their running duel – fast becoming a walkover – and, although McPhail seemed to stumble and fall as his feet touched the ground, he was quicker off the mark than the lumbering Ranger and was soon racing 'half the length of the field' through the inside-right channel and into the Rangers penalty area. McPhail held off one attempt to dispossess him, and then slotted the ball, almost disdainfully, past the advancing Niven from about ten yards to give Celtic an undreamt-of 6–1 lead.

Billy McPhail remembers Neilly Mochan, who always celebrated Celtic goals exuberantly, rushing towards him 'pumped up with glee' and exclaiming, 'What a goal! What a goal!'

Glee was an emotion which had long since been driven from the traumatised psyches of the Rangers supporters, who had earlier massed behind the goal McPhail had just scored into. Their ranks were thinner now, but some of those still present had seen enough. Perhaps they were also inflamed by the flaunting of an Irish tricolour at the opposite end, as has been claimed in some circles, but there can be no justification for what followed, no matter which club's supporters are involved. Within seconds of McPhail completing his hat-trick, fighting broke out among the more disgruntled element on the west terracing. Bottles and stones began to fly, and large gaps appeared at the front of the terracing as fans ran to safety beyond the perimeter wall. The *Evening Times*'s final sports edition, which appeared a few hours later, seems to have captured the events accurately enough:

> Just after Celtic scored their sixth goal ten minutes from the end of the League Cup final, a large section of the spectators at the Rangers end of the terracing jumped the terracing wall and rushed on to the field. It was not a break-in, but obviously an escape from trouble high up on the terracing. Police reinforcements appeared as if by magic from nowhere, and they went in like an infantry platoon to the half-deserted terracing. At the end of the scene, which lasted for a full two minutes – with play still going on on the field – the police bundled three men from the terracing.

If it is clear that the disturbance did not signify any intent to have the match abandoned, a dispirited Rangers side must surely have been hoping by this stage that the slaughter could be prematurely concluded. But their players and supporters could expect no mercy from the referee who, unlike his counterpart in a boxing ring who intervenes to save one of the contestants from further punishment, is not authorised to call a halt before the regulation 90 minutes have elapsed. Certainly Rangers' defence was punch-drunk, reeling under constant pressure – pressure that could not be relieved by a forward line which was getting no change from a resolute Celtic defence. Celtic's half-back line had completely subdued Rangers' vaunted inside trio with sharp, determined tackling and swift covering. It has to be said, though, that the defensive task facing Fernie, Evans and Peacock was rendered simpler by an Ibrox attack devoid of invention or subtlety. Simpson, Murray and Baird – inside-forwards who had been praised for their attacking thrust in recent press articles – were, on the day, reduced to little more than honest grafters. Baird would be generally picked out as the best – if only in the sense of the most determined – Rangers performer. But the loss of any rhythm or purpose in Rangers' front line was perhaps due to the fact that almost from the beginning, Celtic's superior football had been sapping the Ibrox side of its collective and individual self-belief, a verdict voiced by Bertie Peacock 40 years on: 'Football is a confidence game – as we grew in it, Rangers began to lose it, and the goals came freely as we started to penetrate their defence early on.' Making matters even more difficult for Rangers, their only real threat on the day – that posed by wingers Scott and Hubbard – had been progressively snuffed out by effective marking and positional play on the part of Donnelly and Fallon, although their task was rendered easier by the fact that any meaningful supply of the ball to the wingers had become a casualty of the mayhem which reigned for most of the match in Rangers' rearguard. Nevertheless, John Donnelly must receive credit for the maturity and tactical awareness by which he foiled his veteran opponent Hubbard, illustrated by his clever method of boxing-in the wily South African and so giving the Ranger no scope for his favourite ploy of cutting inside. John recalls the tricky left-winger trying to impose himself on his young opponent early on in the match: 'Out near the corner flag he put his foot on the ball and kept it there, inviting me into the tackle.' But Donnelly stood his ground and then thwarted Hubbard's attempt to 'nutmeg' him after the failure of the original ploy. One of Rangers' most potent threats, the nippiness and thrust of the South African, was thus gradually nullified. Meanwhile, Sean Fallon on the opposite flank kept tabs on the dangerous Alec Scott by means of patient jockeying – 'He could be a real handful, a bit of a flyer,' recalls Fallon, 'and you had to be wary not to dive in and let him get away from you, for there was no sweeper or the like in those days.' Jack Harkness, writing in the *Sunday Post*, was simple and succinct in his analysis of these individual contests: 'Scott and Hubbard were to have been so much superior to Tully and Mochan. What a faulty forecast that turned out to be! Donnelly and Fallon put Hubbard and Scott in their hip-pockets, while Tully and Mochan were creating all sorts of panic around Rangers' goal.' (20 October 1957)

At no time in the game were Rangers allowed to build up any momentum, and this had alarming consequences for their defence, which was denied 'any respite the longer the game went on', as John Loch wrote for the *Edinburgh Evening Dispatch*. Commenting on 'a conclusive victory for purely scientific football over strength and determination', he highlighted the strain on the creaking Ibrox defences in the closing stages by citing the case of the overworked veteran Ian McColl. Earlier in the second half McColl had been seen with his arms outstretched, a captain beseeching his colleagues to pull themselves together. But now he looked 'to have shot his bolt. He looked tired of it all and long before the end he appeared to give it up completely' (21 October 1957). That observation touches obliquely on a much-overlooked factor in Rangers' reduction to a leaden-footed rabble, slow of thought and movement compared to the fluent Celts – namely, the Parkhead side's superior fitness. At least this was the feeling in the Celtic camp, to judge by the fact that the club's self-effacing trainer, Willie Johnstone, was publicly singled out for congratulations at the post-match victory banquet held in Ferrari's restaurant in the city centre that evening. Writing in his regular column for the *Evening Citizen* a week later, Charlie Tully spoke of Johnstone as 'a hard man at times, bringing us back most afternoons, but he is for us. And we respond by giving him all we've got at training and on the field. Some of the boys actually turned up at Parkhead last Sunday' [i.e. the day after the final].

Certainly, such was the physical and mental exhaustion in Rangers' ranks latterly that Sean Fallon's impression of the final stages was of 'finding it so easy that we took our foot off the pedal, though that's something that often happens in football when one side is so far in front and the other has given up. The Rangers players had their heads down and they were totally disorganised – and that was most unlike them in those days!' Four decades later, his full-back partner, John Donnelly, reflecting on the 'unreality' of it all, recalls how 'Rangers just gave up the ghost when it was 4–1 or so. We were confident of victory, but you don't think of winning 7–1 – you just don't believe that sort of thing will happen.' Sammy Wilson, described by his captain as 'no mean performer' that day, believes that Rangers were increasingly in the grip of a 'state of shock' at having been so comprehensively outplayed. After all, it was a rare experience for them, particularly at the hands of their greatest rivals in the 1940s and 1950s when Celtic were generally, and accurately, considered the underdogs in Old Firm encounters. And although Donnelly had to clear one shot from the goal-line with the score at 6–1, Sean Fallon's recollection of Celtic easing up late on in the match is confirmed by the *Sporting Post's* observation (again using the present tense) that 'Celtic are at half-cock'. There was now no question as to where the cup was headed.

'Rex' of the *Sunday Mail* had no doubt about how it had been won: 'The fact that must stick in Rangers' throats is that they were flattened by the very thing they themselves so badly lack – PURE, UNADULTERATED FOOTBALL.' He continued in an obvious 'dig' at the Ibrox club's penchant for more robust methods: 'Mark that word "unadulterated". Celtic kept playing the *ball* all the time. That stemmed from confidence in themselves' (20 October 1957). Celtic's players had demonstrated a fearless belief in their own skills and talents, thus rendering the 'power-play' tactics in vogue elsewhere – decried by the *Glasgow Herald's* Cyril Horne as a 'disfiguring weakness in the sport' – as unnecessary as they were unattractive.

Equally as stunned by the outcome as the Rangers players were the Celtic supporters. Their delighted surprise was turning into delirium as they tried to assure themselves and one another that it was now really six goals their team had scored. In the words of one of them, Tom O'Neill of Dumbarton, they revelled in the spectacle of Celtic 'seeming to score every time they ran up the pitch'. Insofar as they were capable at this stage of reflecting on what they had so far witnessed, they probably focused on the performances of Celtic's attacking stars – Tully,

Mochan, McPhail and Fernie – who had all played 'blinders'.

The contributions of Tully and, on the other flank, Mochan, so prodigious in this game, highlighted the fact that this was an era when the need for wingers to unlock defences went virtually unquestioned in British football – when in fact they were so *de rigueur* that the pairings fielded by various clubs could be recited as a litany by most supporters. The Old Firm apart, there were Smith and Ormond of Hibs, Herd and Ring of Clyde, Leggat and Hather of Aberdeen, Hunter and Weir of Motherwell, McKenzie and Ewing of Partick Thistle, and so on. It was, after all, a time when tactics were basic and unsophisticated, worked out not by managers or coaches but by the players themselves, relying on their own invention, and discussed and practised informally as and when they felt so inclined. Neither Jimmy McGrory of Celtic nor Scot Symon, his opposite number at Ibrox, was ever a manager noted for indulging in sophisticated pre-match planning. Their pep-talks were merely that – simple words of encouragement and exhortation.

Hence if Celtic's football in this League Cup final was largely off-the-cuff, it owed its success on the day to the Parkhead club's more talented performers all approaching or attaining their very best form. The two wingers were running amok, the centre-forward was giving a display of aerial brilliance bordering on the fantastic, and – most significantly of all – the right-half was choosing this occasion to live up fully to his team-mate Billy McPhail's description of him as 'the perfect athlete, a player who has the ideal build – especially the thighs – for a footballer'! On this beautiful afternoon, Willie Fernie was simply majestic.

The Celtic FC Supporters Association Handbook (1958–59), looking back on the game, stated, rightly, 'Each and every cog in the Celtic machine functioned perfectly that glorious day and it would be unfair to single out individuals for special mention.' But after the final, chairman Bob Kelly, a man who rarely bestowed compliments on individual Celts – and who could not see beyond his idol Patsy Gallacher as the ultimate footballer – was nevertheless moved to concede that Fernie had turned in an exhibition almost as good 'as Patsy at his best'. That Fernie was the man of the match brooked little contradiction, despite McPhail's hat-trick. Fernie ran Rangers ragged with repeated, devastating surges out of defence that gave his opponents no relief as they struggled to regroup in the face of a Celtic team which seemed to come at them from all angles, like the many-headed Hydra.

It was thus fitting that the task of putting the final seal on a marvellous team performance should fall to Fernie, who had reached a pinnacle of brilliance in his personal display. The seventh and final goal was netted from the penalty spot in the last minute after a desperate lunge from Shearer brought McPhail crashing down well inside the penalty area just as the latter was threatening a repeat of his previous goal. Mr Mowat had annoyed Celtic supporters in two earlier cup-ties against Rangers in 1957 by refusing strong penalty claims (the Scottish Cup second-round replay in February, and the Glasgow Cup match in August). But on this occasion he had no hesitation in awarding a spot-kick. McPhail declined the opportunity to cap a personal triumph with a fourth goal.[4] And so, appropriately enough in the light of his contribution to the victory, Willie Fernie stepped up to face Niven. He stroked the ball home as if he were taking a penalty in a practice match, placing his shot neatly along the ground into the corner of the net, to the right of the hapless Niven.

That made the final score: Celtic 7, Rangers 1.

BILLY McPHAIL

Billy McPhail's all-too-brief career at Parkhead was a triumph against the odds. After all, had not Clyde, in May 1956, let the player join Celtic for a mere £2,500, a symptom of his unenviable reputation for injury-proneness? And wasn't his new club resigned to the fact that the transaction was in the nature of a gamble? Here was a player who in little more than a decade in top-class football would suffer cartilage trouble, a broken collarbone and a fractured jaw, as well as ankle and knee problems. His many admirers would wince when the slimly built McPhail was subjected to the rough-house tactics which were the norm in Scottish football during the period. But almost invariably his aficionados would be compensated for their anguish by an exhibition of the deft touches that made him such a compelling centre-forward to watch. Above all, they were entranced by his ability to soar above his markers to plant a firm header in the net or direct a subtler nod down to a better-placed colleague shaping for a volley – aerial techniques which reached their apotheosis in his partnership with inside-forward Sammy Wilson in those early months of the 1957–58 season. Even when not in the vicinity of the opposition goal, the pair could combine to initiate attacks completed by others, as was the case with Mochan's astonishing goal just on half-time in the League Cup final.

Sean Fallon recalls McPhail as possessing 'the great knack of seeming to hang in the air', while another former team-mate waxes more lyrical with a soaring metaphor: 'Billy could get up there among the pigeons.' But, paradoxically, McPhail's early years in senior football did not hint at such a striking role. He joined Queen's Park in the autumn of 1944, as World War II was drawing to a close, and played for his school team (St Mungo's Academy, Glasgow) on the Saturday morning and a Queen's Park side in the afternoon. A contemporary of a (very!) young Ronnie Simpson at Hampden, he never featured in Queen's Park's first team at centre-forward, being fielded as an inside-forward, a winger and a left-half instead. At that time the number nine position was held down by such useful performers as Tony Harris, Andy Aitken and Bobby Kerr. This was a period when Queen's had a strong squad of players, available – or recruited – during the transition from wartime to full-time competitive football. (In dressing-room banter, Harris would comment on McPhail's slender frame by jokingly referring to him as 'Muscles'.)

Celtic's interest in McPhail was a long-standing one, it is typical of the Parkhead club's reputation for parsimony in that era that, when he joined Clyde in May 1947, the Shawfield club had offered a signing-on fee that was four times greater than that which their more illustrious neighbours were prepared to pay. Indeed, McPhail might never have ended up at Celtic Park had Manchester City pursued their interest in November 1952, by which time Billy was established at centre-forward in a fine Clyde team whose left wing consisted of two future Scottish internationalists, Archie Robertson and Tommy Ring. However, McPhail's career in such distinguished company was to be overshadowed by an injury inflicted in December 1953 which was to dog his playing career (and, indeed, effectively end it less than five years later). Back helping out in defence against Airdrie at Broomfield, he was caught up in a goalmouth mêlée. He was helped off, but later resumed, limping. Despite treatment, his future was blighted to the extent that he missed the opportunity to partake in a piece of Scottish Cup history, that of the same family providing the opposing centre-forwards in a final, his elder brother John being the spearhead in Celtic's line-up for the 1955 showdown with Clyde. (Sadly for him, too, Billy was thus denied a winner's medal.)

Billy virtually entered the front door at Parkhead just as his brother was leaving it a year later. But even though McPhail's two goals in the 1956 League Cup final against Partick Thistle were instrumental in ending a decade of ignominious Celtic failures in the competition, it is both surprising and instructive to recall that the full approval of the Celtic support was still being withheld almost on the eve of McPhail's greatest triumph in a green and white jersey. Early in season 1957–58, Celtic fans were complaining that his fitness was now so suspect that 'he couldn't last two or three games' (this overheard on the terracing after he missed the opening league match at Falkirk). And there had already been grumbles about his failure to make an impact on the Rangers defence in the Glasgow Cup tie at Ibrox in mid-August 1957, a performance which drew a mild rebuke from one of his foremost admirers in the press corps, Cyril Horne of the *Glasgow Herald*: 'McPhail was sadly remiss, however; he seemed to have no zest for the physical side of the game.' Indeed, criticism of the striker reached such a pitch that one letter-writer to the 'Stick out your neck' column of Glasgow's *Evening Citizen* (a Mr McFarlane of Greenock) appealed to fellow supporters to get off McPhail's back and not go out of their way to barrack the player with cries of 'He's only a ghost of his brother!' (7 September 1957). Only six weeks later, one of the cleverest centre-forwards ever to grace the

Scottish game finally emerged from that imagined shadow in the most sublime of fashions. In doing so, he vindicated the judgement of his earliest mentor, Jacky Gardiner at Queen's Park, who was forever encouraging him with the tag of being 'God's gift to football'. However challenging was the bestowal of that accolade, Celtic supporters have always suspected McPhail of being a chosen vehicle of divine intervention on 19 October 1957.

WILLIE FERNIE
This 'Wizard of the Weave' broke into the Celtic team in the spring of 1950, and impressed enough to be fielded in the Charity Cup final when a young Celtic side saw off Shaw, Woodburn, Cox and co. at a sundrenched Hampden. His appearances were irregular, however, until the 1952–53 season at the end of which he picked up another Charity Cup medal and then took the place of an injured Charlie Tully at outside-left against Hibs in the Coronation Cup final. His reward for a fine display was a more permanent slot in the 'Double'-winning side of '54, which in turn brought him international recognition at the World Cup in Switzerland that summer. By the mid-1950s, Fernie was being recognised as a ball-player of genius, both by his many admirers and by uncompromising, often cynical opponents who used any means, fair or foul, to stop him from doing what he was best at – terrorising the opposition with runs of unmatched style and verve.

But Willie Fernie's career with Celtic was at a crossroads as the start of season 1957–58 loomed. He was embroiled in a wage dispute with the club – a situation exacerbated by the fact that he had just bought a new house and his wife Audrey (formerly a secretary of Celtic manager Jimmy McGrory) was about to give birth to a son. Jimmy McGrory, indeed, refused to expand on the club's stance on the matter beyond a rather perfunctory statement: 'We do not differentiate between the wages of our first-team full-time players.' Fernie resolved his differences with the club by re-signing on 1 August, this at a time when Newcastle United were expressing an interest in acquiring his services. The Tyneside club had in fact been trying to sign him for around six months or so, and they later tabled a formal bid of £18,000. Chairman Bob Kelly reacted to the offer by claiming, rather self-righteously, 'We are not prepared to entertain approaches for any player until the man concerned approaches the management,' while an unnamed Celtic official insisted that 'negotiations never got to the length of price discussions'. Nevertheless, this public stance clashed rather discordantly with the English club manager's statement that they had been put off by Celtic's demand for a sum nearer £20,000. Whatever the real truth behind these avowals, it was thought that Newcastle would still have first option on the player if he became available, although in the event it was their north-east rivals

Middlesbrough who took Fernie south the following season (for a reported fee of £17,500) – a scenario already envisaged by Fernie's former team-mate John McPhail in his capacity as a sportswriter for the *Daily Record*. McPhail had written as early as 30 July 1957: 'Do not be surprised if the popular Celt ultimately looks to England for his future.'

Symptomatic perhaps of this unsettled period of his Celtic career was a semi-public dispute about Fernie's best position in the team. With Bobby Evans, the regular right-half, being asked to fill the pivot's role – a problem position for Celtic since Jock Stein's ankle injury and subsequent enforced retirement as of January 1957 – the Celtic hierarchy (as it was revealingly described then) had decided to experiment with Willie Fernie in the red-head's former berth. One writer reported the seemingly far-fetched theory that the management had *always* envisaged Fernie as a wing-half, and Jimmy McGrory, on being asked how he thought the experiment was proceeding, replied with a grin, 'What experiment?' He went on to add, 'You know, you could almost say that playing him at inside-forward was the experiment. We played him there in the past few seasons only because of the shortage of first-class men for the job. But we have always considered that Willie was really a wing-half.' (Interview with Harry Andrew for the *Scottish Sunday Express*, 6 October 1957.) The manager's smile, however, betrayed the fact that in the best part of a decade with the club, Fernie had only turned out in the half-back line on a handful of occasions (although he had been fielded there in the reserves when he first came to Parkhead). And in fact, it seems that an unspoken time-limit of the six League Cup sectional matches at the start of the new season had been placed on the switch to test its long-term suitability. For one thing, there were doubts as to whether the player's temperament was suited to such a transition, carrying as it did a greater burden of defensive duties. His critics in the press and on the terracing might have acknowledged him as Scotland's premier ball-artiste (his team-mate Sean Fallon recalls that 'in training it was impossible to get the ball off him'), but they also saw Fernie as a mercurial player with a habit of holding on to the ball a fraction too long instead of passing it to a colleague in a scoring position. And, as one of the authors overheard a denizen of 'The Jungle' expostulate around that time, 'He couldnae tackle tae save himself.'

There appeared to be a touch of hesitancy and unease on Fernie's part too at the outset of the experiment, for it was noticed during the second of the club's pre-season public trials that he seemed restrained when operating in the 'semi-defensive wing-half position' and took a keener interest in proceedings when moving forward with the ball. Essentially, of course, he was, like Bobby Collins, a prototype of the attacking midfielder (a term not yet in vogue). But as the new season got under way, some observers remained unconvinced about the value of the switch.

Commenting on Celtic's struggle to overcome Airdrieonians in the opening League Cup tie, Tommy Allan of the *Scottish Sunday Express* pooh-poohed the notion that Fernie (whom he called 'Celtic's problem boy') could ever make it as a right-half. Allan added that even before Fernie was knocked out by the ball and taken off temporarily before resuming at outside-left, he 'was not in the same class as Price for half-back play'. A fortnight later, with Celtic's fate in the tournament hanging in the balance, Fernie delivered a magnificent riposte to his critics in the return match with Airdrie at Broomfield Park. With the game evenly poised at 1–1 halfway through the second half, he suddenly cut loose, giving a dazzling display of ball control on the greasy surface, and clinching victory with a thudding first-time volley. He had not only negotiated a tricky hurdle for Celtic (and perhaps himself), he was limbering up for the final itself.

THE SUPPORTERS
After the final whistle had sounded at Hampden, Bertie Peacock collected the League Cup and held it aloft for the supporters to see. There follows a series of reminiscences on the game and its immediate aftermath from supporters who witnessed it, or who soon heard about it.

Jimmy Jordan (now resident in San Francisco) recalls:

> Forty years have passed since I last saw Celtic in a big game . . . the Scottish League Cup final of 1957. I emigrated to San Francisco a few months after this match. Although there were over 82,000 at the game, there seemed to be room in the ground as my good friend Johnny Hughes (from Scotstoun) and I made our way around the terracing and took up positions in the North Enclosure directly opposite the main stand. We were about twenty rows up and almost at midfield.
>
> Jack Mowat, regarded as one of Scotland's top referees at that period, was in charge. Celtic defended the west (Mount Florida) goal at the Rangers end. Celtic took over this game from the start, but the woodwork prevented them from going ahead on two occasions. It wasn't until midway through the half that Celtic took the lead – Billy McPhail headed the ball down to Sammy Wilson, who wasted no time in hitting a great shot into the net. Neil Mochan scored an opportune goal just before half-time – much to the delight of most of the spectators around us in the terracing. Shortly after half-time, Billy McPhail added a third goal.
>
> Although Billy Simpson scored for Rangers, this was Celtic's day and Charlie Tully was in complete charge of the game. He appeared to be around the centre-circle most of the second half, conducting his troops as they advanced on the Rangers goal. It took me back to nine years earlier (25 September 1948) when Charlie was starting his career

with Celtic . . . Celtic had defeated Rangers in a League Cup game at Parkhead by 3–1, and the headline in the *Sunday Mail* above the by-line of 'Rex' (R.E. Kingsley – Scotland's leading football writer) read: '21 NOVICES DANCE THE IRISH JIG.' Charlie had been in sensational form.

As each goal was scored the Celtic crowd got merrier, but behind the west goal (the Rangers end) disturbances started to break out, and some of their supporters started to come over the retaining wall. Charlie Tully had the ball near the centre spot, and pointed out the disturbances to referee Mowat . . . by this time not too many of Rangers' supporters remained in the stadium.

Celtic's seventh goal came in the last minute. It was a penalty kick taken by Willie Fernie. It was rumoured afterwards that George Niven, Rangers' goalkeeper, asked Fernie to miss the penalty.

Charlie Harvey recalls:

The first ten minutes of 'The 7–1' saw this potentially great team at its best – and it got better – and ever better as the minutes ticked away. The ball was stroked along the deck into open spaces that the Celts, but seldom the 'Gers, had anticipated. They went through a tough Rangers defence like a knife through butter. Don't let anyone kid you, Rangers were taken apart by the appliance of pure football science. But oh, the frustration of that first 15 or 20 minutes! Woodwork was struck three or four times, on one occasion denying Tully what would undoubtedly have been the best goal of all time. At the angle of the penalty box, over on the stand side, he stood with his right foot on the ball as two worried 'Gers defenders sprinted towards him. They went in different directions as Charlie waggled his arse while moving the ball forward, back, and then sideways. It was done on about one yard square of turf. Never famous for his shot, he took a couple of steps forward and hit a rocket that beat Niven at his near post. The ball struck the inside of the upright, travelled the length of the goal-line, hit the other post and came out. At that moment many a devout man uttered very bad sweary words.

John Eadie recalls:

Anyway, coming up to this game, Rangers were always winning this and winning that. And then we heard about this big lad Valentine . . .

My brother Ed, he was in the railways, and he got transferred down to London. He went for the big money. He'd maybe been down there about two or three months. So he came back up and we had a helluva drink on the Friday night, talking about the game. We met in The Tavern pub where the Parnell Celtic Supporters Club met, at the

150

corner of Florence Street and Ballater Street (in the Gorbals). John Adams owned it; he was a Catholic, and he came and took it over – it was called McVey's in the early 1950s – and done it up, and had all the Celtic supporters in there. He was a real good guy. Anyway, Ed had brought whisky with him up from London, and he'd been drinking all day and carried on when we went for a drink in The Tavern. He was drinking heavily and spending money galore – he always did that. So we went to the game. And you always have that thing in the back of your mind, when you see that Blue coming out: Rangers, they're gonnae do it again, you think.

But Sammy Wilson scored that goal, and Mochan got the second goal just before half-time. Ed must have seen about three or four goals. Ed kept saying, 'Gie's another drink.' And then Billy scored, Billy McPhail. Then Simpson, was it, he got one back? 3–1. When that went in, I went, 'Aw naw, this is them coming back into it again,' you know? But then Billy scored again, and then Mochan got the fifth goal – a long ball over, and then he hit it, right in the net. And Ed by this time was sitting down on the terrace. He was just sitting there – totally drunk. I said, 'Ed! Ed! It's 5–1!' And he just moaned, 'Naw, naw.' I said, 'Naw, it's 5–1, Ed, Mochan's just scored!' Then the next thing – Billy scores again, the one he just flicked round Valentine then slotted past the keeper – six! And I said, 'Ed! Ed! Come on, Ed! It's six, it's six!' And we're all going forward, and everybody's going crazy, and I'm shouting, 'Ed! Ed! It's 6–1!' And Ed just said, 'Yer joking.' And the others kept saying, 'Naw, it's 6–1, ye've got tae get up, ye've got tae see them!' 'Naw, naw, I don't believe ye!' he was saying. He was sitting down on the terracing, real drunk he was. Then we got the penalty kick. Somebody close by said, 'Aw, they'll probably miss it, they won't make it seven – they won't take a liberty' – right? But Fernie just came up – bang! Ha ha ha! I shouted again, 'Ed! Ed! It's SEVEN, Ed, it's SEVEN, Ed – it's f****** SEVEN! Get up, Ed! It's SEVEN! Get up, get up!' And then he said, 'Whit? WHIT? Make it EIGHT!' And he jumped up shouting, 'Make it EIGHT, MAKE IT EIGHT, MAKE IT EIGHT!'

I'll never forget that; everybody was talking about it afterwards. The next day we were all still going on about how he jumped up and shouted, 'MAKE IT EIGHT!'[5]

It was unbelievable – 7–1 against Rangers! Rangers had a good team at the time too; the only one that was a diddy was big Valentine, and he didn't play again for them. But 7–1! This was the greatest thing that ever happened! We walked back, just walked, singing. The Rangers fans, they must have gone up to Carmunnock or something like that, because we never met any of them going down the road. Ha ha ha!

We went back to The Tavern, and then we all had a sing-song back at the house. And on the Sunday . . . reading all the papers.

Mochan had been dropped a couple of weeks before. On the Saturday morning in one newspaper they said that Mochan was back – 'M-Plan for Rangers'. That's when I thought we had a chance, because Mochan was back.

My mate Jimmy Price was in Australia at the time. He bought a paper – saw the score: 7–1. He threw it down – couldnae believe it! Said, 'Och, it's a mistake.' So then he bought another paper. Saw it again – 7–1. Threw that one away. Couldn't believe it. Then he bought a third paper. Still the same score – 7–1. Later I asked him, 'Jimmy, how many papers did you buy?' 'Seven!' he said. Ha ha ha ha ha! Jimmy's got 'Celtic 7' on his car. He's always had that. Every car he's had, it's got 'Celtic 7' on it! Ha ha ha ha! I called Jimmy up once to tell him I had a new number – 371-7171. I told him you can pay for it, you can get a number like that. Ha ha ha!

Bill Cassidy (now resident in Ontario, Canada) recalls:

I remember the game like it was yesterday. I was 14 at the time and along with a friend we both went to Hampden expecting another humbling defeat. I don't want to talk too much about the game itself, but I would like to tell the *true* story of my journey home from the game. My friend and I boarded a bus on our way back to Rutherglen. There weren't many on this bus but there were two women sitting at the front. We sat on those long seats just as you went inside a double-decker bus. The women were getting off before us and walked past where we sat, and one of them asked the score of the big match. We promptly replied, '7–1 for Celtic.' She drew us a look and said to her friend, 'That's what's wrong with the youth of today, you can't get a straight answer out of them.' I still remember her face to this day. She must have felt foolish when she learned the result later.

Larry O'Hare (now resident in Australia) recalls:

My brother was in Canniesburn Hospital recuperating from a near miss with God at that time. He was the only 'Tim' in his ward and was getting dog's abuse. At that time dog's abuse was dog's abuse, not like the mild stuff we get nowadays, and, as you know, Celtic were the underdogs. He wasn't looking forward to the result. We visited him that night and it was the first time we had seen him smile for months. The 'Huns' wouldn't look at him and he made a complete recovery. I myself was listening to the game on the radio but can't remember much about it, except that when we were leading 5–1 and Rangers were attacking, I can recall saying, 'Please, God, don't let them score.'

152

Alex Coulter (now resident in Australia) recalls:

I remember this game well as at the time I was playing football and turned up for our game on the Saturday to find out there had been a mix-up and the game had been cancelled. By this time it was too late to head for Hampden so I went home and put the radio on. The BBC commentator, George Davidson, kept saying Rangers were winning 3–0 – possibly wishful thinking. I was baffled, as it was 'all Celtic'; and then it was a free-kick for Rangers and McColl crossed and Simpson scored. I was horrified – 4–0! But then Mr Davidson says, 'I must apologise; one of my colleagues tells me I have been saying Rangers were winning; as a matter of fact the score is 3–1 to Celtic.' Boy, was I happy!

At that time the only other person in the house was my father, who was asleep as he was on nightshift. But when the score reached 5–1 I went into the room and got him out of bed, saying, 'You've got to come and listen to this!'; and at the end of the game he said, 'Why didn't you waken me earlier?' Those were the days!

Gerard Hamill recalls:

The 7–1 match I half-listened to in my uncle Eddie's house, in Ravel Row in Parkhead. My dad and I arrived late for some reason, and I can remember uncle Eddie meeting us on the landing, on the top floor of his three-storey building, in a state of high excitement and utter bile about the commentator, who couldn't seem to handle the very idea that we could be winning. He kept saying it was the other lot who were leading, and having to correct himself. There must have been about seven or eight men listening and rejoicing. The women were out. I was more interested in my cousin Ann's rocking chair. Imagine!

Paul Lusk (now resident in Perth, Western Australia) recalls:

Coming from Auchinleck and being only nine years old at the time, I never really had the opportunity to get to Celtic matches. But I will never forget this particular match, mainly because of Dad's general attitude to Celtic and their performances around that time. Comments of 'Bloody hopeless' and 'They'd cut your hair' were commonplace.

I remember that the second halves of games were all that were ever broadcast at that particular time, and when they crossed to Hampden Celtic were 3–0 up. Shortly after Billy Simpson got one back for Rangers. Comments from my Dad spewed forth – 'Rangers will probably go on and win this!' Well, win they certainly did not, and, of course, Celtic went on to add four more wonderful goals, much to my delight and that of my father. The poor soul had waited so long for something to celebrate. Ahhh – for the good times!

Michael Hutton (High Valleyfield, Fife) recalls:

Although I was not at the game, the memories of that day are still fresh in my mind 40 years later.

I was only eight years old. My father, Patrick, who was a coalminer – a job I was later to follow him into – was Celtic-daft. He used to take me every week to see the Bhoys in our local Celtic supporters' bus. That day in 1957, I knew – even at such an early age – was so important to my father and his brothers. To beat Rangers was everything then – as now. But my father would not go to Old Firm games or listen on the radio – he was a nervous wreck and could not face it.

Our local junior team, Valleyfield Colliery, were at home that day, so he took me to see them play (I can't remember who against). Anyway, my dad said, 'Michael, run to the shop for me.' I said okay – the shop was about 100 yards away, but you could not see it from the park because of some houses. I came out of the shop and the shop-owner's son drew up in his car. It was brand new and had a radio – in 1957 I had never seen one like that before. As I passed he said, 'You'll be happy today, young Hutton. Your team's winning 2–0.' I stood beside his car and listened to the game. He was not kidding me on!

I sprinted down to the park, shouting, 'Dad, Dad, Celtic are winning 2–0!' I don't think he believed me. I then told him I was going back up to listen to the game and that if Celtic scored again, I would shout and jump up and down as a signal. So away I went. The third goal went in. I ran back to where my dad could see me and screamed to him, 'It's three!' – and away back to the car. The same thing at four, five, six, then seven. I got back to the park as the game was finishing. 'Dad, they won!' I was jumping up and down shouting, 'It's 7–1, it's 7–1!' Not one man there believed me. I can remember them all ridiculing me and me saying, 'Dad, honest, it's true!'

One of the Valleyfield players whom my dad knew asked, 'Pat, what's Michael saying?' and my dad told him I was saying Celtic had won 7–1. He ran over to me and asked, 'Is that true?' – to which I replied, 'Honest to God, it's true.' He grabbed me then and did a wee jig.

To get to our house we took a short cut through some woods. I don't think my father still could take in what I was saying. I was so excited. I recall saying that Fernie had scored the last goal with a penalty. Anyway, we were soon home. My dad switched on the TV. We sat, eyes fixed to the screen. I mind him looking at me and smiling. Then it came up on the screen: RANGERS 1 CELTIC 7. It was a black screen with white letters. Dad grabbed me and flung me in the air screaming and shouting, and we danced all round the room. My mother came in and asked, 'What's happened?' My dad and I were dancing and shouting with delight, and she joined in. What a day! Forty years later I can still remember it all so clearly in my mind.

Seamus Murphy recalls:

The day of the match, we were docked in Haifa, Israel, and we were all round the wireless listening for the result on the BBC World Service . . . Celtic 7 Rangers 1. The 'Huns' just sat there with sheer disbelief on their faces. As for me, it was the happiest moment of my life. I'd have happily gone to my Maker at that moment.

Tom Campbell recalls:

I was in Ottawa at the time, and the evening edition of the *Toronto Telegram* used to carry the football scores from the UK (the time difference made this possible). I bought the paper in a corner store in Dalhousie Street, near the Farmers' Market, and was almost afraid to open it. I saw the score and couldn't believe it; in fact, I was convinced it was a misprint for '1–1' and went to bed half-thinking that was the result. I bought the Sunday edition the next day and saw on the sports pages a little square with the headline 'Celtic 7, Rangers 1' – and a paragraph which indicated that the switchboard at the newspaper had received 'hundreds of calls' asking to verify this scoreline. The paragraph also carried a comment to the effect that this clarification would make a lot of people happy – and a lot of people unhappy. I was one of those who were very happy!

Tommy Lanigan recalls:

The game itself is well documented. Imagination would have to be applied to the limit if anyone wants to picture the joy at the Celtic end as we witnessed the undreamt-of destruction of the 'invincible' Rangers and the 'Iron Curtain'. Many people had to turn their backs as Fernie approached the penalty spot to stroke home number seven. They just couldn't absorb any more. We had never known anything like it, or even thought it possible. Older people had reared us on stories of heroes like Jimmy Quinn, Patsy Gallacher and Jimmy McGrory. We knew by heart of the great deeds the Celts had done, but we had no hope of seeing any real Celtic glory in our day . . . After the final whistle we stood singing and dancing for 20 minutes, reluctant to leave.

The police had the routes back to the East End well segregated. Rangers fans went home via Polmadie and Shawfield. We went through Toryglen and Rutherglen. I'll never forget the sight in Prospecthill Road. Traffic was at a standstill. Road and pavements were a seething mass of rejoicing green and white. The Rangers crowd had arrived in Bridgeton well before us and when we reached The George we saw that every window had been smashed. Sweeping up began as we started the party of all parties. We weren't the least bit bothered about the 'Billy Boys' returning – we had plenty of hard men too!

In normal circumstances silly behaviour was frowned upon in Bridgeton, but that night the attitude was 'Anything goes'. It was like Hogmanay and VE night [Victory in Europe, 1945] combined, only a hundred times better. We sang – conduct unheard of in a Glasgow pub, which could get you the jail and lose Charlie Deeney his licence. We even danced on the tables. To go on after hours would certainly have cost Charlie his pub, so we left voluntarily at closing time. Celebrations went on in houses all over the East End until five or six in the morning. To get into any party all that was required was Celtic allegiance. In fact, the celebrations went on for weeks and weeks and weeks.

Andy Gillen (now resident in Berkshire) relates: 'My father George Gillen was actually married on the great day – and his mates who had to attend the wedding have never forgiven him for missing the match.' George Gillen (Cumnock) himself takes up the story:

It was a special day for me as I was married in St Mirin's Cathedral in Paisley and honeymooned in Dublin. I don't think my wedding friends (Celtic supporters) have really ever forgiven me! En route to the air terminal we were engulfed by the football crowd in Glasgow. I asked the Rangers supporters the score. Needless to say their answer was not repeatable. However, the Celtic supporters answered, to my delight and joy, '7–1 for the Bhoys.' A day I certainly will remember!

His son Andy comments, 'I couldn't help laughing at his closing line – I wonder if he remembers it because it is his wedding anniversary or because of the result?'

Tommy Bole (now resident in Los Angeles) recalls:

When Fernie scored the seventh goal I was standing – in tears with the emotion of it all – at the very top of the King's Park end terracing. I was getting ready to leave since I had to go to a wedding reception. The guy getting married was Billy Jones, and the reception was going to be that evening at the St Mungo's Halls in the Gorbals. I kept thinking, 'I wonder what it's gonnae be like tonight.' It was a mixed wedding, you see. When I got there, one lot were celebrating like mad, the other lot were very, very quiet.

Willie Goldie (ex-Celtic goalkeeper, at the time an Airdrie player) recalls:

Another incident on that particular day – I was playing next door at Cathkin (a reserve match), and we were aware of eight roars, but it was impossible to tell from what section of the ground they were coming, and the consensus of opinion among the players at corner kicks and throw-ins etc. was that it was 4–4. What a pleasant surprise for three men in the Airdrie team ('Tims') to learn the truth! I remember some other 14 or 15 shocked and angry faces in the Airdrie party.

Captain of the Lisbon Lions, Billy McNeill, recalls:

At that time I used to take the train back home after playing football with a friend of mine, a goalkeeper called Bert Gebbie. Before we went our separate ways I remember we got the *Evening Citizen*, the early edition, and it had 'STOP PRESS: Celtic 7 Rangers 1'. We stared at it in amazement, and Bert, who was, shall we say, not a Celtic man, wouldn't believe it. He kept saying, 'Naw, naw, it's a misprint – it's got to be a misprint.'

[McNeill learned of Celtic's sensational victory after his junior club, Blantyre Victoria, had suffered a first-round Scottish Junior Cup replay home defeat at the hands of the romantically named Douglas Water Thistle at Castle Park, Blantyre. McNeill was playing at the time in the left-half position. 'Willie McNeill' (as the press called him at the time) was described in one newspaper article as being 'quite a discovery' in that berth. He had been 'farmed out' to the Blantyre side after signing for Celtic two months earlier. Gebbie, incidentally, had made some outstanding saves as his team went down 2–1.]

Betty Solis (Govan) recalls:

I was 12 and living in Pollok on the day of 'The 7–1'. The news had gone round 'the scheme' and it was all that people were talking about. It didn't mean anything to me except that something bad had happened to Rangers. I was 'hinging oot the windae' when I saw my greatest enemy, Colin, coming home from Hampden with his dad. It was the only time I saw him without a Rangers scarf. Colin was a snob and didn't associate with the Catholic kids. His head was buried in his chest and his dad was even more solemn and sad-looking than usual. As they approached the close I shouted with fiendish glee, 'SEVEN WAN, SEVEN WAN!' His dad ignored me but Colin looked up and I could see him crying. I've never forgotten the happiness this gave me – and I'm still not interested in football!

Mary Harvey (Simshill) recalls:

I was ten years old at the time of 'The 7–1' and didn't even know there was a football match on that day. It would be about seven o'clock in the evening and I was in Croftfoot Drive, near Hampden, with my pal, Dorothy. We were going to confession at St Bartholomew's. In the distance I could see a wee drunk man swaying from side to side and heard him repeat the word 'seven' non-stop. He stopped alongside us and said in a happy but incredulous tone, 'Seven, we beat them SEVEN WAN.' He was so happy we weren't the least bit scared of him. As he disappeared we could still hear him:

'Seven, seven, seven . . .'

Gerry Heaney watched the match from the Rangers end that day, and recalls the scene:

As the game progressed the atmosphere of antipathy and hostility increased. The singing and chanting was loud and bigoted. The leader of the choir in our area was a big fella who was decked out in a hand-knitted sweater complete with the knitted figure of 'King Billy' on the front. The 'Sash' was belted out time and time again, as was 'No Surrender'. I can remember a few verses of those songs to this day! At one point we mouthed the verse quietly to kid on we were on their side!

My memories of the game are sketchy (perhaps because we were scared), but I do recall several things:

1. McPhail and Wilson were a dynamic duo. They played off each other so well. This is borne out by their goals and assists 'stats' in 1957–58, and Sammy did not produce as well when Billy retired in '58.

2. Willie Fernie was a wizard of the dribble. His body swerve was classical and left defenders swinging at the air. Like Jinky [Jimmy Johnstone], he at times overdid it and tried to take on too many defenders. Di Canio reminds me of Fernie in some ways, but Paolo has more pace and can finish better.

3. The skill of Celtic – passing, dribbling, heading, shooting – was far superior to the 'Gers', and proved that discipline in defence, plus creativity and directness in attack, is superior to power and force. The score could easily have been 12–1 or 13–1.

I remember the Celtic end erupting after every goal, but there was not anything like the amount of green and white colours being waved as in the late '60s and '70s. I don't think scarves, hats and banners were so much in vogue back then. You saw very few people wearing these except at games, and even there it was a minority who did so, mainly kids. The cheering was as spontaneous and as enthusiastic as I remember in later years, but there was not the singing of team songs or songs/chants for individual players like there is now.

There was a lot of cheering at the Rangers end when Rangers scored, but it was not sustained. There was a lot of drinking around us and this perhaps led to their optimism for a comeback, which did not transpire.

My final memory of the 7–1 game was the bottle-throwing and mass exodus of The Forces of Darkness. Hundreds of fans threw bottles down from the top and middle of the terraces towards the field, but they landed mainly on their own fans – youngsters, for the most part. I saw many people jumping out on to the track bordering the field to escape the rain of glass missiles from above. Most of the terracing was clear of fans after goal number five. At that point John and I 'came out of the closet' and cheered loudly as Celts scored two more goals. At the end of the game we stayed with the rest of the Celtic fans, waving our scarves happily and cheering till we were hoarse. What an experience! What a team! Those heroes are legends in my mind and I hope my sons will live to see a Celtic side of that quality.

The long walk back to Rutherglen that day was like the end of a pilgrimage – we waved our scarves proudly at every passing bus and car and chanted the magic number: 'SEVEN, SEVEN, SEVEN, SEVEN . . . !'

The euphoria continued over to school on Monday. We reviewed each goal with much detail and I was a bit of a celebrity because of my account of our foray into the Rangers end. I may have embellished the account somewhat, but it added to the excitement that we all felt on that day. I also remember going to Mass on the Sunday after the game and seeing Sean Fallon there (he was in our parish – St Columbkille's, Rutherglen). Years later when I saw him he looked his normal size and build – about 5ft 8ins, 170lbs. But on that day after the 7–1 game he seemed like G.I. Joe the super-hero. To us he attained legendary status as a result of that game, as did the rest of the squad. The goalie that day was Beattie, and a few years later he was involved in the bribery scandal in England. I resisted criticising him then because he had been part of that band of stalwarts in '57.

Interestingly, ten years later, in 1967, I played for Third Lanark in what was to be tragically their last season as a club. The manager was Bobby Shearer, who had played in that game for Rangers. He was a nice man and not a 'Hun-worshipper' as some would have believed. He

159

was a hard player, a journeyman and not your classic full-back, although he and Eric Caldow were the full-backs for Scotland for a time. When I once asked him about the 7–1 game he replied in his inimitable and forthright manner, 'They were unstoppable.'

I liked Bobby – he was a player's man. For example, Thirds' owner, Bill Hiddleston, owed the players several weeks' wages and was messing us about. We had decided that enough was enough, so on the day we were due to play Morton at Cappielow we told Bobby we would not play till we got our back pay. This was about an hour before kick-off. He acknowledged our request and remained neutral when the owner threatened us unsuccessfully. There were about 6,000 fans in the park and we used this as a lever. We got our cash and Bobby retained our respect.

Edmund Burns also recalls watching the game from the Rangers end, and then returning home:

The weather was perfect. Maybe the Rangers fans showed some resentment at Valentine, but basically the victory was down to Celtic – 11 players all fit and all on form. Near the end of the game the crowd at that end had thinned out considerably, and suddenly I heard a shout: 'Burns, what the hell are you doing at this end?' It was a neighbour of mine from 'The Sheddens' in Busby, Alec Cain, with his wife Sheila. They weren't especially big Rangers fans, but they attended all the big events together, football, whatever. Anyway, we watched the rest of the game together, and I think when the cup was presented, we were the only three people left in that end of the ground.

After the game I walked back via Queen's Park and along Victoria Road. I went into a few pubs on the way home – for example, the Star Bar at Eglinton Toll and the Kiloran Bar in Eglinton Street. Then I got the subway from Bridge Street. I meant to get off at St George's Cross, but got off at Cowcaddens by mistake. I remember as I went up the stairs the ticket collector shouted out, 'What was the score?' I was halfway up the stairs at the time. I shouted back, 'Rangers one' – he was all smiles. When I got to the top, I belted out, 'Celtic seven!'

I had picked up the keys that morning for a new flat I was moving into on Great Western Road. So I walked to George's Cross from Cowcaddens. I stopped in for another wee drink at Divers' Bar and Bell's Bar at George's Cross. My wife was staying nearby at my in-laws' flat in Windsor Street. I didn't think it was 'safe' to go there straight away, so I just went up to the Great Western Road flat (still unfurnished, of course) and flopped down there. Then I got up about 2 a.m. and went over to the wife's parents' flat. What did I have to drink that night? Seven halfs and one beer!

160

On the Monday morning I went into work. Most of the other employees were Rangers supporters and usually on a Monday there would be a bit of banter about the weekend's football. Not that Monday. No comment – they were shellshocked! But I walked in 7ft 1in tall!

Fourteen years later Alec Cain paid a visit one Friday night. The next day Celtic were playing Raith Rovers in the Scottish Cup at Parkhead, so we decided to go to the game together. It was the only other time I watched a football match with Alec Cain. And do you know what the score was? 7–1 to Celtic, again!

Ian Murphy (now resident in Kilbirnie) recalls:

Me and Pat Byrne went along to the Celtic end, and couldn't get in, so went along to the Rangers end. We left at 5–1, got to the train station and found we'd scored seven . . .

Tom Carruthers (Perth, Western Australia) relates an unusual tale from the day of the final:

'Dad, can I go to the game with you?'

'No, sorry son – I've got two tickets, one for myself and one for your Uncle Robert.'

Well, that was that, I would just have to spend some time with my pigeons and listen to the game on the wireless. Before I knew it, Celtic were 3–0 up. I ran in to tell my mother who was 'gasbagging' to the woman next door. 'Away you go, you must have got it wrong,' they both said in tandem; 'Celtic'll no be beating Rangers by that score.' They must have thought, 'What's he drinking in that pigeon loft?' especially when I told them the final score.

However, the proof came walking, or should I say staggering, up the road at about 7.30 p.m. in the form of my old man. When he got level with the front door, but still out on the pavement, he must have decided that was far enough, and sideways over our little garden fence and hedge he went, coming to rest on the front lawn. Naturally enough the words of wisdom came flowing from my mother's silken tongue. 'How did you get yourself into that state?' Well, needless to say it was the next day before we got the full story. All he kept saying was, 'It was that minister's fault.' It turned out that my uncle never showed up and, believe it or not, my Dad gave his spare ticket to a man of the cloth – but not 'one of ours', one of 'theirs' (perhaps thinking that he would thus earn some brownie points from the man upstairs).

Well, he got more than brownie points! Every time Celtic scored, out came a bottle for a drink to drown the minister's sorrows – and one for Dad to celebrate. By full-time my Dad reckons he must have almost had him 'converted'! That picture of my Dad staggering up the road and falling over into the front garden and the look of exaltation expressed on his face are etched in my memory forever. I don't know whether it was because the Bhoys had thumped the Gers 7–1 or whether it was because he had drunk the minister's whisky – probably a combination of both! Anyway, thanks for the memory, Dad! The garden he fell into was at 116 Barshaw Road, Penilee, Glasgow, some 40 years ago.

Robert McAulay continues his father's tale:

My dad couldn't remember all that much about the actual game but he recalled that the sense of euphoria amongst the Celtic fans was almost overwhelming as the goals went in, and this was in contrast to the Mount Florida end which emptied a little more every time the Rangers net rippled. Dad was often puzzled why the Celtic side of this era, which contained many fine players, didn't do better. He singled out Evans, Collins and Fernie as being as good as anything he had seen before.

After the match came the walk back through Toryglen and Polmadie to Norman Street in Bridgeton. If you don't know this area, Norman Street was the home of the 'Norman Conks', a famous or infamous Glasgow gang of the 1930s who regularly fought with the 'Billy Boys' from Bridgeton Cross. In the 1950s Norman Street was a wee Catholic enclave in the heart of Protestant Bridgeton. In that decade immigrant Irish workers would come over the water and work in places like Cowan's sweet factory or Templeton's carpet factory. They would stay for six months and get tax-free wages and then head off back to Ireland.

Anyway, it was among a lot of these people that my dad and his brothers spent the post-match celebrations. John and James Mitchell were the proprietors of Mitchell's Bar in Norman Street, and it was here the Bridgeton Emmet Celtic Supporters Club would congregate – the Emmet also had a highly successful juvenile football team who wore green and white hoops. The celebrations lasted as long as the licensing laws would allow and then it was off to 'The Hut', a dance hall just along the street. And before my dad realised it, his ten bob from selling the match programmes was gone! As my dad explained, a victory such as this was once-in-a-lifetime and ensured that the vast majority of Celtic fans had, for a short time, an escape from the miserable social conditions that were their existence. In 1957 he still lived with his mother and five brothers in relative poverty in a room and kitchen with an outside toilet. In his words, 'It brought a wee chink of light into the darkness of our working-class life.'

John Boyle (now resident in Los Angeles) recalls missing the match and then learning of Celtic's progress in the final:

I was going to buy shoes and then go to the game. But on the bus I met a boy I knew, John Donaghy. He played for Bridgeton Waverley. He wanted to know how to get to Rosebery Park, home of Shawfield Juniors, as he had a match there that day. So it ended up that I never got the shoes and instead took him to Rosebery Park. And since I knew a lot of the players, instead of going to Hampden I stayed to watch the juniors' match. During the game we could hear the roars from Hampden. Then I went away to check what the score was on the radio. They announced it was now 4–1 for Celtic. So I raced back to the ground with the good news. John Donaghy was playing on the wing for Bridgeton Waverley, so I was near enough to tell him the score. Well, he did a somersault, right there on the park. I can still see it! The funny thing was – Bridgeton Waverley were playing in blue jerseys!

John McKechnie recalls:

I was very fortunate to be at the Celtic end that day as a 15-year-old, and made full use of a healthy pair of lungs. I can still recite the team by heart, and will always remember the fantastic performance of Willie Fernie – as if the ball was tied to his boot. He had us in stitches, and to this day I've never seen anything to compare with Willie's ball control that day. It's even more amazing when you think that the bookmakers had Rangers as favourites to win, which made this victory all the more enjoyable for us. Billy McPhail, who scored that wonderful hat-trick – what a clever signing by Jimmy McGrory!

Joe Connelly, who had placed a £40 bet on Celtic to win, recalls his feelings about the match and the money he had riding on the outcome:

We entered Hampden and stood at the Celtic end (east terracing). The game soon started and Celtic were kicking towards us. We saw plenty of the game as Celtic were almost permanently parked in the 'Gers' penalty area. In the first 20 minutes Collins and Tully struck the woodwork and we began to think, 'It's the same old story; we turn them inside out, and they'll break away and score.' However, we were being too pessimistic . . .

When the ball was lobbed into the area, Billy McPhail leapt high and won it, but instead of heading it goalwards, he headed the ball back towards the edge of the penalty area and Sammy Wilson took it on the volley. The ball screamed past Niven, and the Celtic end erupted. But better was to come . . . Half-time was ten minutes of joy and celebration and my mind fleetingly went back to my £40 bet . . . and just for a minute I thought, 'I wish it was time-up.' Oh ye of little faith!

The only blip was a Simpson goal for Rangers, a very good header, but we were soon back singing and dancing under that fine blue sky . . . It was all so unbelievable. When Shearer pulled down McPhail in the last minute, it was the only time in my life that I was not too bothered about whether we were awarded a penalty or not.

We left Hampden singing, hugging and kissing complete strangers. The walk back into the town, we seemed to float on air. It's at times like that you wonder about the effect an institution like Celtic FC can have on your life. It plays such a dominating, powerful role. When we arrived back into town, half a dozen people, seeing my Celtic scarf, enquired, 'What was the score, son?' When I told them, I got the same reply from them all: 'WHIT?' I know it seemed unbelievable, but I was there and I know it happened.

I left my money till the Monday (my £40 at 7–4), and I gave my late mother £50 as a gift. She always spoke of the finest weekend of her life: 'Joe gave me £50 to buy myself something new, and Celtic beat the Rangers 7–1.'

David Potter, then living in Forfar, recalls the day vividly:

Even in those early days I experienced a gnawing away at my vitals (something which I have never lost), of knowing that the game is on and worrying what the score is. My mother would always say, 'He gets intae an awfu' state about a futba' match.' Forty years later my wife and daughters say the same!

I was indeed in an 'awfu' state as I half walked, half ran up the road. Years later I remember doing a Latin prose which began 'An uncertain rumour, as usually happens . . .', and this was precisely what happened that day. A boy on a bike passed shouting 'seven'; someone's radio was on and I heard the commentator saying something like 'It's one of the most remarkable results in Scottish football history'; but the honour of telling me the score fell to Betty Black.

Betty lived with her father, husband and son in a household not dissimilar to my own. Her father, old Frank – a favourite character of my boyhood – supported Celtic, but Betty had married Nelson Diplexcito. Nelson, another favourite character of my boyhood, had lost a leg on D-Day, and like the rest of his family he had a complex about being half-Italian. You would have thought that leaving a leg on Juno Beach as the Black Watch charged off landing craft would have been enough to deflect racist jibes about being an 'Eyetie', a 'Wop' or a 'Catholic'. It was the last one that hurt, so the Diplexcito family all had to support Rangers. Rumour even had it that they voted Tory as well, in an attempt to be more British than the British.

Anyway, poor Betty had her problems, but she also had a mischievous sense of humour; and when she shouted to me that Celtic had won 7–1, I wasn't sure whether to take it seriously. Mature thought (I was only nine), however, indicated quite correctly that you didn't joke about things like that. So I charged up the road to be met by my gibbering, incoherent father and was told that the score was indeed 7–1. The Diplexcitos avoided me for days afterwards.

It wouldn't have mattered that we did not have a TV in 1957, for the BBC failed to show the highlights in full that night. Sadly for my family, Uncle Fred died the day afterwards, and this always soured my father's talk of that great game. But I needed to enjoy that success, because it would be a long time before I experienced another.

George Sheridan (Glasgow) recalls:

I well remember that day. My pals and I stayed in Wilton Street, a long goal-kick from Firhill, and we just used to go up there and get lifted over. Hampden was the other side of the world for us, we were too young, and our parents were highly responsible adults.

I vividly remember going along the top of the terracing at the city end of Firhill (where the 'Piggery' was) at full-time. Usual snail's pace exit. It was a big stout policeman who was telling the crowd, 'Aye, it was 7–1 for Celtic.' We couldn't believe it. It would take us less than five minutes to get home, but we must have made it in five seconds! Our joyous parents confirmed the score and the weekend was spent reading all the papers, some of which I still have.

Father Lawrence Byrne recalls one moment from the final in particular:

My most abiding memory of that famous game was the goal scored by the late Neilly Mochan. It was Celtic's second goal of the match and came shortly before half-time. To this day I can still see it in my mind's eye. Neilly was cutting in from the left wing and I'm sure it was Shearer, Rangers' uncompromising right-back of the time, who was chasing him. About eight feet from the byline and 25 yards from goal (the years might have added a few yards!), directly in line with where I was standing, Neilly hit the ball (the old brown leather ball which must have been twice as heavy as the footballs of today) with his ferocious left foot. I stood there mesmerised as I watched it curl in high at the right-hand side of Niven's goal. It was long before we thought the Brazilians and Italians were the only ones who could do that! The angle at which he hit the ball and the ferocity of the shot will remain with me forever. Over the years I have seen Neilly many times in and around Celtic Park – unfortunately always at a distance – but each and every time I automatically recalled that wonderful goal he scored so many years ago.

As you can imagine, the dancing and the singing on the terraces at half-time was unbelievable. The day was completed for me when Dick Beattie, our goalkeeper, at the end of the game turned to the Celtic end and held up seven fingers. It was a scoreline we had to live on for a long time until the arrival of the great Jock Stein as manager.

Peter Sweeney concludes the story of the day his wife was expecting their first child:

As the game progressed we couldn't believe our eyes as Celtic were so much on top. Soon it was 4–1, then 5–1. I said to John, 'Let's try to make it to the back of the terracing.' That was easier said than done. Can you imagine Celtic supporters wanting to leave *this* game early? As we pushed our way to the top, we were subjected to taunts of 'You Huns had enough?' and so on. After a long time we made it to the top of the terracing and started down a long flight of stairs. When we were halfway down, the Celtic end erupted. We raced back and, sure enough, it was now 6–1. We started down the stairs once again, and this time we reached the bottom when a huge roar went up: 'Penalty!' We looked at each other, and without saying anything we both raced back up the stairs. John could not see anything, but on my tiptoes I just managed to see Willie Fernie stroke home number seven.

This time there was a sea of Celtic fans leaving, no doubt mindful of the revenge the 'Derry Boys' might inflict on unsuspecting Celtic supporters. We made it to Aitkenhead Road and were waved on to a passing trolley bus by the conductor, even though the bus was already crowded. At one stage he fell off the platform and had to be hauled back on by the fans. He never even took one fare for that trip. I often wondered if he lost his job.

The bus was moving so slowly, we soon found we were leading a spontaneous victory parade with scarves at every window and everyone singing. The good news had gone ahead of us because as we reached the Gorbals people were lining the pavements, waving and cheering. From house windows appeared scarves, banners, tablecloths and towels, anything with green on it. What a sight it was!

We had waited a long, long time for this day. I swear it was as if the whole scene had been planned in advance.

Climbing over bodies I managed to get off the bus at Glasgow Cross. John said it was just the same all the way to the Springburn terminus. Nobody got off the bus, they just turned it round and headed back into town. Bus inspectors and police just kept waving it on. Next day, John was so hoarse he could hardly talk.

With my mother-in-law, I headed for the hospital with the comments of our families and friends ringing in our ears, to the effect, 'The baby has just got to be born today.' Nothing had changed at the Maternity and my wife Barbara was beginning to feel guilty at disappointing so many people. The visiting over, we had to leave, but were told to phone later, as 'you never know'.

After several fruitless calls from a nearby telephone box, I tried once again at 11.30 p.m. The phone seemed to ring forever. Eventually a doctor answered and apologised, saying that they had all been very busy delivering our daughter Linda Anne. She made it with 25 minutes to spare.[6] I had a double celebration now!

I often wonder what I would have called the baby if it had been a boy – maybe Charles Patrick Tully Sweeney. My father Hugh always said, 'Nobody will ever argue with you as to the date of the 7–1 game.' He was right.

I never got to see Bertie Peacock presented with the cup, but it was still an unforgettable day.

Jim Kavanagh (Glasgow) recounts:

The following is definitely true. A man called John Reilly was a neighbour of mine. He took me to the matches as a boy. He died a couple of years ago [1995] aged about 72. He was a remarkable character. His non-sectarian view of Celtic was admirable. He was a member of the Kinning Park CSC (Stanley Bar). Apart from his wedding day, John Reilly only missed one Celtic game in Scotland (and few elsewhere!) and that was the day his daughter was born – the very same day Celtic beat Rangers 7–1! The daughter in question sits behind me on match-days at Celtic Park, as do his son and grandson. I believe the journalist Chick Young and ex-Old Firm players Derek Johnstone and Danny McGrain were at his funeral.

*   *   *

One impressive measure of the euphoria and elation that day is recounted by Harry Conway, now a member of the San Francisco Celtic Supporters Club. In 1957, he and a friend named John Sawers were both members of the 'San-Toy' (a gang from the Calton). After the match, they were invited for a drink by 'Tarzan', the leader of their mortal enemies the 'Cumbie' (a gang from the Gorbals), at the latter's favourite watering-hole, the Wheatsheaf Bar in Crown Street. It was the first time ever that 'San-Toy' and 'Cumbie' boys had ever got together for a friendly tipple.

ENDNOTES

1 In 1957 it was still the custom for each team to run out on to the pitch at a gallop, and separately, even at cup finals. It would be some years before the teams came on to the field walking side by side. Presumably the more recent custom was introduced as a better symbol of sporting friendship.

2 No substitutes were allowed at that time, it being nearly a decade away from their introduction into Scottish football. But Celtic did have two travelling reserves should there be any late call-offs among the chosen XI – the somewhat mercurial forward Alec Byrne, who could be fielded on either wing or at centre-forward, and the versatile Eric Smith, who could play in most forward positions as well as in the half-back line.

3 It is often forgotten that the less dashing figure of Sammy Wilson would actually end that season as Celtic's top scorer with 32 goals in the major competitions, albeit the subtler talents of McPhail were missing for a lengthy spell on account of injury. It should be noted that newspaper accounts of Celtic's first goal do not tally, and so our description is based on the black and white film cited in the endnote number two to chapter six, albeit there is an irritating break in the footage at one stage in the build-up to the goal.

4 The feat of scoring four goals in an Old Firm match has only been achieved once in competition. George T. Livingstone scored four times for Celtic in a 5–0 defeat of Rangers in an Inter-City League match at Ibrox on 1 March 1902.

5 A curious coincidence occurred when one of the authors was first being told this story, not by Mr Eadie himself, but by another Los Angeles Celt, Joe Bole, at the 1996 Convention of the North American Federation of Celtic Supporters Clubs in Las Vegas, Nevada. As Mr Bole was telling the story, a visiting Celtic supporter from Glasgow, Jimmy Divers, was present, waiting to tell *his* story of 'The 7–1'. Mr Divers hadn't met Mr Bole before, he thought. But the story he was waiting to tell was precisely the same one – Jimmy had been a witness to this event, standing just a few yards away on the terracing at the time.

6 Mr Sweeney kindly supplied one of the authors with a photocopy of Linda Anne's birth certificate, detailing the date and time of her arrival.

CHAPTER SIX

Aftermath

Now here is Mochan on the ball;
He runs around poor Ian McColl.
Wee George Niven takes a daring dive
But Smiler Mochan makes it Number Five.

Among the newspaper headlines telling of Celtic's astounding victory were the following:

'GERS WERE LUCKY NOT TO LOSE TEN' (*Sunday Mail*, 20 October)
'SCIENTIFIC CELTS SMASH THEIR GREATEST RIVALS' (*Sunday Post*, 20 October)
'RANGERS DINNED DOWN TO IGNOMINY' (*The Scotsman*, 21 October)
'CELTIC'S SEVEN-GOAL TRIUMPH IN LEAGUE CUP FINAL' (*Glasgow Herald*, 21 October)
'CELTIC – YOU WERE WORTH ALL SEVEN!' (*Daily Record*, 21 October)

On the night of the match itself, early and later editions of the *Evening Times* headlined the match report by Gair Henderson as follows:

'RANGERS REEL . . . Celts pile on pressure – score twice'
'ALL HAIL, McPHAIL 7-goal Celts humble Light Blues'

Its rival, the *Evening Citizen,* carried the headline:
'HAMPDEN "PARADISE" FOR THOSE CELTS . . . Sixty glorious
minutes keep League Cup'

Celtic's players left the field after their magnificent triumph fully redeemed
in the eyes of their overjoyed supporters who, only a few months
previously, had unreservedly condemned their favourites for being 'a
lifeless lot' in the Scottish Cup semi-final defeat by Kilmarnock, and 'an
uninspired, lacklustre team, some of whose members could not even agree
among themselves' as they went down to defeat against Rangers in the
Charity Cup shortly afterwards. The extent of the turnaround can perhaps
be judged by the comments in the Rangers Supporters Association annual,
published not long after a final at whose conclusion Ibrox fans had
departed mentally scarred by what they had witnessed:

> It is not the intention of this annual to criticise the Rangers players
> in a derogatory manner, but it is hard to find anything about this
> game that would be otherwise, if the game has to be reported from
> the 'Rangers End'. Many a heart was sore around 4.30 that
> afternoon, and I heard one sorrowing fan say, as I left the park, 'No
> team should be able to beat Rangers 7–1. It just should not be
> possible.' That may or may not be true, but nevertheless Celtic
> proved that it can be done, and they have also proved, twice this
> year to Rangers, that the true art of football will triumph in face of
> all opposition.

A handsome, indeed generous, tribute, but by the time it was published
the recriminations had already begun. Indeed, one suspects that they
were already under way in the dressing-room after the Rangers players
trudged disconsolately off the Hampden pitch – in stark contrast to the
jubilation in the Celtic party.

Bertie Peacock, Celtic's captain on the great day, recalls a gesture
reflective of the euphoria felt within the Parkhead ranks. It was made
immediately after the match by chairman Bob Kelly and was by no means
uncharacteristic, suggesting as it did a basic kindness of disposition that
was often hidden under a gruff exterior. Kelly invited two friends of Peacock
who had been over from Coleraine, Johnny Burns and Mick McColgan, into
the Celtic dressing-room and gave them four or five Celtic jerseys as
souvenirs. But if goodwill reigned within the Celtic camp, the same could
not be said about the club they had humiliated. In particular, the spirit of
generosity would not be extended by the Rangers management to the
luckless John Valentine.

THE SCAPEGOAT

The heat of battle had barely died down when the knives were out for Rangers' recently signed centre-half. In truth, he had never been completely comfortable at Ibrox, unsuited to the out-and-out 'stopper' role required of him by Rangers. One of his opponents in the final is rather blunter, saying, 'Let's be frank, Valentine didn't suit Rangers because he wasn't a kicker!' Ironically, before joining the Govan club Valentine had been a target for Celtic, who saw in him a potential successor to Jock Stein after the latter's ankle injury forced him to retire from playing football in early 1957.

Cyril Horne of the *Glasgow Herald* put his finger on Valentine's unease when, in a postscript on the nightmare that the player had undergone, he stated that the former 'Spider' had, in a Rangers jersey, become unrecognisable as the 'consistently impressive' performer for Queen's Park he had been: 'Valentine seems to be playing these days without a particle of confidence; strangest of all, his known ability in the air – there was no surer header of a ball for several seasons – seems to have disappeared' (22 October 1957).

Tommy Gallacher, a son of the peerless Patsy of Celtic fame and himself a noted player with Queen's Park and Dundee prior to embarking on a career in journalism, accurately predicted in the (Dundee) *Courier and Advertiser* 'the repercussions of Rangers' humiliation' for one of their players. Noting that 'As a rule, when the Light Blues have an exceptionally bad result, somebody's head rolls', he instanced from recent memory the fate of a distinguished Rangers goalkeeper (and Scottish internationalist), Bobby Brown, who was sidelined for a season after an opening-day 5–0 defeat by Hearts in 1952. Gallacher went on to suggest that in view of the Ibrox club's track record in such circumstances, 'This time it appears that former Queen's Park man John Valentine may take the brunt of the blame for the defeat.' (21 October 1957) In the following day's issue, in an interview with Gallacher, Valentine admitted that, subconsciously, his trying to fill the boots of the mighty George Young may have affected his play, although he insisted that he had signed for Rangers 'with my eyes open. I knew just what to expect if things didn't work out. At Ibrox, if you lose a game it's a minor tragedy. And Saturday's defeat was anything but a minor one!' When asked about the Rangers players' reaction to the defeat, he replied, 'I must say they took it a lot better than some of the supporters.' However, although he was clearly striving to retain a sense of proportion about the crushing loss, he owned up to being uncertain about his personal future: 'I don't know. All I do know is that Rangers and Mr Symon couldn't have been nicer to me. The sooner I repay them by striking my true form, the better I'll be pleased.'

He never got the chance. His place in the first team was initially taken by young Willie Moles and then by Willie Telfer, signed the month after the cup final from St Mirren. Valentine was to drift into obscurity, being transferred to St Johnstone, then a Second Division club, a year later. He was simply the most prominent victim of one of the blackest days in Rangers' history, one whose resonance is still such that Bob Crampsey, the eminent football historian and broadcaster, has his doubts as to whether writers to his 'Now You Know' column in Glasgow's *Evening Times*, ostensibly seeking information on this particular match, are genuine seekers of knowledge. It is more likely, he believes, that in nine cases out of ten, correspondents are indulging in the seemingly endless capacity for mischief for which Old Firm fans are well known, albeit mischief of the more harmless variety: 'Virtually all of those writing in about the 7–1 game are all too aware of the details (in fact, if asked, could quote you chapter and verse) – they just relish seeing them in print!' It works both ways, of course. When he was mine host of The Bank restaurant in Glasgow's Queen Street in the 1940s and 1950s, the former Celtic manager Willie Maley was profoundly irritated by questioners who asked if he remembered the biggest defeat suffered by Celtic in a competitive match (8–0 at Motherwell, April 1937). Maley's brusque reply ran along the lines of, 'I'm not likely to forget it as long as there are people like you to remind me.' Glasgow football fans have long memories . . .

Willie Allison, a man who had barely hidden his allegiance in a 40-year career in journalism (mostly as a sportswriter) and with whom the defeat still rankled nearly a decade later, gave his point of view in his book, *Rangers, the New Era, 1873–1966*: 'There were passages in the match which brought about Celtic's goal-flood that might easily have taken a different shape had the breaks gone with us when we needed them. We would, however, withhold nothing from the merit of Celtic's success.' This rather bizarre interpretation of the course of the final is all too indicative of the importance invested by the partisans of both clubs in clashes which always carry overtones of the socio-religious divide in the West of Scotland – passions which had once again generated terracing mayhem which most people in the nation preferred quietly to ignore.

THE SECTARIAN PROBLEM

The 1950s were quite possibly the most troubled period in Old Firm history as regards the problem of hooliganism at football matches, a problem whose roots lay in sectarian divisions within Scottish society at large. Following the latest outbreak of violence at Hampden – five of the reported 17 persons arrested on the occasion of this final received sentences ranging from one to three months at Glasgow Sheriff Court a few days later – the authorities, predictably, preferred to sweep the underlying tensions under the carpet while self-righteously condemning the symptoms. Yet, rather hypocritically, they recoiled from taking any action themselves. Bailie Richard McCutcheon concluded, without benefit of evidence, that the attendance had fallen short of the anticipated 100,000 due to 'many people . . . keeping away because of the fear of bottle-throwing', while his colleague Bailie John Blackwood, Glasgow's senior magistrate, contented himself with the observation that control inside the ground was a matter for the clubs, in co-operation with the police: 'Magistrates do not license football grounds as we license dance halls or cinemas, and for that reason we have little control over what happens within the grounds.' Mr Blackwood, however, gave no indication of any eagerness to seek such powers. Only one of the city magistrates, the rather aptly named Jeremiah O'Sullivan, was in favour of 'banning Old Firm games until the fans learn to behave more sanely', a prospect which the domestic game's governing body reacted to with studied indifference. Willie Allan, secretary of the SFA, smugly observed that 'since the crowd did not go on to the playing pitch and the game was not interrupted, it is unlikely that the referee, Mr J.A. Mowat, will make any reference to the disturbances in his report'. (This was in stark contrast to the rather more severe attitude taken by the authorities on the occasion of previous outbreaks of trouble at Old Firm matches only a few years earlier.)

Other observers were not so sanguine. Gair Henderson of the *Evening Times*, in a postscript to the match, demanded that the police be given powers to 'remove by all necessary force not only every single banner [but] every single spectator who dares to flaunt one at future Celtic–Rangers games'. Insisting that only prompt action by the police had prevented the 'five minutes of terror' on the west terracing (Rangers end) from leading to a 'full-scale riot', he denounced a 'few of the sweepings of Glasgow's gutters' for marring a great football occasion: 'Not for a long time have I seen such phoney patriotism as was displayed by the vast array of Union Jacks, red, white and blue banners, and solid orange squares which were brandished from the Rangers end of the field. And not for an equal length of time have I seen so many tricolours, harps and shamrocks flourishing outside the country of their origin' (21 October 1957). 'Rex' of the *Sunday Mail* waded into both sets of fans too: 'The behaviour of some terracing louts parading as Rangers supporters has been rightly condemned by all decent people, but the first insult to our decency happened at the other end before the game even began. The Celtic team has been justifiably extolled for its superlative discipline, even under severe provocation. I wonder what the Celtic fellows thought as they stood to attention before the kick-off and heard a section of hoodlums parading as *their* supporters bawling and singing and shouting to drown the National Anthem' (27 October 1957).

The two correspondents were soon joined in their distaste for these demonstrations by an anonymous writer of an article headed 'Colour bar in . . . Scottish football' (already referred to in chapter one). This piece appeared in the Christmas 1957 issue of *Life and Work*, the Church of Scotland magazine. Referring to the 'willing and eager segregation of the greens and the blues', the writer deplored 'the flaunting of Union Jacks and Irish flags. Fights, flying bottles. Filthy language. Simultaneous singing of the National Anthem and "Faith of Our Fathers" [a popular Catholic hymn of the time]. In the stand, pockets of supporters sit silent during the National Anthem.' 'G.G.', however, then went on to cause deep offence to Celtic supporters with his assertion that religion had entered football with the founding of Celtic FC, and that there were still reminders of that with the flying of the Irish flag at Celtic Park, where 'rows of priests in the stand make it a "church occasion". He carried his attack even further by questioning the legitimacy of having a club in Scottish football with predominantly Irish Catholic links which, he claimed, only served to fuel religious bigotry. The writer did toss in the suggestion that the undercurrent of feeling on show at the League Cup final evidenced bigotry among Protestants too; and he put forward as a solution a programme of measures comprising 'a lot of hard work by both Churches among their supporters on how to play the game of life' and, in the short term, 'the licensing of all football grounds by the magistrates and police'. But despite these reasonable points, the article produced an outraged reaction among Celtic supporters who detected a hidden agenda – one designed to collectively brand them, and their club, as riven with religious bigotry.

In the *Sunday Mail* of 1 December 1957, the general secretary of the Celtic FC Supporters Association, Hugh Delaney, condemned the article, describing it as 'grossly unfair and prejudiced'. 'We are,' he wrote, 'completely non-sectarian. Scores of our branch officials are Protestants. I know of not one branch that discourages Protestants from becoming members – let alone prohibits them.' (The Association's 1957–58 Handbook had contained a tribute to the late chairman of the Thornliebank branch, James Fry, who had also been a former vice-president of the Association: 'Unlike the majority of Celtic followers [he] had no national or sectarian ties to influence him in his choice of football favourites.') Another protester against the offending article, 'C. McG' of Blantyre, claimed that Rangers had not been the first club 'to show intolerance towards Celtic. The great Queen's Park, arriving at Celtic Park for their first game [at that venue, in 1888], refused to strip in the Celtic pavilion. They stripped in their horse brake because they "would not mix with those Irish".'

Such reactions on the part of Celtic supporters accurately reflected a sense of alienation from the wider Scottish society in which they lived, a feeling which may have seemed remarkable for mid-twentieth-century

Britain, but one that was hardly surprising in view of the attitudes that prevailed in Scotland (or at least the West of Scotland) at the time, even in respectable academic circles. In his article on 'Community Life' in *The Third Statistical Account of Scotland – Glasgow* (1958), one John A. Mack, a lecturer in citizenship at Glasgow University, made a point of stating:

> It is still the case – a matter generally glossed over in discussions of crime in Glasgow – that the poorer members of that [large Roman Catholic Irish] community contribute to the crime totals, and notably to the juvenile crime totals, more proportionately to their numbers in the total population than are proved against Protestant children . . . It would be highly unscientific as well as unmannerly to deduce any causal connection here. It is primarily a matter of social and economic conditions. In other countries, or other parts of this country, where Roman Catholics are not predominantly drawn from the lower-income groups, they are correspondingly non-delinquent. These figures indicate simply that a high proportion of children and adults, living in Glasgow, in those conditions of comparative poverty and squalor which conduce to high delinquency, happen to be Roman Catholic. But this is not all. There is also the element of culture-conflict. Besides being comparatively poor, they are mostly Irish by blood and sentiment; and this national difference, with its overtones of historical antagonism to England and to Protestant Scotland, has undoubtedly contributed among many of the more recently settled groups to a certain sympathy or at least tolerance for whoever is against authority. Even the settled community – as recorded elsewhere in this book, the Irish in Glasgow are now largely third and fourth generation and have contributed notably to civic welfare – is still to some extent on its guard.

'Authority' seemed to share such perceptions. As an English BBC television sports commentator testified in his book *Sports Special*, published shortly after he was despatched north to cover the 1955 Scottish Cup final between Celtic and Clyde (the first to be televised live), he was struck by the heavy police presence that was so evident from his commentary position, and was told, 'Just you wait until those Celtic fans get going, and then you'll realise why we need so many police. And by the way, don't kid yourself that the Celtic fervour has anything to do with football.' After stating that 'Never have I heard such a din as I heard from the Celtic fans that day – banners, flags, whistles, songs, the lot', the commentator, Kenneth Wolstenholme, added, 'These Celtic fans were frightening, and when one is constantly told that their demonstrations are religious and racial and have nothing to do with sport, one has a feeling of unpleasantness.' Even though Wolstenholme concluded that

'The real Celtic fan is a decent enough citizen', he cited a Celtic player who, anonymously, told him that 'We have good supporters, but unfortunately the mob makes itself so conspicuous that people think all our fans are mobsters'.

With such a poor image, or rather stereotyping, the Celtic support might well have come to regard itself as some sort of underclass, a sense of alienation from their social surroundings that the most famous myth surrounding the 1957 League Cup final can only have served to reinforce.

THE CASE OF THE MISSING FILM

The durability of that myth is such that, nearly four decades on, David Leggat, in an 'Old Firm Special' issue of the *Evening Times*, claimed that the BBC's failure to show full highlights of the 1957 League Cup final 'is something which still rankles with the Parkhead club. The Beeb claimed it was one of the biggest boobs in the history of sports broadcasting. But Celtic, suspecting a bias against them at the BBC sports department of that era, felt there were darker motives at work' (6 November 1996). 'The Case of the Missing Film', as the affair has been dubbed, can now be unravelled fully as the result of some detective work on the part of one of the authors.

At 10 p.m. on 19 October 1957, Celtic fans – many doubtless having hurried home from the pub after celebrating a momentous victory – huddled expectantly around their TV sets to watch edition number 73 of *Sports Special*, a production of the BBC's recently formed 'Sportsview' unit. After a brief introduction by the presenter, Kenneth Wolstenholme, from the Lime Grove (Shepherd's Bush) studio in London, viewers throughout Britain were shown almost 11½ minutes of highlights of the Wales v. England international match played that afternoon at Cardiff before Wolstenholme gave the next item a big build-up:

> Now to Scotland, and what a game they had there – Celtic v. Rangers in the Scottish League Cup final at Hampden Park. Not for 29 years had these famous teams met in a final of a senior competition – that's hard to believe, isn't it? – and they brought all the glamour of the great occasion to Hampden this afternoon. For where will you find two greater rivals than Celtic and Rangers? *Sports Special* cameras just couldn't miss this great tussle, so take a grandstand seat at Hampden Park as Celtic and Rangers meet in the final of the Scottish League Cup. Our commentator is Peter Thomson . . .

According to the file on the affair stored in the BBC's Written Archives Centre at Caversham Park in Reading, just over seven minutes of footage – of the first half – of the final was broadcast. At that point the stations at Birmingham, Bristol, Cardiff and Glasgow 'opted out' for their own programmes. In the case of Glasgow this was for their regular programme, *Talking Sport*, a ten-minute round-up of the day's sporting events in Scotland presented by Peter Thomson and George Davidson. It is not clear from BBC records whether Scottish viewers were able to hear before the 'opt-out' Kenneth Wolstenholme's remark (at least that attributed to him in the programme script) that 'Our film unit had to leave before the real explosion came, for in the second half Celtic went wild and slaughtered their great rivals. It will take Rangers years to live down the memory of that 7–1 defeat – by Celtic!' But, apparently, Peter Thomson told those watching in Scotland at the outset of *Talking Sport* that no second-half footage of the final could be screened because of a studio fault in London. It can safely be assumed that shortly afterwards the BBC's switchboard in Glasgow lit up like a Christmas tree with phone calls from irate Celtic supporters who felt that the blame really lay in a conspiracy hatched in the sports department of the BBC's Glasgow operation, which they regarded as being staffed by closet Rangers fans (Peter Thomson being the chief suspect), and believed that these same 'Bluenoses' were simply anxious to prevent the screening of 'their' team's annihilation by Celtic. These callers assuredly did *not* subscribe to the less damning theory of a letter-writer to the *Weekly News* who suggested that the BBC may not have wished 'to show pictures that might include the riot scenes. The first lot of pictures certainly showed the banner-wavers were out in force' (26 October 1957). Many Celtic supporters have since maintained that the film of the second half was deliberately destroyed on the orders of the aforesaid Peter Thomson (who was the most prominent figure in the BBC's sports output in Scotland at the time).

The truth can now be revealed in full, and it is quite different from the situation alleged in the conspiracy theory. The BBC in Glasgow were innocent victims of the outrage and abuse directed at them. In fact, the greatest irony of the whole episode is that the match was not even initially scheduled to be covered on television at all. According to a contemporary internal BBC memo, it was only on Thursday afternoon, 17 October (48 hours before the final), that the decision was taken – after 'the strong representations of Scotland' to London – to cover the match by means of the closed-circuit telerecording system 'because of the difficulties they [i.e. BBC Scotland] are experiencing with developing [film] locally'.[1] Thus, the final would be filmed by an outside broadcast unit at Hampden Park which would transmit the match electronically ('down the line', as it were) to the BBC studios at Lime Grove in London, where a telerecording machine would record the proceedings for editing purposes prior to the highlights being shown on *Sports Special*. The process, which had pronounced technical limitations, involved filming the pictures as they appeared on a television screen – videotape recording was not introduced until the following year. But, unfortunately, the operator of this device in the Lime Grove studio, perhaps anxious to keep dust off the lens of the camera, put a lens cap on it at half-time and forgot to remove it in time for the coverage of the second half.

The then editor of *Sports Special*, Paul (now Sir Paul) Fox, one of the most distinguished figures in the history of British television (he later held top posts at the BBC, ITV and Channel 4), recalls watching early pictures of the match as they came through from Glasgow to Lime Grove and remembers the moment, later that afternoon, when 'a chap came to me ashen-faced to say he had nothing of the second half'. An embarrassing blunder, no doubt about it, but such glitches were by no means uncommon in what were, as Sir Paul Fox points out, essentially pioneering days in British television: 'We were working with primitive technology by modern standards, equipment which was often heavy and cumbersome.' He might have added that facilities in Lime Grove were far from ideal, for the investigation into this particular mishap makes reference to 'everyone working in very cramped conditions'. Bob Crampsey concurs with this assessment of the difficulties faced by television broadcasters in the 1950s. He sprang to prominence as a commentator with Scottish Television (STV) shortly after its *Scotsport* programme was inaugurated in 1957, and recalls the susceptibility of film cameras covering football matches (and other sporting events) to jamming and to bad lighting: 'The industrial fog that descended suddenly on central Scotland in those days often rendered the film we took for *Scotsport* unusable.' In addition, the clumsy and unsophisticated nature of these cameras meant that, for example, deflected shots during matches could 'throw' the operators of the equipment, earning the resulting footage the unflattering tag of 'Montford's Mad Movies' (after the *Scotsport* presenter, Arthur Montford).

However, despite the difficulties produced by primitive working conditions and equipment, Paul Fox was far from sanguine about what had happened. Professional pride apart, he was only too aware of the likely impact in Glasgow. He had fond memories of its hospitable citizens from the time he spent there in 1943 when based at Maryhill Barracks for general army induction (he became a paratrooper), but that stay also brought to his attention the intensity of the 'Old Firm' rivalry. Thus, before he left his Lime Grove office that evening, he dictated a furious memo to the telerecording machine operator's boss, James Redmond, the Assistant Superintendent Engineer, Television Film (a memo reproduced at the end of this chapter). That was followed, less than 48 hours later on the Monday morning (21 October), by clear evidence of the angry reaction of Celtic supporters (and perhaps club officials) in the shape of a terse message to the Controller of BBC Scotland from S.J. de Lotbinière, the Controller of Programme Services, Television, which was despatched from Television Centre in London:

'Saturday's telecine supervisor has been called in from his day off and will be on the mat at 12 noon. Will report thereafter.' The upshot of that showdown was revealed that same day when James Redmond replied to Paul Fox's memo by confirming what had happened and outlining steps to prevent a recurrence:

> The operator concerned fitted a lens cap during the period when he was changing magazines at half-time and omitted to remove it afterwards. As a result of this, of course, nothing was telerecorded during the second half. There was no reason why the operator should have fitted the lens cap as this is not a necessary part of the changeover routine. The offending lens cap has been removed from the area so that it cannot be used again and the operator concerned has been removed from telerecording duties. [This document is also reproduced in full at the end of this chapter.]

James Redmond recovered from this temporary career blip to become the BBC's Director of Engineering a decade later, but at his retirement dinner, shortly before he too was knighted (in 1979), he reflected ruefully in his speech on how Paul Fox had given him the 'biggest bollocking' of his life way back in 1957.

Clearly, then, 'The Case of the Missing Film' lodged deep not only in the memory of Celtic fans. But perhaps now that the truth has been exposed it will no longer be justifiable to act like the newspaper editor in John Ford's film *The Man Who Shot Liberty Valance* when he says, 'When the legend becomes fact, print the legend.'[2]

THE REST OF THE SEASON
Sadly, the League Cup triumph was really the last hurrah for a fundamentally ageing side which contained a number of stalwarts whose contribution to the Celtic cause was drawing to a close, as one of them, Bertie Peacock, the captain, acknowledges: 'That 7–1 team was a really good side, but even at the time I sensed that the club was nearing a stage of change.' Its pace would be accelerated by a combination of injury and enforced retiral, leaving little but heartbreak to follow in the slipstream of a sensational victory. The stunning win over the then reigning Scottish league champions ('Sure now, that was a day!' beamed Charlie Tully as he left Hampden Park) was regarded by the Celtic players as a boost to the club's hopes of bringing the league flag back to Parkhead after an absence of four years, so providing an opportunity to take part for the first time in the newly established European Champions' Cup, a competition which was that autumn boosting Rangers' coffers to an extent that engendered envy and alarm among the Celtic directors. Bertie Peacock articulated the team's ambition when he emerged from the Celtic dressing-room after the

final to speak to waiting pressmen: 'That is the first of the big cups. Now we're after the others.'

Celtic seemed well set to sweep the boards. They followed up their Hampden success with maximum points gained (without losing a goal) in league matches at Cathkin against Third Lanark (with Collins scoring twice) and at home to Kilmarnock before an appreciative 35,000 crowd (Mochan 2, Wilson and McPhail – 'the most damaging and profitable centre in Scotland' – were the scorers). They then travelled to Methil knowing that a victory over East Fife would leave them primed to take over eventually at the top of the league from current leaders Hearts if they won their three games in hand (Celtic were five points behind Hearts prior to the East Fife match). Willie Allison, reporting on the Kilmarnock match for the *Sunday Mail*, had noted that McPhail 'in his present mood of subtlety and consummate skill with his head . . . could lead Scotland's attack with distinction' (3 November 1957). Both Celtic and McPhail were on a roll; it was as if their fortunes were intertwined.

Seamus Murphy recalls this period in Celtic's league campaign:

> By the end of October we were docked in Liverpool. I was paid off and couldn't wait to get back to Glasgow. At the time I lived in Townhead, and my local pub was Willie Miller's round the corner in Taylor Street [where mine host was the ex-Celtic goalkeeper], and, believe me, they were still celebrating that famous victory! I met up with my pals and did some more celebrating. Then on the Saturday we went to 'Paradise' to see the Bhoys thrash Kilmarnock 4–0 and, remember, Killie were a good side in those days.

Against East Fife the defence once again held firm, as McPhail scored twice in the last five minutes to increase the margin of victory to three goals (3–0). That left Celtic unbeaten in the league, with 11 points from six matches, and Hearts' five-point advantage could be nullified if the Parkhead men kept on the winning trail. But the victory at Methil was to prove a costly one. During the first half McPhail emerged from a tackle feeling a twinge of pain which he didn't pay much attention to at the time. But, later on, the same ankle received a further knock in a clash with East Fife keeper Allan. Although it did not prevent McPhail from making sure of both points for his team, the ankle, he remembers, 'ballooned' after the game, enforcing his withdrawal from the Scottish team due to play Wales at Hampden in the Home International match the following Wednesday. Sadly this robbed the player of his only full international cap. Evans, Fernie and Collins all played in the representative match and the last-named scored Scotland's goal in a 1–1 draw, but also took a knock which kept him out of the league encounter with St Mirren at Celtic Park three days later, on 16 November. In the event, McPhail 'recovered' in time to make the Celtic team for that match, while Collins's place was taken by the 17-year-old John Divers.

Whether or not the enforced changes and McPhail perhaps not being 100 per cent fit had an effect, the match against St Mirren disclosed an Achilles' heel which was repeatedly to blight Celtic's championship aspirations, namely their surprising vulnerability when playing at home. Celtic dropped a point in a 2–2 draw after twice being in front (Divers had opened the scoring).[3] Two fine victories then followed at Easter Road over Hibs ('Dick Beattie was just fantastic,' said one report on the 1–0 win) and at Broomfield (5–2 against Airdrie), but the earlier type of slip-up was repeated on 7 December when a goalless draw with Dundee at Parkhead marked the first occasion on which the Celts had failed to score in 17 competitive matches since their Glasgow Cup loss at Ibrox in mid-August. The Dens Park side had goalkeeper Brown to thank on numerous occasions for their point, although one reporter remarked that the home team's centre-half commanded his penalty area so well during Dundee's first-half pressure that 'It is phooey to suggest that Evans is not the complete pivot'. But, ominously for Celtic, Dundee – recovering from their horrendous opening to the league season – had been content to absorb Celtic's frantic second-half onslaught. Also significant was the absence of Tully, still suffering from the effects of a strained muscle incurred the previous Saturday in Celtic's away win over Airdrie.

Tully had been paid a compliment after that Broomfield match by a distinguished spectator who indicated to a reporter afterwards that Celtic might miss the Irishman's prompting. The great Uruguayan inside-forward Juan Schiaffino, fresh from helping AC Milan to rout Rangers at Ibrox in the European Cup – and taking in a Scottish match before flying out to play for Italy in a World Cup qualifier in Belfast (he had Italian parentage) – knew a fellow schemer when he saw one and opined that even a handicapped Tully was a menace to opposing teams: 'With one good leg, he still made many fine moves and clever passes.' Tully's injury gave an opportunity for another promising youngster, the 18-year-old Mike Jackson, to make his first-team debut in the Dundee match, while the Irish magician, now well into his 34th year, was obliged to seek the attentions of a specialist. He would not resume first-team duty until early March 1958, by which time his club's league-title hopes had all but vanished.

Although the Dundee result had been a warning to Celtic that their unconvincing home form had to improve (only one league match had been won out of four at Celtic Park to date that season), they were still installed as championship favourites. Yet the club was about to embark on a sombre period on and off the pitch. Four days after Dundee had exposed the shortcomings of a Tully-less Celtic, the League Cup holders were humbled by a 6–1 margin at Middlesbrough (of England's Second Division). A precocious young striker called Brian Clough scored four goals as Celtic went down to a defeat so embarrassing that it is perhaps not surprising that it was somehow omitted from the results of 'Friendly Matches' in the next issue of the annual *Celtic Football Guide*. (The ex-Celt-turned-journalist John McPhail, reporting on 'a bitter, bitter lesson to Celtic', highlighted the apparent difference in standards between the two leagues by remarking in his *Daily Record* report on the Teessiders' ability to vary the pace of the game: 'Middlesbrough used the ball, sharp and precise, conserving their energy for the quick burst through that left Celtic's defence floundering in the rear.') A chastened Celtic headed back north for a league match three days later which was to be overshadowed by tragedy.

On 14 December 1957, six minutes into the match between Clyde and Celtic at Shawfield, a 30-foot section of a four-foot-high barricade wall collapsed, the outcome, according to the *Sunday Post*, of a section of the 26,000 crowd swaying forward 'like a tidal wave' in the excitement which followed Celtic's opening goal. In the aftermath of the accident, ambulances ran a shuttle service – 'bells ringing to cleave their way through the dense Christmas traffic' – between the ground and the various city infirmaries. One 12-year-old boy, Jimmy Ryan of Green Street, Bridgeton, was killed, and 48 boys and men were injured. Some of the players were involved in carrying those hurt in the disaster to safety. Play was resumed after almost half an hour and Celtic won the match 6–3, but the result would have been the last thing on the minds of anxious relatives who rushed to the ground as news of the accident spread in the surrounding district.

'Larry Marshall, star of STV's *One O'Clock Gang*, rushed to the Victoria Infirmary when he heard of the tragedy. Two of his nephews – Peter Tomasso and Victor Thomson – were trapped under the wall.

'Peter and Victor – both nine – were at the match with their fathers, Mr Victor Thomson, 21 Southview Avenue, and Mr Ernest Tomasso, 25 Mossgiel Crescent, Busby.

'"It's the worst experience I've ever had," said Mr Thomson. "We shouted for our boys, but we couldn't find them. Youngsters lay, trapped by the wall. Some said there were boys right underneath the wall. Men tried frantically to move the wall, but they couldn't move it."

'Peter was taken to the Victoria with face cuts and a crushed foot. Last night he underwent an operation. Victor was taken to the Royal with a suspected fractured pelvis.' (*Sunday Post*, 15 December 1957)[4]

Despite the victory – a somewhat irrelevant statistic in light of the tragedy – the fates had begun to conspire against Celtic. A week later Partick Thistle visited Parkhead and inflicted on Celtic their first defeat (3–2) in all competitions since mid-August, and only their third in 23 competitive matches since the start of the season. As if that were not enough, the setback was exacerbated by injuries to two more key players: Fernie, helped off the field with a leg injury, missed the entire second half and was out of action for five weeks, while McPhail, hurt in a clash with goalkeeper Thomson, also needed assistance to depart the pitch after the interval. Although McPhail (described by one newspaper as 'Scotland's unluckiest footballer') resumed, limping badly on the wing, he was sidelined for nine weeks, a period during which one Celtic player pleaded privately, and unavailingly, with the management that an attempt be made to strengthen the squad and sustain the league challenge by making a move to sign the 'King of Tynecastle', Willie Bauld. Bauld, a famous centre-forward and member of the Edinburgh club's celebrated 'Terrible Trio', was being kept out of the Hearts line-up at that stage by the brilliance of Alex Young.[5]

Celtic had now lost the record of being Britain's only unbeaten league side that season, but worse was to follow – and with bewildering rapidity. With three of the major stars of the League Cup final missing (Fernie, Tully and McPhail), there followed three further successive home defeats, giving the phrase 'festive season' a rather hollow ring where Celtic was concerned. Queen of the South's 2–1 victory on Christmas Day was followed a few days later by a 2–0 win for a Hearts side now beginning to stamp its authority on the championship race (Collins missed a vital penalty for Celtic); and, in the Ne'erday 1958 clash with Rangers, the Ibrox club rubbed salt into the wounds when they extracted a modicum of revenge for their recent humiliation at the hands of their greatest rivals, Scott scoring the only goal of a game played on an icy surface.

John Donnelly had dropped out of the side after the defeat by Queen of the South, with Fallon switching to right-back and Jim Kennedy coming in to fill the other full-back position. (Kennedy, incidentally, typified the 'jersey' player Celtic had on tap until the 1980s and the influx of the 'mercenaries'. At the time of his signing in 1955, it was noted that the new recruit was 'a great Celtic supporter, [who] would rather go and see them than play for his junior club, Duntocher Hibs'.)

Changes up front were rather more dramatic. Eric Smith had regained the outside-right position after Mike Jackson's debut, only to lose it to Jim Conway for the match with Hearts. Conway in turn was replaced by Matt McVittie for the clash with Rangers (McVittie was prevented from equalising in that game only by a remarkable save by Ritchie in the Rangers goal). At inside-right, Bobby Collins was not fit to play in the New Year derby, and his place was taken by John Colrain, making his debut in senior football. Yet another young player, Vince Ryan (from the Dublin club Home Farm), had been fielded at centre-forward for the game against Hearts and kept his place for the Rangers match (a game, unfortunately, which would be an unhappy experience for him in front of goal). With so much chopping and changing and rank inexperience in the forward line, the results were perhaps not surprising in retrospect. But the fact remained that Celtic were now hopelessly adrift of the eventual champions Hearts, a team long considered to be lacking in the steel and consistency essential to a title-winning team. But the Tynecastle club proved capable of putting to rest a 61-year hoodoo in the most emphatic manner, amassing a Scottish league record haul of 132 goals, netted during a 34-match programme.

Although Celtic's home form improved and they were only to lose another three out of 19 league matches (all defeats away from home), the damage had been done: they could only finish in third place on 46 points, a distant 16 points behind the champions (and three behind second-placed Rangers). To add to the disappointment, on 1 March 1958 they went down to Clyde (the eventual winners) in the Scottish Cup in a match which was officially an away tie, but moved to Celtic Park because of understandable concerns over the safety of Shawfield (65,000 attended the match at Parkhead). Although Fernie was back in time for this match, Tully and McPhail were both unavailable, and Celtic could make little headway after falling behind early in the tie to goals by Ring and Currie. It was a sad result which effectively ended a season that had in late October looked to be the most promising in several years.

JOHN DONNELLY

John Donnelly was very much the 'quiet man' of the 1957 League Cup-winning side, at least in terms of publicity, as this perfunctory profile of the new signing in the *Celtic Football Guide* for 1956–57 suggests: 'A centre-half from Armadale. Showed great promise with his Junior club last season.' The 20-year-old Donnelly got the chance to establish himself in Celtic's first team after the veteran Mike Haughney decided to emigrate to the United States in the summer of 1957. Donnelly took over the right-back spot on Celtic's tour of that country after assistant trainer Jimmy Gribben suggested that he be tried out in Haughney's former berth. He came into the team in the last three matches of a close-season tour which was enjoyable enough, although mixed in playing terms, Celtic losing three out of their four meetings with Tottenham Hotspur. Donnelly's first-team competitive debut was not long in coming. He was Frank Meechan's replacement for the Glasgow Cup tie at Ibrox played on 19 August 1957, and although it was a losing experience, the youngster acquitted himself well. Cyril Horne of the *Glasgow Herald* noted that Celtic could take consolation from the fact that 'Donnelly, playing in his first senior Old

Firm match, was intelligent and successful throughout against Hubbard, who has rarely been so subdued by fair methods' (20 August 1957).

John underlined his growing reputation as a quick learner when, a month later at the same venue, he secured a rare post-war Celtic victory at Ibrox (rare up till that point at least) by blocking Hubbard's point-blank scoring attempt after Murray's header had hit the base of the post and careered along the goal-line with Beattie spread-eagled. This piece of alert defending was also very timely, for it occurred when Rangers, having made some headway in reducing a two-goal deficit, were launching strenuous efforts to force a late equaliser.

Sean Fallon rates Donnelly as 'a sound, clean full-back who was a good kicker of the ball, and a player who was improving with every game'. Donnelly's willingness to work on his game was a trait which probably owed something to the influence of, and interest taken by, his father, himself a former professional with Albion Rovers, Luton and Charlton Athletic. His son, a part-timer, trained at Celtic Park on Tuesday and Thursday evenings; but every Wednesday he was taken out by Donnelly senior to a piece of vacant ground near the family home in Broxburn for a spot of coaching. Not only that, but Mr Donnelly was his son's severest critic, pointing out the flaws and errors in his offspring's play after every match, although the criticism was delivered with a constructive emphasis, and plenty of encouragement.

Sadly, a lengthy career at Celtic never materialised for this youthful hero of '57. His appearances were curtailed first by National Service. This involved round trips of four hours or so by public transport to Celtic Park for evening training sessions on top of military obligations which could include night guard duty on his return from Glasgow to Penicuik, near Edinburgh, where he was stationed. This schedule could be 'very exhausting', Donnelly recalls, and did his Celtic career 'no good at all'. Later his opportunities for first-team action were severely limited on account of the irresistible claims being staked for the position by Duncan MacKay, a competitor who was arguably the finest Celtic right-back in living memory, Jim Craig and Danny McGrain included.

DICK BEATTIE
The most criticised player in the Celtic side during the two seasons prior to the 'October Revolution', Dick Beattie was blamed (said Jack Harkness, a sportswriter who had himself been a goalkeeper of international distinction) for 'letting the odd "daft" one slip into the net'. That charitable interpretation was not shared at the start of the 1957–58 campaign by the many Celtic supporters who were still suffering nightmares as a result of Beattie's bizarre lapses in the previous spring's Scottish Cup semi-final replay against Kilmarnock. They recoiled in horror when recalling the moment that Beattie had raced from his goal to

the 18-yard line to nudge Curlett out of the way and so concede a penalty (converted by Mays after the Celt had saved his first attempt); the psychological blow sustained on the stroke of half-time when, with the score at 1–1, Beattie allowed a cross from Curlett to 'float over his fingers', giving Mays the simple task of restoring the Ayrshire side's lead; and the manner in which he had compounded these errors shortly after the interval when he again rushed out of his goal to intercept the opposing forward Bertie Black, only to lose possession in a tussle for the ball, leaving Black with an open goal. It should be said that Celtic's management (which meant in effect the chairman, Bob Kelly) had contributed to the débâcle by swapping the two wingers, Higgins and Collins, after only five minutes of the match and, during the interval, reversing the positions of Alec Byrne and Neil Mochan, initially fielded at centre-forward and inside-left respectively (nor, indeed, were their starting positions the most profitable ones for either player). Perhaps these obvious signs of panic had communicated a similar lack of confidence to the goalkeeper.

At any rate, Beattie entered season 1957–58 with a big question mark against his future as Celtic's number one. But within seven weeks of its start, Jack Harkness was maintaining that there was no better keeper in the country, indeed, that Beattie had been the main reason for Celtic starting the season with a bang. Harkness's assessment seemed to receive some justification when Beattie's level of performance earned him a place in the Scottish League side for the match with the Irish League at Ibrox on 9 October, though only as a replacement for Bill Brown of Dundee, who had to call off injured. Nonetheless, Harkness claimed that Beattie was only reaping the dividends of hard work done in the close season. He revealed that while Celtic were on their close-season tour of North America (which Beattie missed through injury), the goalkeeper had reported to the ground on his own every other night for training and 'had accepted invitations right and left' to keep goal at charity fêtes on Saturday afternoons and evenings. Not only that: 'For his fortnight's summer holidays he literally took up residence at Celtic Park.' These welcome signs of dedication – which in the authors' view are indicative of a more general seriousness of purpose and higher degree of resolution pervading the club that summer – would soon be amply rewarded.

POSTSCRIPT
Seamus Murphy concludes his memories of this era:

> Sad to say, I'm the only one left alive in my group of pals. We had all been in the orphanage together during, and just after, the war – a great bunch of lads. We used to go into the Stirling Castle pub in Cathedral Street which was 'half and half', I seem to remember. The landlord was

a rank Rangers man, but his son was Celtic-daft, so he used to ask us to take him to Celtic Park now and again. Before my leave was up, we went along to Garngad to the local Celtic Supporters Club who were showing a film of the 7–1 match – in technicolour, as I recall. I remember a couple of Celtic players were present, including a young Mike Jackson. Many years later, when Celtic Films visited my local Celtic Supporters Club in Luton, I asked them if they knew anything about that film. They told me that it hadn't survived the years (too much wear and tear, I should think!).

PS – One of the first things I did when I came home from the Mediterranean was to go to the *Daily Record* offices in Hope Street to get photographs of all seven goals. Then, on my last trip to sea in August 1962 – I was coming home to get married – I was packing my gear, stuffing everything in, and came to my collection of photos. I had nearly a hundred taken over the years from every part of the world, plus my Celtic ones. I thought to myself, 'I don't need these any more.' I opened the porthole and threw them out into the sea. It's only now, after all these years, that I wish I'd held on to them. What a fool!

From: Mr. Paul Fox, Editor, "Sportsview" Unit, E.302 T.S.

Subject: 16 mm TELERECORDING OF CELTIC v. RANGERS: 19th OCTOBER.

To: A.S.E.Tel.Film   19th October, 1957.

        Copies to: C.P.S.Tel.
                                                               H.O.B.Tel.
                                                               E.i.C. Telecine & Telerecording
                                                               Mr. Ivor Smith
                                                               A.H.S.P.II
                                                               Mr. Peter Thomson
                                                               Mr. Harry Govan

I am sure I don't have to underline the seriousness of the situation that arose this evening due to the faulty handling of the 16 mm telerecording of the Celtic v. Rangers match. As you probably know by now, the whole of the second half of this Scottish League Cup Final was ruined because the operator had left the lens cap on in changing magazines at half-time.

I should explain that Scotland went to tremendous pains to get a Unit into Hampden Park for this occasion and that many special arrangements had to be made so that the game could be covered as fully as possible for this most important match for Scotland. The transmission was perfect, the game was a tremendous thriller – quite apart from the importance of the match – and all the good action happened in the second half.

I am just trying to explain the background to the game so that the seriousness of the situation may be fully understood. Quite apart from ruining tonight's edition of *Sports Special*, it also made us look extremely foolish to everyone in Scotland. I am quite sure that you are investigating exactly what happened and I hope that measures will be taken so that this sort of situation never occurs again. I think I would be wrong in not pointing out, at the same time, that the telerecording machine was not ready until a minute before the kick-off because the film had not been loaded and I feel altogether that the handling of the machine was carried out in far too lax a manner. I would have thought it vital that whoever is in charge should be present when the magazine is changed at half-time.

I am sorry that the 16 mm telerecording routine, which has been going so well until now, should receive such a serious setback.

                                                               (Paul Fox)

From: Assistant Superintendent Engineer, Television Film   (TS 106 & 34)

21st October 1957

Subject: 16 MM TELERECORDING OF CELTIC v. RANGERS:

To: Mr. Paul Fox, Editor, "Sportsview" Unit.

Copies to: C.P.S.Tel
H.O.B.Tel
E.i.C Telecine & Telerecording
T.O.M. Telerecording
A.H.S.P.II
Mr. Peter Thomson
Mr. Harry Govan

I very much regret the operational error which caused you to lose the second half of the Celtic v. Rangers match on Saturday 19th October. The operator concerned fitted a lens cap during the period when he was changing magazines at half-time and omitted to remove it afterwards. As a result of this, of course, nothing was telerecorded during the second half. There was no reason why the operator should have fitted the lens cap as this is not a necessary part of the changeover routine. The offending lens cap has been removed from the area so that it cannot be used again and the operator concerned has been removed from telerecording duties.

Our operating instructions have been amended to ensure that in future a check is always made that light is falling on the film in the gate of the camera and we are also instituting a double check system in an attempt to ensure that any mistake on the part of one operator is observed by a second.

I am also making arrangements to provide you and all other editors with viewing facilities elsewhere than in the telerecording room to ensure that the telerecording operator interests himself entirely in his operating problems and is not distracted from them by the activities of anyone else.

May I apologise once again for this operational error for which there is absolutely no excuse. Please accept my assurances that I am doing everything possible to prevent any similar accident in the future.

SH   (J. Redmond)

ABOVE AND LEFT: The text of the relevant documents in 'The Case of the Missing Film' – The 'Conspiracy Theory' rebutted. (Courtesy of the BBC Written Archive Centre, Reading)

ENDNOTES

1 The transmission of highlights of the Scottish League Cup final replaced the original, scheduled highlights of the Manchester United v. Portsmouth league clash at Old Trafford. It should be noted that in 1957 there were no regular TV highlights of Scottish football matches (the football authorities were worried about the possible impact on attendances).

   The reference to the 'strong representations of Scotland' reflects the sensitive nature of the relationship between the London headquarters of the BBC and its 'regions', as they were called. The accommodation reached in this instance is in stark contrast, for example, to a chilly exchange almost four years earlier, when the Controller of Light Programmes (Radio) demanded an explanation for the failure of the Glasgow office to let London know of a rearranged, later kick-off for the Scotland v. Wales match on the afternoon of 4 November 1953. It was an oversight which led to 'overrunning' of the live radio transmission throughout the UK of the second half of the match, and thus the postponement of *Mrs Dale's Diary*, a programme which was virtually an institution in the South of England. In his reply, while acknowledging Glasgow's inexcusable failure to check the kick-off time, the Head of Scottish Programmes pointed in mitigation to the Scottish Football Association's omitting to notify the BBC of the change in kick-off time and ended by noting that it was the first such 'misunderstanding' in the course of ten years. Although the listeners had received good value for their licence money by way of an exciting second half which incorporated four goals and a gallant Welsh fightback (from 3–1 down they came away with a 3–3 draw), the Controller of Light Programmes was not mollified by this response, firing back a curt, one-sentence acknowledgement of the explanation.

   The two cases illustrate in their different ways the exacting, perfectionist standards demanded by the world's most famous and respected broadcasting organisation, as well as the practical inevitability, in television's early days, of occasional failures to meet them.

2 Black and white film of the 7–1 match does still exist, and can be seen in a number of Celtic videos produced in recent years (e.g. the official Centenary video). It is not, of course, the 'missing film' which the BBC had intended to show, but one apparently taken by an enthusiast from the press box. The film shows all the goals except Celtic's sixth. A shot is shown which a later editor of the film clearly and understandably thought was that goal, but careful scrutiny reveals that the ball goes wide, and in any case the shot is struck from a position which does not tally with all the contemporary accounts of McPhail's hat-trick counter.

3 Celtic were denied a penalty 12 minutes from the end of this match, and Billy McPhail was cautioned for protesting too vehemently to the referee, Jack

Mowat (once again). The official left the field to a chorus of loud boos from the home support.

4 The two boys mentioned in this report, both of them relatives of one of the authors, happily made a full recovery and continued to support Celtic in later years.

5 The two other members of the famous inside trio were Alfie Conn, father of Alfie of Old Firm fame, and Jimmy Wardhaugh, a fearsome striker of the ball.

CHAPTER SEVEN

A Grand Old Team

Down the middle runs Billy McPhail
With big John Valentine on his tail.
With a shot along the ground
The Cup's at Parkhead safe and sound.

SONGS, POETRY AND JOKES
Naturally enough, 'The 7–1' was soon being commemorated in the popular Celtic-minded subculture which thrived in Glasgow and its environs at the time. The most famous song celebrating the great victory is the one from which this book takes its title. It in turn was a parody of a calypso number which had been in the top ten of the British charts since August 1957, namely 'Island in the Sun' (the theme song from a film of that name) sung by Harry Belafonte, a New Yorker styled the 'King of Calypso'.[1] The first line of the film theme was 'Oh, island in the sun . . . '

The lyrics of 'Oh, Hampden in the Sun' were written, according to a profile written by Jim Friel (of whom more anon), by one Mick McLaughlan, who wrote under the pen-name 'Mick Garngad', after the district in the north of Glasgow (adjacent to those of Townhead and Provanmill) where he was born around the turn of the century. Irish navvies engaged in the digging of canals and the building of railway lines had settled in the tenements which became Garngad in the late nineteenth century, giving the district its nickname of 'Little Ireland'. McLaughlan himself was of Irish descent, and, like many in the city, of Donegal stock. He became well known as a raconteur, poet and song-writer, his talents making him much in demand at the traditional wakes which were a feature of the district until the demise of that community (or at least of 'old Garngad') in the late 1950s and early 1960s, a result of

193

the redevelopment then beginning to transform the face of Glasgow. (The district is now called Royston, a change of name decreed by the City Fathers because of Garngad's 'unfortunate reputation' – apparently youngsters from there experienced difficulties when applying for jobs once their place of residence became known – and because the district was much altered by new buildings.)

Although 'Mick Garngad' was essentially a chronicler of the locality he loved (the Garngad–Townhead quarter), his bardic craft extended to the wider Glasgow area and events beyond these shores. For example, at the age of 14 he wrote a poem entitled 'The Sinking of the *Titanic*', and, as World War II drew to its end, he penned 'The Forgotten Army', a tribute to the troops still fighting the Japanese in Burma (now Myanmar) after hostilities had ceased in the European theatre. Unsurprisingly, the bold Mick was a fanatical supporter of Celtic FC, taking great pride in the players born in his native district who appeared in the green and white – Jimmy McGrory, Malcolm MacDonald and Steve Chalmers – and in the feats of the club itself, notably chronicled in 'Oh, Hampden in the Sun' and, earlier, the Coronation Cup victory song (1953), which begins, 'Said Lizzie to Philip . . . ' Given his reputation as a prankster, practical joker and general 'patter merchant', it is no surprise that Jim Friel, a native of Garngad (and historian of the local junior club, St Roch's) – to whom the authors are indebted for information on this remarkable character – should note that a man 'bearing an uncanny resemblance' to Mick could occasionally be seen at Ibrox stadium, brandishing song-sheets relating to Rangers FC, signed by one 'Blue Knight'!

One suspects that the demolition of the old Garngad – and the decanting of its inhabitants to the outlying housing schemes which were central to the planners' vision of a new Glasgow – must have broken Mick's heart. He penned an evocative 'Farewell to Garngad', an elegy for an area of the city which – in parallel with the 1950s itself – now seems like a vanished world. However, had he still been alive (he apparently died in the early 1960s), how he would have relished seeing the inimitable Dorothy Paul's rendition of his classic 'Oh, Hampden in the Sun', sung with great verve and gusto during the two-month run of the play *The Celtic Story* at the Pavilion Theatre, Glasgow, in early summer 1988.

*   *   *

Another, less well-known, song of rejoicing has as its chorus the following lines (unfortunately the authors have been unable to trace its author):

> *Another goal for Glasgow Celtic,*
> *Another victory for the cause,*

Another reason to be giving
Another cheer just for the Bhoys.
For if I live to be a hundred,
I'll never ever have such fun
As the day that Glasgow Celtic
Beat the Rangers seven-one.

*   *   *

Yet another song of celebration is a parody of a Lonnie Donegan single of the time, which had been riding high in the charts during the summer and autumn of 1957:

I'll tell you of a story that fills my heart with joy;
It happened one day at Hampden Park when I was just a boy.
The Scottish League Cup final,
The score it came from heaven,
Celtic played the Rangers – Celtic scored the seven!

Oh . . . puttin' on the agony,
Puttin' on the style;
1–2–3–4–5–6–7, scorin' all the while.
I've never seen anything like it,
And I've travelled as many a mile.
Is watchin' the Glasgow Celtic puttin' on the style!

(Again, the authors have not been able to discover the identity of the person who penned this version of the lyrics.)

*   *   *

Seamus Murphy wrote a whimsical song – as if from a would-be Rangers supporter's point of view – entitled simply 'Celtic 7, Rangers 1' (to the tune of 'The Wild Colonial Boy').

I took a stroll, down Hampden way,
One sunny Saturday,
To see the famous Rangers club,
Against the Celtic play,
For me, they are the finest side
The world has ever seen,
And they're here to play, and win the day,
And thrash the White and Green.

And as I joined that happy throng,
Of loyal fans so true,
We sang the praises of the Gers,
The cream, in royal blue;
We sang 'The Sash My Father Wore'
And 'Follow, Follow' too,
And the tears couldn't hide,
When we sang with pride,
Of the red, the white, and blue.

But from the start, we all lost heart
As the Celts began to play,
With Fernie, Mochan and McPhail,
They looked winners all the way;
When Wilson scored, and the Fenians roared,
We knew our fate was sealed,
Then with Mochan's first, poor Shearer cursed,
As he lay stretched on the field.

And then King Billy, of the Celts,
Began to run amok,
He scored a hat-trick on the day
And left the Gers in shock;
Poor Valentine, he died the death,
As he tried to stem the tide,
But it was plain to me, he was all at sea,
And was easily swept aside.

Poor Niven in the Rangers goal,
Sure, he never stood a chance,
Five times the ball hit the back of the net,
And left him in a trance;
When McPhail struck in number six,
It was plain for all to see,
Then the star of the game, Willie Fernie by name
Wrapped it up with a penalty.

And as I left the joyful scene,
Where the mighty Rangers fell,
My thoughts were with those men in green
Whose brilliance had me 'neath their spell;
I threw away my scarf of blue,
And Ibrox, no more be seen,
As from that day, I'm happy to say,
I've been wearin' of the Green.

The official Supporters Association was also not slow in paying homage to the heroes of October. In its Handbook for 1958–59, the following poem appeared:

WINNERS OF THE SCOTTISH LEAGUE CUP
1957–58

A tribute to the boys who wore the Celtic green and white

> *O fair the day, and bright the sun,*
> *That shone o'er Hampden's green,*
> *Well nigh one hundred thousand hearts*
> *Throbbed 'neath a sky serene.*
>
> *This was the hour, that would proclaim*
> *To thousands staunch and true,*
> *Who had the best right to the silver prize*
> *The Green or the Royal Blue.*
>
> *The men in blue stride to the field*
> *To a thunder of fierce acclaim,*
> *The thunder that greets the men in green*
> *Puts the tempests' roar to shame.*
>
> *The fray begun – now history extols*
> *That day of sweet renown,*
> *How victory went to the men in green,*
> *How the men in blue went down.*
>
> *Seven times flashed a lance of green,*
> *Launched at a rival line,*
> *Seven times pierced, the ranks of blue*
> *Broke in the bright sunshine.*
>
> *Here's to the men who won the day*
> *And earned eternal fame,*
> *Here's to the men in green who gained*
> *New lustre for Celtic's name.*
>
> *Beattie, the tall, to whom was given*
> *The rear, to watch and guard,*
> *Discharged his trust with matchless skill*
> *Maintained his blameless ward.*

Donnelly, the youth, for whom this hour
Would make or mar his fate;
Know then, young John, right well you earned
A place among the great.

Fallon, the strong, who undismayed,
Fronted the hostile roar,
Staunch as the rugged rocks that guard
His native Sligo's shore.

Fernie, the happy rambler,
Supreme in every wile,
Trailed in his wake the baffled ones,
The victims of his guile.

Evans, with the restless urge,
That knew not halt or rein,
His one resolve – no raider's foot,
Would tread his loved domain.

Peacock with a master's touch,
The craftsman's art portrayed,
His deadly thrust, saw rivals reel,
Frustrated and dismayed.

Tully, the merry schemer,
Dire purpose dressed in glee,
Elusive as a leprechaun,
Round a fairy thorn tree.

Collins, the eager warrior,
His aim – to strive, to win,
Whose sturdy frame could scarce contain
The mighty heart within.

McPhail, the tall and slender,
Borne like a bird on wing,
Thrice did he cast a fatal dart,
Thrice did the heavens ring.
Wilson, the ever ready,
To make or bar the way,
He struck the blow that marked the road,
To final victory.

Mochan, the ever smiling,
The last, but not the least,
Shod with the deadly thunderbolt,
He crowned the Celtic feast.

Thus do we sing your praises,
To honour the lasting fame,
That raised once more to starry heights
The beloved Celtic name.

Time shall not dim your lustre,
And none your right gainsay,
To measure your feat with the brightest page,
In Celtic history.[2]

*   *   *

Another poem that made its appearance that autumn took as its inspiration not only the winning of the Scottish League Cup, but also the recent launch of the Soviet space satellite known as 'Sputnik' into orbit.

Twinkle, twinkle little Sputnik;
You are sure a dirty tricknik.
Up above the world so high,
Making zig-zags in the sky.

How the hell can people sleep,
When all night you go 'Beep-beep-beep'.
Telling all the Tims in Heaven,
Rangers one, and Celtic seven?

*   *   *

John Lindsay (Bearsden) recalls a variant on one well-worn joke:
'I was a pupil at St Mungo's Academy (Glasgow) from 1955 on. I remember a teacher there known as 'Farmer' Kelly, and his exceptional teaching methods. When taking the register he insisted on using a Parker pen with Quink ink, and counted the class as follows: "One, two, three, four, five, six, seven past Niven, eight . . . "'

Joe Connelly remembers a humorous version of the Rangers line-up:
'David Niven, Moira Shearer, Eric Caldow, R.S. McColl, Dickie Valentine, Bette Davis, Lizabeth Scott, Mrs Simpson, Ruby Murray, John Logie Baird, and Old Mother Hubbard.'

Various contributors suggested the story of the Rangers players on a sports quiz panel who, fed up with all the questions being about Celtic, request one on Rangers. 'All right,' says the quizmaster. 'Who scored Rangers' goal when they lost to Celtic 7–1 in the League Cup final?'

CELTIC IN THE 1950S: THE FANS PERSPECTIVE
Charlie Harvey:

Celtic's team of the '50s should have been world-beaters. Even the greybeards admitted that they'd never seen so much football talent in one team. Craftsmen like Tully, Fernie, Collins, Evans, Baillie, Peacock. Occasionally this talent gelled and the football was a joy to behold. Poetry in motion. A lot was missing, though: confidence and leadership, among other things. What a difference a Matt Busby would have made! He had been rejected by a Celtic management who preferred the compliant type – like Jimmy McGrory. It was frustrating for the support, although we found it hard to stay angry with a classy team – even one that won few trophies.

Roy McGuinness:

In the '50s, in addition to Tully, we had non-stop players: Bobby Evans, Bertie Peacock, wee Bobby Collins and Neil Mochan ('The Rocket'). Of course Billy McPhail came later, but prior to that we had his brother John ('Hooky') McPhail. Jimmy Walsh, who could put the ball round a defender one way, go around him another, and meet the ball at the defender's back – what a swerve! The great Willie Fernie, arguably the greatest dribbler of a ba'. Jock Weir, a speed merchant, so fast he sometimes ran away withoot the ba'.

Hughie Corbett:

'Oh, Hampden in the Sun' – yes, yes, yes, 7–1! But then came the lean years for me and my scarf under that tight-fisted so-and-so Kelly. If you ever see a photograph of the lynch mob, I'm the one with the rope. Then came The Big Man. Under him I was privileged to have years of watching attacking soccer at its best.

Tom Campbell:

In the 1950s, Celtic had great individuals capable of marvellous individual performances. But too often there was a lack of teamwork. Couldn't anyone in authority see this? Off the field, there was a pettiness about much of the way the club's affairs were handled. For example, Celtic programmes – pathetic little black and white pamphlets costing 3d [approximately 1½ pence]. They used to have the half-time scores in the middle – A: Aberdeen v. Clyde, B: Dundee v. St Mirren, etc. Nobody bought the programme apart from the odd fan (although everybody in the ground made sure he found out which letter was the Rangers fixture). One afternoon, for some reason – perhaps the size of the crowd – the man couldn't get to the scoreboard to put the scores up by hand. Celtic announced the scores over the tannoy: 'A: 1–0, B: 1–1,' etc!

Celtic at that time always appeared to be three players short of challenging for honours, especially in defence – goalkeeper and full-back were particularly problematic positions. This was a perennial problem – we attempted to play attractive, attacking football, but had basic weaknesses in defence. Also, there were some players who were not prepared to work hard at their trade – there were some poor trainers among them. Celtic would get things right in spectacular style – the Coronation Cup, the 'Double' in '53–'54, the two League Cups – but generally only for short periods. They tended to fail in the long run through lack of method. Apart from those moments of brilliance – as in the Coronation Cup – Celtic were too often an earnest, plodding, unimaginative side relying on inspiration which came infrequently.

I think Bob Kelly ruined the careers of several promising players during the 'seven lean years'. These youths were too often left to fend for themselves on the field. The pressure was too much for many of them. They lacked guidance and support. The air around Parkhead in those days was one of casual paternalism. I think Kelly genuinely confused Celtic's best interests with his own at times. His autocratic control over team selection – remember, he'd never played the game professionally himself (only at junior level) – was a form of arrogance. As if he and only he knew what was best for Celtic! Also, in dealing with the authorities, he expected the worst and got it, which allowed him to play the martyr's role. I think that he was more comfortable psychologically with the status of being a loser with a grievance. In football terms, I think he revelled in the 'moral victory'. Too often the only real protest against shabby treatment came in the annual Celtic guide, where he was essentially preaching to the converted.

Willie Goldie recalls the humorously bleak outlook of some among the Celtic support in the '50s:

When I was about 16, and had just started serving my time as an apprentice, I could sometimes be found on the toilet in 'The Jungle', praying for the Celts, and in those days we had to pray pretty hard, because the Lord seemed to be 'slinging a deafie'. This particular time I went to a Celtic v. Hibs match at Parkhead, with an absolute Celtic fanatic workmate. Hibs were winning 2–1 with two minutes to go, when the ball went past for a goal-kick. The wee ball-boy ran after it, but because it was so far past, he couldn't throw it back that distance, so he decided to kick it back. But he 'sclaffed' the ball away to the side, and my friend Tommy said, in abject exasperation, 'That's the worst set of ball-boys in Britain!'

*   *   *

With all the injuries and retirements at Celtic Park in the late 1950s, the management turned to youth to see the club into the next decade. It was a policy which – despite later claims that it had all been part of a master plan – in some ways the club's management fell into, rather than consciously thought out in advance. There appeared to be an element in the transition of making a virtue out of necessity. But once reliance on young talent was an ongoing reality, Celtic, in the person of Bob Kelly especially, decided that it was the right way forward. It was a decision which would prove extremely controversial for several years, as Celtic seemed destined to be a club of serial failures.

YOUTH POLICY?

Being outgunned, as it were, for the 1957–58 league title by a team with such an impressive record as Hearts' was of little consolation to Celtic followers who were about to witness the break-up of a team which had recently, and so spectacularly, done much to restore the club's pre-eminence in Scottish football. Before the following season (1958–59) had even got under way, both Billy McPhail and Sean Fallon had received injuries in the first public trial match which, following medical advice, necessitated their retiral from the game they had played with a fair measure of success. Before Christmas, the club transferred two of its biggest stars, Bobby Collins and Willie Fernie, to Everton and Middlesbrough respectively for the barely disguised purpose of funding the installation of floodlighting. Unsurprisingly, minus almost half the team which had brought silverware to Parkhead in the previous two seasons, Celtic finished a distant sixth in the championship, and the major cup trophies eluded them after two defeats at the semi-final stage (to Partick Thistle in the League Cup and to St Mirren in the Scottish Cup). This set a pattern which was to last until the mid-1960s and the appointment of Jock Stein as manager.

In late 1957 Lanarkshire was on the brink of discovering that its citizens, particularly the female ones, had been the target of a man soon to be unmasked as Scotland's most notorious serial killer. In May of the following year, Peter Manuel, a 32-year-old born in New York (to Scottish emigrants) who grew up possessing an unhealthy obsession with famous American gangsters, was sentenced to death at Glasgow's High Court for the murder of seven people (he was also probably responsible for two more). During a trial which created enormous public interest – queues for places in the courtroom's public benches formed 14 hours before the proceedings commenced – Manuel conducted his own defence with no mean skill (his presentation was described by the presiding judge, Lord Cameron, in his summing-up as 'quite remarkable'). All to no avail, for, in the words of one account, in July 1958 – after his appeal was dismissed – Manuel 'took the 12 paces from the condemned cell to the execution chamber at Barlinnie Prison, and one minute later he was dead . . .'

By the end of the 1958–59 season the evergreen Charlie Tully was announcing his retirement as a Celtic player, and the exodus from Parkhead was soon added to by Dick Beattie, Bobby Evans, Sammy Wilson, Bertie Peacock, Neil Mochan and lastly (in 1962) John Donnelly.

* * *

Despite the turmoil affecting the playing personnel at Celtic Park towards and just after the turn of the decade, the seeds of future greatness were already being sown within months of Jock Stein's appointment as reserve-team coach in the summer of 1957, shortly after his own playing days had been truncated by a stubborn ankle injury which left him with a permanent limp. The 'Off the Peg' column of the *Evening Times* was soon describing Stein as the most popular personality inside Parkhead, 'the idol of the Celtic youngsters, and, believe me, these youngsters are the Celtic goods. Jock has been given sole charge of the Celtic stars of the years to come. He looks after the lads like McNeill, Donnelly, Colrain, Conroy and Kennedy. And what does Jock do? He gives his youngsters the same handsome treatment handed out to the men of the first team. Last Sunday, for instance, he took them all down to Seamill for a day in the sun and the sea. The "kids" loved it. Now they worship Jock and are dead keen to make the big-time grade. Smart move by Celtic? Yes!' (pink sports edition, 10 August 1957). Another item in the same column hinted at the quality of material Stein was recruiting and working with. The Celtic dressing-room, it said, had been 'agog' on the evening of the club's second pre-season public trial: 'The "man" who caused most of the excitement was Willie McNeill, the 17-year-old centre-half who played 45 great minutes when John Jack was pulled off at half-time. In the bath Bobby Collins told his team-mates: "That's the greatest discovery Celtic have made in years. He's 6ft 1in – a Goliath compared to this David – and I've never seen a better-looking player." Manager Jimmy McGrory also thinks that the boy from Our Lady's High has a reasonable chance of making the grade if he is not spoiled by too much praise early on.'

The promise, too, of Bertie Auld was already being identified. Signed in April 1955, a few weeks before Stein would captain Celtic for the last time in a major cup final, he had briefly been loaned out to Second Division Dumbarton and was now, as a 19-year-old, challenging for a permanent first-team berth after making his debut against Rangers in the Charity Cup in May 1957. He caught the eye of Harry Andrew of the *Scottish Sunday Express* in the League Cup against Airdrie at Broomfield, even though he was 'starved' of the ball for much of the match: 'His corner-kicking was deadly, and he is also a ball-worker in the Parkhead tradition' (25 August 1957). Indeed, one suspects that Auld may have been a candidate for the outside-left slot ahead of Neil Mochan to face Rangers in the League Cup final two months later but for question-marks about his temperament. He appeared to have had something of a running feud with Scottish international full-back Alex Parker during Celtic's league victory over Falkirk at Brockville in early September. Auld was eventually cautioned by Mr Barclay of Kirkcaldy, who also 'pointed to the pavilion as a warning'. Significantly, perhaps, the young winger wasn't fielded in any of the four Old Firm clashes that season, matches where Celtic's team selection was dictated by a chairman who regarded games with Rangers as potential 'flashpoints', although Auld's first-team appearances were also limited by Neil Mochan's re-emergence as a regular. Harry Andrew's assessment of Auld's promise was shared by Jock Stein.

Stein, with his insatiable curiosity about everything happening on the Scottish football scene, doubtless also noticed the impact already being made by a 19-year-old forward with Kilmarnock (a part-timer employed, aptly, as it would turn out, as a precision instrument maker). Joe McBride, who was to become Stein's first major signing for Celtic when the latter returned to Parkhead as manager in 1965, would (along with McNeill and Auld) be a member of the immortal 'Lisbon Lions' squad during season 1966–67 – a campaign in which he finished the club's top scorer in major domestic competitions despite playing his last match before Christmas. Nine seasons earlier he was widely regarded in football circles as the major factor in Kilmarnock's gates at second XI matches being the highest in the Ayrshire club's history, according to the *Sunday Post* of 17 November 1957. The newspaper noted that in his first season in the senior ranks McBride had already notched 24 goals in reserve football.

Sadly, Stein's progressive outlook was not matched by an appreciation of the realities of professional football on the part of the Celtic directorate, with the result that the adoption of a youth policy – whether by accident or design – in the late 1950s led to a succession of teams being overloaded with youngsters pitched in at the deep end. All too often Celtic teams of this period would take the field without the appropriate leavening of experienced personnel. Almost inevitably, as a consequence, disappointment followed upon disappointment for several seasons as Celtic set off on a long, fruitless quest for the major honours. After three years success still showed no sign of beckoning, and perhaps there was a hint of self-questioning and doubt about the path down which he had taken the club lurking behind the chairman's remarks, aimed at the increasingly disgruntled Celtic support, in the *Celtic Football Guide* for the 1961–62 season: 'I am sure that all of us [management and supporters alike] are in agreement that the promise of our many young players is almost at the stage of fulfilment.' In the event, this 'almost' meant that those same supporters had to wait another four years for that fulfilment to be achieved. But during the proverbial 'seven lean years' between the League Cup triumph of 1957 and the momentous recapture of the Scottish Cup in 1965, they at least had the comfort blanket of the former famous victory to sustain them – something they could hurl defiantly at the Rangers legions who stood opposite at Parkhead, Ibrox or Hampden.

A SACRED FLAME

That 7–1 scoreline was wont to be scrawled too on a multitude of walls and buildings in Glasgow and its vicinity – as John McGuire recalls:

> I was a kid at the time of the 7–1 victory, being brought up in an area called Burnbank (part of Hamilton) which was infamous for its Protestant sectarianism, similar to the reputation of the equally infamous Larkhall. It was a time when 'Tims' were strictly second-class. Very, very few 'Tims' were in the professions or had any of the skilled jobs (I can talk *ad nauseam* on this).
>
> Anyway, in Burnbank, on the way to my school there appeared in large green numerals '7–1'. This remained there for many years, being occasionally touched up. I left the West of Scotland in the mid-'70s and only returned there for funerals. Two or three years ago, I went back to the street where the '7–1' had been painted. It was still there about 35 years after the event – and clearly still being regularly touched up.

I was too young to go to the game in '57, but the 7–1 victory gave all Celtic supporters a great lift until the good times arrived in the mid-1960s. I only ever remember my relatives talking about the game in reverential tones until I bought the Centenary video and saw the goals. When I was about five or six my uncle, who helped run the Hamilton Celtic Supporters Club, gave me a football programme autographed by Charlie Tully. I didn't appreciate the significance at the time and lost the programme; but whenever I see the highlights on video, it brings a tear to the eye.

Eileen Lanigan recalls:

If I'd heard of 'The 7–1', I must have forgotten about it by the time the following happened. I was at Bridgeton Cross one Saturday afternoon in 1959 along with my sister, Margaret, and my wee brother Thomas who was three months old. He's 37 now. Rangers supporters' buses were passing the Cross. The 'Bluenoses' were going crazy, shouting and stamping because they had beaten Celtic. My sister started to taunt them. She brandished seven fingers (palms outwards) and chanted, 'Seven—seven—seven—seven . . . ' I thought we were dead! The crowd on one bus tried to get to us but they couldn't get the door open in a hurry. What saved us was the traffic light going to green and the driver getting away sharpish.

At matches the fans got their practice in early, with Cyril Horne commenting on 'The regular, if hardly rhythmic, chant of "Seven, seven, seven" which developed at the covered enclosure end of the ground' in February 1959 during a Scottish Cup tie with Rangers at Parkhead (the 'Rangers' end was still uncovered at that time). A young Celtic side had fielded only one survivor from the '7–1 team' in its forward line, the 27-year-old Sammy Wilson at inside-left. But despite their obvious lack of experience of big-time football, the young Celts harassed the favourites into a 2–1 defeat and, indeed, the margin of victory might well have been greater had the eager youths in the Celtic attack shown more composure in front of goal.[3] Horne was rather dismissive of the Celtic supporters' constant recitation of the magic number ('wildly vainglorious') in his match report for the *Glasgow Herald*. Doubtless he also deplored the accompanying mock-Churchillian gesture of seven fully-stretched-out fingers being raised in the general direction of the Rangers support, an admittedly rude adaptation of a celebratory action by goalkeeper Dick Beattie, who had turned in triumph to the *Celtic* support massed behind his goal after Fernie's conversion of the penalty kick on a glorious afternoon 18 months previously.

That afternoon in October 1957 is one which many older supporters especially still regard, Lisbon notwithstanding, as the greatest of all days. In the aforesaid report, Cyril Horne had to admit that 'the League Cup final of last season has for some an irresistible and indestructible appeal'. Timeless, in fact – as any self-respecting Celtic man or woman will tell you.

*   *   *

Here comes Fernie cool and slick;
He ambles up to take the kick.
He hits it hard and low past Niven.
The Tims are in their seventh heaven.

ENDNOTES

1 Belafonte later that year had a Christmas hit entitled 'Mary's Boy-child', which was the first record to sell a million copies in Britain. It topped the charts for seven weeks from late November.
2 This poem was provided to the authors courtesy of Frank Glencross of Dalbeattie.
3 Neil Mochan was also in the line-up, but at left-back. Evans and Peacock were in their usual positions in the half-back line.

APPENDIX ONE

Where Are They Now?

Dick Beattie left for Portsmouth in August 1959, and later played for Peterborough. At the beginning of 1963 he returned to Scotland and turned out for St Mirren at Celtic Park in March of that year. Sadly, his sojourn in England was to have a sting in the tail. Later he worked as a welder with Yarrow's and John Brown's (shipbuilding firms on Clydeside). He died on 15 August 1990.

John Donnelly was called up to do his stint of National Service in the summer of 1958. He found it nigh-on impossible to break back into the team thereafter and left for Preston North End in 1962, finishing his career with the Lancashire club four years later. He later emigrated to South Africa.

Sean Fallon seemed to be well positioned to succeed Jimmy McGrory as team manager after his retirement as a player. As McGrory's assistant, he was instrumental in bringing Bertie Auld back to Celtic Park from Birmingham shortly before the appointment of Stein as manager, and later he was at The Big Man's right hand throughout the glory years, playing a crucial role in the signing of many future Celtic stars. When Stein was injured in a near-fatal car crash, Fallon took over the reins for a season. He later held posts with Dumbarton and Clyde. He still lives in Glasgow (and was recently present at the 30th Anniversary celebrations with the Lisbon Lions in Las Vegas, Nevada, sponsored by the North American Federation of Celtic Supporters Clubs).

After his spell with Middlesbrough, Willie Fernie returned to Celtic in a blaze of publicity and hope in October 1960. Just over a year later he moved to St Mirren and was instrumental in knocking Celtic out of the

Scottish Cup in late March 1962 at Ibrox. Stein invited him to coach at Celtic Park in later years, after which he had several seasons in charge of Kilmarnock. He is now in the taxi business in the Glasgow area.

Bobby Evans left Celtic Park in rather acrimonious circumstances in 1960. He subsequently turned out for Chelsea and, later, Raith Rovers. He lives near Glasgow.

Bertie Peacock was player-manager of Coleraine before serving for five years as team manager of Northern Ireland in the mid-1960s. In 1974 he managed Coleraine when they won their first-ever Irish League championship. He still lives in Northern Ireland and has been honoured for his services to football in that province.

Charlie Tully was given an enthusiastic welcome when he appeared for the League of Ireland versus the Scottish League at Parkhead in October 1960 following his move to Cork Hibs. He had spells managing Bangor and Portadown, and was present in Lisbon on 25 May 1967. (When asked if he would have got a game in Celtic's European Cup-winning side, he replied, 'Sure, now, I could have taken the corners.') He died in his sleep on 27 July 1971, soon after celebrating his 47th birthday.

Bobby Collins joined Everton from Celtic in 1958, ironically the club he had rejected in acrimonious circumstances nearly ten years before. In 1962 he moved to Leeds and was so successful there that he was recalled to the Scottish international team and played at Wembley against England in 1965. Thereafter he travelled widely in a coaching capacity, and currently resides in the north of England.

Billy McPhail's playing days ended at Celtic Park. He was subsequently involved in the hairdressing and restaurant businesses, and still lives in Glasgow.

Sammy Wilson was freed by Celtic in the summer of 1959 and was snapped up by Millwall. After a couple of years in England, he returned to Scotland and had a spell managing Brora Rangers. He has now made his home in Ross-shire.

After departing from Celtic in 1960, Neil Mochan had spells playing with Dundee United and Raith Rovers before returning to Celtic Park as trainer/coach in February 1964. He was on the bench in Lisbon (and, indeed, on the pitch attending injured Celts), and was a (much-loved) fixture at Parkhead until his untimely death in Falkirk on 28 August 1994.

APPENDIX TWO

Celtic's Competitive Record in Season 1957–58

N.B. Celtic score/goal tally appears first in each result

League

September	7	1957	Falkirk	(a)	1–0	Fernie
	21		Rangers	(a)	3–2	Collins, McPhail, Wilson
October	12		Raith Rovers	(h)	1–1	Mochan
	26		Third Lanark	(a)	2–0	Collins 2
November	2		Kilmarnock	(h)	4–0	Mochan 2, Wilson, McPhail
	9		East Fife	(a)	3–0	McPhail 2,Mochan
	16		St Mirren	(h)	2–2	Divers, Wilson
	23		Hibernian	(a)	1–0	Wilson
	30		Airdrie	(a)	5–2	Collins 2 (incl. 1 pen., Wilson 2, Peacock
December	7		Dundee	(h)	0–0	–
	14		Clyde	(a)	6–3	McPhail 2, Smith 2, Wilson, Mochan/Clinton*
	21		Partick Thistle	(h)	2–3	Mochan 2
	25		Queen of the South	(h)	1–2	Conway
	28		Heart of Midlothian	(h)	0–2	–
January	1	1958	Rangers	(h)	0–1	–
	2		Queen's Park	(a)	3–0	Wilson 2, McVittie
	4		Falkirk	(h)	2–2	Byrne, Colrain

211

	11	Motherwell	(a)	3–1	Mochan, Collins, Holton (o.g.)
	18	Aberdeen	(h)	1–1	Collins
	25	Raith Rovers	(a)	2–1	Collins, Byrne
February	22	Kilmarnock	(a)	1–1	Wilson
March	5	East Fife	(h)	4–0	Byrne 3, Collins
	8	St Mirren	(a)	1–1	Collins (pen.)
	14	Heart of Midlothian	(a)	3–5	Byrne, Collins (pen.), Smith
	19	Hibernian	(h)	4–0	Wilson 3, McPhail
	22	Airdrie	(h)	4–2	Collins 3 (incl. 1 pen.), Byrne
	29	Dundee	(a)	3–5	Collins (pen.), McVittie, Wilson
April	5	Aberdeen	(a)	1–0	Byrne
	7	Queen's Park	(h)	5–1	Wilson 2, McVittie, Byrne, Smith
	9	Clyde	(h)	6–2	Collins 2, McVittie, McPhail, Fernie, Wilson
	12	Partick Thistle	(a)	1–0	Collins
	16	Queen of the South	(a)	3–4	Wilson 2, McPhail
	21	Motherwell	(h)	2–2	Wilson 2
	30	Third Lanark	(h)	4–1	Wilson 2, Peacock, Collins (pen.)

<u>84–47</u>

Played 34 – won 19, lost 7, drew 8
Points total – 46
Celtic finished in third position, 16 points behind the champions, Heart of Midlothian (who scored 132 goals)
Celtic's top scorer in the league – Wilson, with 23 goals from 33 matches.

*Match v. Clyde at Shawfield on 14 December 1957 – Celtic's third goal was result of Clyde defender Clinton deflecting Mochan's shot into his own net.

League Cup
Section 3:

August	10	*1957*	Airdrie	(h)	3–2	McPhail, Mochan, Peacock
	14		East Fife	(a)	4–1	McPhail 2, Collins, Mochan
	17		Hibernian	(a)	1–3	Collins
	24		Airdrie	(a)	2–1	Smith, Fernie
	28		East Fife	(h)	6–1	McPhail 2, Wilson 2, Auld, Collins

212

31		Hibernian	(h)	2–0	Wilson, McPhail

18–8

Celtic qualified for next stage, the quarter-finals, by topping the section with 10 points, three more than runners-up Hibernian.

September	11	*1957*	Third Lanark	(h)	6–1	McPhail 2, Collins 2, Wilson, Auld
qtr-final first leg						
September	14		Third Lanark	(a)	3–0	Collins, McPhail, Wilson
qtr-final second leg						

Celtic qualified for the semi-finals on a 9–1 aggregate.

September	28	*1957*	Clyde (at Ibrox)	4–2	Wilson, McPhail, Collins, Fernie
semi-final					

October	19	*1957*	Rangers (at Hampden)	7–1	McPhail 3, Mochan 2, Wilson, Fernie (pen.)
final					

38–12

Played 10 – Won 9, Lost 1
Celtic's top scorer in the League Cup – McPhail, with 13 goals in 10 matches

Scottish Cup

February	1	*1958*	Airdrie	(a)	4–3	Byrne 2, Collins, Fernie
February	15		Stirling Albion	(h)	7–2	Byrne 2, Smith 2, Wilson 2, Mochan
*March	1		Clyde	(h)	0–2	–

*drawn as a home tie for Clyde, but the tie was switched to Celtic Park for safety reasons following the wall collapse at Shawfield during the Clyde v. Celtic league match on 14 December 1957.

Played 3 – won 2, lost 1.
Celtic's top scorer in the Scottish Cup – Byrne, with 4 goals from 3 matches.

Glasgow Cup

August	19	*1957*	Rangers	(a)	0–2	–

Glasgow Charity Cup

May	3	*1958*	Partick Thistle	(h)	1–0	Wilson
	8		Rangers	(a)	1–1*	Peacock

*Score at end of regulation 90 minutes, following which Rangers qualified for the final by winning the toss of the coin. There was no extra time.